Praise for *Dat*

"The first edition of *Data Wise* provided educa............._der-standable way to make sense of data in school di:........_and classrooms. Readers of this revised and expanded edition will value the opportunity to discover new ways of thinking about what students should learn, why they should learn it, and how they should be taught."

—Tom Payzant, former superintendent, Boston Public Schools, and professor of practice, Harvard Graduate School of Education

"*Data Wise* has been a central ingredient in our school turnaround. The model has helped us take a comprehensive approach to using data to inform instructional practice and provides a framework for all school improvement efforts. By combining this model with the hard work of an exceptional faculty, our student body has seen some of the largest student achievement gains in Massachusetts and across the nation."

—Ben Klompus, BART Charter Public School, Adams, Massachusetts

"Demystify that data! A powerful asset to data-driven inquiry and improvement . . . *Data Wise* guides schools and school systems through the growth of comprehensive data systems that encompass classroom work samples as well as standardized tests. With a sympathetic understanding of the inevitable limits on staff time, the authors discuss the best ways to structure collaborative faculty time and include protocols to involve faculty and staff in gaining insight from data."

—*Horace*

"Turning a culture of never using data to data-driven instruction is not an easy feat. Although our school district furthered teachers and administrators with plenty of data sources, teachers needed a framework and a system to utilize data in the most efficient way. By implementing the Data Wise process at the district level, instructional coaches and administrators were able to look at data, classroom practices, and student work effectively. They finally understand the function of data-driven instruction and how that is tied into planning, practices, and student work."

—Beverly Enriquez, director, curriculum and federal programs, Douglas Unified School District, Douglas, Arizona

"*Data Wise* is practical and based on experiences in real schools; therefore, it achieves one of its goals of helping school leaders understand how to use student assessments to improve teaching and learning. . . . *Data Wise: A Step-by Step Guide to Using Assessment Results to Improve Teaching and Learning* is a nice contribution to how to get assessment data used by those who are leading and teaching in our schools."

—*Teachers College Record*

"The step-by-step process described in this invaluable book has helped me engage my faculty in lively, frank, and productive discussions about our student assessment results. Now we are able to make the connections between data and instruction in ways that improve teaching and learning systematically throughout the school."

—Janet Palmer Owens, principal,
Mason Pilot Elementary School, Boston

"A masterful example of what can happen when great scholars confront real-world problems. This book should be required reading for anyone interested in moving beyond the tiresome arguments over the pros and cons of testing."

—Michael J. Feuer, dean and professor at the Graduate School of Education
and Human Development, The George Washington University

"The book is well organized and would serve as a great tool for school and district improvement teams. Of special interest to superintendents is the chapter devoted to the role of the central office in becoming data wise."

—*The School Administrator*

"For any team of educators needing to implement a coherent instructional plan, to identify the learning needs of every student, and to meet those needs, this book will be very helpful. The reviewer believes that if the goal of a school is to review student assessment results to improve teaching and learning, following this book would be beneficial."

—*Education Review*

Data Wise

Data Wise

A Step-by-Step Guide
to Using Assessment Results
to Improve Teaching
and Learning

Revised and Expanded Edition

EDITED BY
Kathryn Parker Boudett
Elizabeth A. City
Richard J. Murnane

Harvard Education Press
Cambridge, Massachusetts

Library of Congress Control Number 2012951226

Paperback ISBN 978-1-61250-521-3
Library Edition ISBN 978-1-61250-522-0

Published by Harvard Education Press,
an imprint of the Harvard Education Publishing Group

Harvard Education Press
8 Story Street
Cambridge, Massachusetts 02138

Cover design: Sarah Henderson
Koru and silver fern illustrations: Laurel Cook Lhowe

The typefaces used in this book are Minion Pro, Myriad Pro, Gill Sans, and Museo Slab.

CONTENTS

PREFACE

to the Revised and Expanded Edition

CONTINUOUS IMPROVEMENT IS COMPELLING. Once you get a taste of what can happen when you work hard with people you respect on something important *and see real results*, there is no turning back. This is what teachers, principals, and coaches tell us about using data to improve learning and teaching.

And this is how we feel at the Data Wise Project at the Harvard Graduate School of Education. From day one, we realized that the only way we could be credible teachers of collaborative improvement would be to commit to practicing what we preach. Fortunately, we have had lots of opportunities to collect a wide range of data on what happens when educators interact with our materials. This information has helped us serve our mission, which is *to support a community of researchers and practitioners in developing and using resources for working collaboratively to use data to make real and lasting improvements in teaching and learning.*

SOURCES OF INSPIRATION

After we published *Data Wise*, we began welcoming over a hundred people a year to our week-long Data Wise Summer Institute. Since then, our institute has brought teams of educators from around the United States and the world to Cambridge for intensive training on how to inspire true collaborative improvement back in their schools and districts. We have learned much from these teams. Their appetite for real-world examples showing the struggles and successes of schools doing this work led us to work closely with practitioners to write *Data Wise in Action: Stories of Schools Using Data to Improve Teaching and Learning* (Harvard Education Press, 2007) as well as two teaching cases: *Data Wise at Poe Middle School in San Antonio, Texas* and *Data Wise District-Wide in Evansville, Indiana* (Harvard Education Press, 2013). Participants' demand for specific resources to support the most challenging (and arguably most important) step of the Data Wise Improvement Process, Examining Instruction, inspired us to bring video cameras into classrooms and meeting rooms in a high-functioning urban school. From this effort we created *Key Elements of Observing Practice: A Data Wise DVD and Facilitator's Guide* (Harvard Education Press, 2010). We have also channeled what we learned from institute participants into the development of degree-program courses here at Harvard and online courses that make our content available around the globe. In the spring of 2012, we began hosting the Data Wise Impact Workshop, where we create a forum for practitioners who are using the Data Wise Improvement Process to share and deepen their work. Each of these programs helps us stay connected to educators who are doing this work. We are pleased to use all royalties from this book to fund research and development of additional resources that support educators in using data wisely.

CHANGING TIMES IN EDUCATION

So much has happened in the world since we published *Data Wise* back in 2005! At that time, finding ways to make effective use of the growing piles of assessment reports felt like a new challenge. Around the world, people were just beginning to harness the power of technology to collect and analyze fine-grained data and support using real-time collaboration via shared documents and video. In the United States, educators at all levels of the system were trying to figure out how to respond to the demands of making Adequate Yearly Progress under the recently authorized No Child Left Behind Act. At the Harvard Graduate School of Education, there was a growing awareness of the need to help the education sector improve, but no clearly articulated strategy about how to do so.

Now data are an established component of educational policy worldwide. An increasing number of educators have access to data warehouses that generate score reports and charts that instantly provide powerful information. There is more systematic use of interim or benchmark assessments for tracking student progress, and there are more policies mandating that educators track student progress, set goals, identify action steps, and implement them. Creating and instantly sharing videos of meetings, lessons, and conversations is now easy and nearly costless.

Today in the United States, current policy initiatives around Common Core State Standards and teacher evaluation present schools with opportunity—and risk. The opportunity is to make more effective use of evidence to inform the education of all of our children. But the risk is falling into the trap that evidence alone will do the job. In working with schools over the years, we've noticed that we no longer have to persuade people that using data is a good idea. However, we are still constantly trying to make the case that data need to be embedded in a *collaborative* improvement process, that the process itself needs constant attention, and that the work will never be finished. This book attempts to show how you can work with your colleague to rise above social pressure to be "nice" (which can sometimes mean avoiding hard truths) and political pressure to be "proficient" (which can sometimes mean prioritizing scores over mastery). Our aim is to support you in harnessing data to chart a course from what is to what could be.

WHAT'S NEW IN THIS EDITION

The goal of this revision is to capture the learning that has taken place since *Data Wise* was first published and to bring our text up-to-date with recent developments in education and technology. The most important thing we have learned in recent years is that using data to improve teaching and learning involves not just adopting an improvement process but committing to cultivating a way of thinking that prioritizes **A**ction, **C**ollaboration, and **E**vidence. We call this way of thinking the "ACE Habits of Mind." We have revised the introduction to describe these habits and explain why they are important—and elusive. To provide concrete ideas for how to support your colleagues in developing the ACE Habits, we have added a section at the end of each chapter showing how each habit can be woven into the work of a particular step of the Data Wise Improvement Process.

We have also completely revised chapter 1, "Organizing for Collaborative Work." Perhaps the biggest change to this chapter is that we put the job of leading the Data Wise Improvement Process squarely into the hands of the school's instructional leadership team, instead of a data team, as we did in our first edition. In working with educators, we came to see that creating a separate entity to spearhead data work could reinforce the idea that data are somehow separable from the day-to-day work of leading learning and teaching—which of course they are not. The content in this chapter has also been reorganized to better reflect the way in which we teach this material and to align to the Data Wise Rubric for assessing your own school's progress. (The Data Wise Rubric is a tool for reflecting on the extent to which your school has integrated the Data Wise Improvement Process into your daily work. For each of the eight steps, the rubric lists several key tasks and describes what it looks like when a school is in each of four stages with respect to that task. For information about this resource, please visit the Data Wise Project website at www.gse.harvard.edu/datawise.)

We made some changes to the chapters in the "Inquire" section of the book. Chapter 3 now makes it clear that it is the job of the instructional leadership team to choose a "focus area" (previously called an "educational question") for the collaborative inquiry. This team is then responsible for facilitating a discussion of data within this focus area in which a broader group identifies a "priority question" to further narrow the scope of the work. We also aligned chapter 5, "Examining Instruction," more closely with *Key Elements of Observing Practice: A Data Wise DVD and Facilitator's Guide* so that readers of both publications will experience consistency between the two resources.

The new edition has also been extensively revised to provide clear and consistent language across the chapters and to ensure that all exhibits reflect our best thinking. We removed document templates and protocols that were no longer central to our teaching, and replaced them with materials that have resonated with school leaders that we work with. Our Selected Protocols section now includes instructions for three additional discussion protocols that have proven to be particularly valuable. We have also added a Resources section that lets you know where to go to get new materials as they are developed, and how to take advantage of the professional learning opportunities that the Data Wise Project now provides.

Finally, we added a new concluding chapter called "How We Improve." Two of the most common questions we get from educators are, "Where do I start?" and "How long will it take?" Chapter 10 addresses these as well as the question of how people learn to do the work of improvement. It describes the importance of starting small, and it explains what happens when you use what you learn to inspire a consistent approach to improvement throughout all the layers of an organization.

ACKNOWLEDGMENTS

Soon after taking the helm at the Harvard Graduate School of Education in 2006, Dean Kathleen McCarthy announced that the mission of the school would be to work at the nexus of practice, policy, and research. She established the Data Wise Project as one of several initiatives in which HGSE faculty and graduate students would work closely with practitioners on efforts designed to impact the place where real change happens: classrooms. We are grateful for her financial and moral support, and for that of her leadership team, including Keith Collar, Jack Jennings, Daphne Layton, and Matt Miller. Their vision has created an opportunity for us to bring the practitioner voice to the fore. We are also thankful to the Spencer Foundation, especially Andrea Bueschel and Paul Goren, for not only funding but also helping to shape exploratory research in the field that we have drawn upon in updating this volume. And we thank Caroline Chauncey, our editor at Harvard Education Press, for championing our ongoing work with such grace and candor. Our sincere thanks go to Fulbright Scholar Ngaire Addis for introducing us to the imagery of the koru, and to Australian educators Penny Vanderkruk and Mark Walker for showing us (both literally and figuratively) the majestic silver fern that the koru can become.

We'll conclude by thanking the many talented and visionary doctoral students and practitioners who have joined the Data Wise team as fellow researchers and teachers over the years. We are grateful to each of you for teaching us so much about what it means to be a team. In particular, we offer special thanks to: Anne Jones, whose extraordinary facilitation skills and educator's instincts helped us take our courses—both in person and online—to the next level; to principal Ben Klompus and all of the educators at the Berkshire Arts and Technology Charter Public School, who shared their practice in a way that has allowed us to fundamentally change our approach to resource development; to David Rease Jr. and Michele Shannon, for drawing upon their deep teaching and administrative experience to articulate an audacious vision for what the Data Wise Project could become—and for making working toward that vision such fun; and to Candice Bocala, whose leadership has guided all our recent work, and whose dedication has made this revised edition of *Data Wise* possible.

PREFACE

to the First Edition

IN AN EFFORT TO DETERMINE how best to prepare school leaders to use student assessment results to improve teaching and learning, a group consisting of faculty and doctoral students at the Harvard Graduate School of Education (HGSE) and school leaders from three Boston public schools worked together for two years. This book is a product of our collective knowledge about what school leaders need to know and do to ensure that the piles of student assessment results landing on their desks are used to improve student learning in their schools.

The contributors to this book are a varied group with quite different experiences and expertise. Three of us are urban public school principals; one of us directs out-of-school programs in an urban public school; several of us are HGSE faculty members, one a statistician, one an economist, one a scholar of assessment issues, and one a public policy analyst. Some of us are HGSE doctoral students, with experience in urban, suburban, and independent schools across the country. All of us have worked in or with urban schools, where we have struggled with the issues that we write about in this book. Most of us have extensive teaching experience; some of us also have worked as guidance counselors, coaches, or administrators. What we share is a commitment to provide all children with a good education, and a belief that thoughtful, systematic, collaborative examination of student assessment results can contribute to this goal.

Forging new knowledge was the core activity that led us to create this book. We met regularly for more than two hours at a time during the school year, engaging frequently in intense conversations about difficult issues. For example, some of our members who had extensive experience as classroom teachers felt it made no sense to spend a lot of time examining results from high-stakes tests. Other members, especially school principals, felt such work was a valuable starting place. Adherents of both positions argued effectively and helped the group appreciate the importance of examining a wide range of data sources.

Another example concerns preparation for tests. Some group members felt it was critical to devote instructional time to preparing students to take high-stakes exams. Others argued that test preparation artificially inflated scores so that the scores did not reflect transferable knowledge. Forging a common understanding between principals who were under intense pressure to improve test scores and assessment experts who were wary of score inflation was a challenge. However, our common commitment to improve the quality of education for urban children led us to seek common ground. The thoughtful suggestions each of us made about the many drafts of every chapter helped us to find it. We frequently came back to the question of whether the content and tone of each chapter would make it useful to school leaders who were focused on improving instruction and increasing student learning.

While we have urban roots, we see our approach to using data and our examples for illuminating it as relevant to educators working in all kinds of schools. We designed the two composite case studies we featured in the book to reflect many of the challenges educators in schools across the country face today.

Many people and organizations contributed to making this book possible. Rather than simply listing them, we provide a brief description of the activities that led to the creation of our seminar group and the people who made it possible.

In spring 2001, Harvard professor Richard Murnane arranged with Boston Public Schools (BPS) superintendent Thomas Payzant to spend the next school year helping the BPS central office improve the support it offered schools in how to learn from student assessment results. One of the first things Murnane learned in planning the year was that several groups were already actively engaged in helping Boston's public schools learn from student assessment results. Of particular importance were the BPS central office staff and the Boston Plan for Excellence (BPE), BPS's external partner.

At BPS, Maryellen Donahue, director of the Office of Research, Assessment, and Evaluation, Al Lau, director of the Office of Information Systems, and Ann Grady, director of the Office of Information Technology, had jointly created a software tool called LIZA (the acronym for Local Intranet Zone for Administrators), which allowed BPS principals to obtain information electronically on the students in their schools. One of LIZA's strengths was that it provided access to student data from the BPS central student database, which was updated every night. This was important, because with a mobile student population, the students enrolled in certain schools in January were quite a different group from the students enrolled there the previous September. One significant limitation of LIZA was that it was not created to support the analysis of patterns in student assessment results, and therefore was difficult to use for that purpose. So while a few computer-savvy principals did use LIZA to download data that they then analyzed in a spreadsheet program, most did not. A second limitation was that teachers did not have access to LIZA.

In response to requests from BPS principals for help in analyzing student assessment results, Ellen Guiney, executive director of the Boston Plan for Excellence, asked Kristan Singleton, then the BPE technology director, to create desktop software dedicated to this purpose. Singleton led a group that created FAST Track, a software with the virtue of being easy to use. By 2001, more than 40 Boston public schools were using the new software to create school-level portraits of student achievement. However, FAST Track also had its limitations. Most importantly, it used student data that the school principals could request from the BPS central office and that a BPE staffer loaded onto each school's desktop computer at the beginning of the school year. Schools with mobile student populations had to repeat this time-consuming process frequently over the school year. A second limitation was that FAST Track updates had to be loaded onto each school's computer by BPE staff, another time-consuming process.

In the process of working with Boston's public schools on data use, the BPS and BPE staffs were learning a lot. So were HGSE doctoral students who were working with selected Boston public schools on data use under the auspices of the Harvard Office of School Partnerships. Yet the groups worked separately and did not learn from each other or pool their knowledge to figure out how to support schools more effectively.

To facilitate such learning, Maryellen Donahue and Richard Murnane invited individuals working on data issues with BPS to participate in a workshop dedicated to learning how to make the work more effective. Approximately 20 people accepted the invitation, and the workshop met for two hours every other week over the school year. Out of the workshop came the realization that BPS needed a data-and-software system that would allow BPS principals and teachers to efficiently examine test scores for their students.

Near the end of the 2001–02 school year, the Boston Plan for Excellence and the Boston Public Schools agreed to pool the knowledge they acquired in developing LIZA and FAST Track and to work together to create such a data system. Moreover, they decided to make the software a part of MyBPS, a comprehensive Web-based system, designed by a team headed by Albert Lau and Alice Santiago, that provided Boston's schools with a wide range of information. The result was MyBPS Assessment, a system that combined the strengths of LIZA and FAST Track and is now used by all Boston schools to analyze student assessment results. Several contributors to this volume worked on this project and learned many of the lessons described in this book.

Once the MyBPS Assessment software became available, the next challenge was to provide support so BPS educators could learn to use it. Again, the Harvard Graduate School of Education, the Boston Public Schools, and the Boston Plan for Excellence worked together to respond to this need. Together they staffed and funded the creation of a year-long course that taught teams of educators from BPS and HGSE students how to make constructive use of student assessment results.

In 2003, Kathryn Boudett became the lead instructor in the data course, with support from HGSE doctoral students Elizabeth City and Liane Moody. Boudett had led a research project for BPE designed to illuminate best practices in data use in Boston. Moody had contributed to this work and had played a key role in developing the MyBPS Assessment software as a member of the BPE staff. City had served as a literacy coach and change coach for BPS and was acutely aware of the challenges urban school faculties faced in learning to make constructive use of student assessment results. Over the next two years the teaching team developed new strategies for teaching critical skills to teams from 17 Boston public schools. Many of the ideas described in this book were developed in the process of planning and teaching this course, including the design of the improvement cycle around which this book is organized.

Before we began concrete work on this book, Thomas Payzant, Maryellen Donahue, Albert Lau, and Ann Grady of the Boston Public Schools had created an environment that made the book project possible. The Boston Plan for Excellence, under the leadership of Executive Director Ellen Guiney, supported the creation of the MyBPS Assessment, the training of BPS educators, and the development of the data course. Kristan Singleton, BPE assistant director, played a critical role in orchestrating BPE's vital contribution to the development of the MyBPS Assessment. Ellen Lagemann, dean of HGSE from 2002 to 2005, helped make the data course and the book seminar possible.

Once we began research and writing, many other individuals made valuable contributions to our work. We extend our sincerest thanks to the many educators who read all or parts of the draft manuscript and provided comments that helped us strengthen the book: Adrienne Chisolm, Hunter Credle, Stefanie Reinhorn, Oscar Santos, and Sara Schwartz Chrismer. These individuals helped us ground our case study schools' approach to improving instruction in sound and realistic practices. We also thank Tim Dugan of Kestrel Heights School in Durham, North Carolina, and Rob Matheson of Apex High School in Apex, North Carolina, for helping us understand their state's student assessment system.

A number of our Harvard colleagues also helped to frame our work. HGSE professor Richard Elmore helped us define and understand the idea of a problem of practice, an important term in chapter 5. HGSE professor Katherine Boles pushed us to think carefully about what it means to write for an audience of school leaders. HGSE professor Robert Schwartz introduced us and our ideas to director Douglas Clayton and assistant director Caroline Chauncey of the Harvard Education Publishing Group. They embraced our ideas for a book and helped us turn it into a reality.

Caroline Chauncey's contributions went beyond providing good ideas for developing the arguments and sharpening the prose. During the 2004–05 school year, she came to our monthly workshop meetings and answered our many questions about how to turn our chapters into a coherent, useful book. Chris City did a marvelous job of editing and improving the manuscript; we are grateful for his dedication to the project during the most intense phase of the writing. Wendy Angus gave critical logistical support for the book seminar and for the book production.

The work that resulted in this book would not have been possible without financial support. Under the guidance of Marshall Smith, a longtime advocate of using data to guide instructional improvement, the William and Flora Hewlett Foundation was an early supporter of both BPE's FAST Track initiative and Murnane's work in Boston. Subsequent critical support for the research that led to this book was provided by the Spencer Foundation and by William and Juliana Thompson. We thank these individuals and organizations for their faith in the value of our unconventional project.

Some of the most important contributors to the ideas described in this book are the many BPS educators and HGSE graduate students who participated in the HGSE-BPS data course and allowed us to learn about the challenges in using assessment results to improve teaching and learning. As an indication of our appreciation for their support, all of the royalties from this book will be donated to the Harvard Graduate School of Education for work with the Boston Public Schools.

INTRODUCTION

Kathryn Parker Boudett, Elizabeth A. City, and Richard J. Murnane

NEWS SPREAD QUICKLY THAT DATA FROM LAST SPRING'S COMPREHENSIVE assessment had gone live on the state's website. When principal Roger Bolton logged on, that news was grim. Franklin High School was listed once again as a school "in need of improvement" for failing to increase the percentage of tenth graders scoring well enough on the English language arts and mathematics exams to receive high school diplomas. Page after page of charts and tables offered the gory details. The sheer volume of information was overwhelming.

Frustrated as a teacher by how little Franklin expected of its students academically, Roger had vowed that when he became principal he would make it his mission to "get the learning up." But now, the newly released assessment results reminded him that he would be judged primarily by whether he could "get the test scores up." He wanted to believe that there was something his faculty could learn from all these numbers that would help them increase student learning and raise the scores. But he didn't know where to start.

Many school leaders across the nation share Roger's frustration—a lack of knowledge about how to transform mountains of data on student achievement into an action plan that will improve instruction and increase student learning. Others have made some progress in responding to this challenge, but have become stymied along the way. Some have learned to identify patterns in student assessment results, but have not figured out what to do next. Some have not been able to convince their

1

colleagues of the value of this work. Others have developed action plans, but have not been able to implement them. Some have implemented plans for improving instruction, but do not know how to evaluate their effectiveness. The goal of this book is to help educators in all these positions to learn how to analyze data in a manner that contributes to improved instruction and increased student learning.

When we use the term "data," we mean not only scores on high-stakes tests administered to monitor state and federal accountability policies, but also the broad array of other information on student skills and knowledge typically available in schools. For example, a growing number of districts administer interim or benchmark assessments to gauge students' readiness for state comprehensive assessments. Some districts also administer end-of-course exams. Many schools assess student achievement with science fairs or exhibitions at which student projects are graded using agreed-upon rubrics. Then, of course, there are the classroom tests, projects, and homework that individual teachers assign to students as they work their way through the curriculum. These are just some of the kinds of data that educators can fruitfully examine in targeting areas for instructional improvement.

When we use the term "school leaders," we mean not only principals, but also the teachers, directors of instruction, department heads, and coaches who are committed to engaging their colleagues in improving instruction at their school. A central premise underlying this book is that a good school is not a collection of good teachers working independently, but a team of skilled educators working together to implement a coherent instructional plan, to identify the learning needs of every student, and to meet those needs. We believe that the process of learning from data contributes to building an effective school and to helping the school continue to improve its performance.

AN ONGOING CHALLENGE

The long-term evidence from the National Assessment of Educational Progress (NAEP) shows that average reading and math scores of today's 9-, 13-, and 17-year-olds are a little higher than they were in the 1970s. This is consistent with the view of most educators that they are working as hard as they can and are accomplishing at least as much as their colleagues did 30 years ago. So why the enormous external pressure to improve schools, as embodied in recent policy shifts toward assessing students on a common core of content and assessing the extent to which teachers help them master that content?

To a large extent, the answer lies in changes in the economy that have dramatically reduced earnings opportunities for Americans who leave school without strong reading, writing, and math skills and the ability to use these skills to acquire new knowledge and solve new problems. These striking long-term changes in the American economy account for much of the pressure American schools face to improve student learning. A complementary concern is the persistent and sizable gaps in the average academic skills of some students compared to others. These gaps often exist among groups of students from different race, income, disability, and language backgrounds. One striking finding from recent research is that while achievement gaps between students of different races and ethnicities have declined somewhat in recent decades, gaps in reading and mathematical skills between children from relatively affluent families and those from relatively low-income families have widened substantially over this time period. Until these gaps are closed, many workers will be denied access to the growing number of jobs that require problem-solving and communication skills and that pay enough to support a family.

One important change in the educational landscape in the United States is that 48 of the country's 50 states have adopted Common Core State Standards specifying the English language arts and mathematics skills that children should master at each grade level. The Common Core State Standards are considerably more demanding than the standards in place in most states and they set goals that substantially exceed the current accomplishments of most American students, especially those from low-income families. Adoption of the Common Core makes sense because they are better aligned than most state standards are today with the skills graduates of American schools will need to earn a decent living. Moreover, adoption of common assessments by most, if not all, states will allow potentially instructive comparisons of the skills of children educated in different states. However, a consequence of the introduction of skill assessments based on the Common Core, which is scheduled to take place no later than 2015, will show even wider income-based gaps in skills than those revealed by current assessments. Closing these gaps poses a momentous challenge to the nation's schools.

We work with educators who are under great pressure to dramatically improve the quality of instruction children receive in school. We believe that the ideas in this book will help educators improve instruction and increase student learning. Moreover, we see this as a worthy goal not only because it will help the next generation of Americans earn enough to support their children, but also because it will give them the skills to contribute to civic life in a democracy beset by a host of problems.

What effective schools look like is not a mystery. They have a coherent instructional program well-aligned with strong standards. They have a community of adults committed to working together to develop the skills and knowledge of all children. They have figured out how to find the time to do this work and are acquiring the skills to do it well. This book is written for those educators who are committed to this work. We maintain that analyzing a variety of student assessment results can contribute to fulfilling their goals, if careful attention is paid to the limitations of tests and the technical challenges in interpreting student responses.

When students receive consistent high-quality instruction, scores on high-stakes tests rise. However, the converse need not be true. Faced with pressure to improve test scores, some educators analyze student assessment results to identify students who need just a few more points to pass a graduation exam, with the intent of improving these students' test-taking skills. Preparing students to pass the exams required for high school graduation is clearly important. However, it is even more important that time be spent helping students develop the skills they will need after graduation.

Some educators examine tests to identify frequently used questions and item formats so they can devote instructional time to helping students do well on particular tests. Familiarizing students with the format of high-stakes tests makes sense. So does explaining strategies to improve scores, such as answering every open-ended response question. However, the line between ensuring that students are test savvy and using up scarce instructional time on preparing for a particular high-stakes test is a thin one. While "drill and kill" may lead to improved scores, it will not prepare students to thrive in our increasingly complex society.

STRUCTURING IMPROVEMENT: A ROAD MAP

For school leaders like principal Roger Bolton, the barriers to constructive, regular use of student assessment data to improve instruction can seem insurmountable. There is just so much data. Where do you start? How do you make time for the work? How do you build your faculty's skill in interpreting data sensibly? How do you build a culture that focuses on improvement, not blame? How do you maintain momentum in the face of all the other demands at your school? This book addresses all of these questions, providing strategies and tools to identify possible explanations for strong and weak student performance, examine the importance of alternative explanations, and plan and execute instructional strategies to improve teaching and learning.

We have found that organizing the work of instructional improvement around a process that has specific, manageable steps helps educators build confidence and skill in using data. This process includes eight distinct activities school leaders engage in to use their student assessment data effectively. Each activity is the focus of one chapter. We see the eight activities as falling into three categories: Prepare, Inquire, and Act.

We use the Data Wise Improvement Process graphic shown here to illustrate the cyclical nature of the work. Initially, schools prepare—they engage in activities that establish a foundation for learning from student assessment results. They then inquire, and subsequently act on what they learned. They then cycle back to further inquiry.

The Data Wise Improvement Process

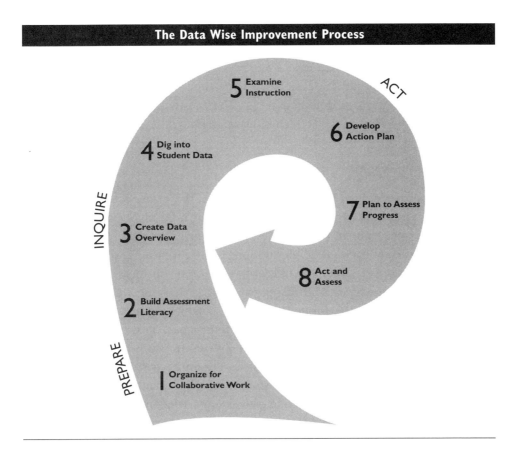

Prepare is about putting in place the structure for data analysis and looking at existing data from standardized tests. Chapter 1 describes tasks involved in organizing for collaborative work, including establishing teams and taking stock of existing data. Chapter 2 explains key elements of assessment literacy that are critical to interpreting test results correctly.

Inquire is about acquiring the knowledge necessary to decide how to increase student learning. Chapter 3 describes the tasks involved in creating a data overview, especially how to construct graphic displays that will allow school faculty to readily identify patterns in the results of standardized assessments. Chapter 4 explains how to dig into student work, first in a single data source and then in other data sources, with the goal of identifying and understanding a learner-centered problem. Chapter 5 shows how to examine instruction in order to understand what current practice looks like and how it relates to effective practice for the learner-centered problem.

Act is about what to do to improve instruction and to assess whether the changes put in place have made a difference. Chapter 6 describes the tasks involved in designing an effective action plan. Chapter 7 addresses planning how to assess whether students are learning more. A key message is that the assessment strategy and the action plan should be developed at the same time. Chapter 8 describes the key tasks involved in making an action plan come alive in classrooms, and in assessing implementation and effectiveness along the way.

THE ACE HABITS OF MIND

One thing we have learned in nearly a decade of working with schools is that real and lasting change entails more than carrying out the tasks involved at each step of the Data Wise Improvement Process. Data Wise is not a "program" to "implement" but rather a means of organizing and bringing coherence to the work of improvement that you already do. We think of it as a way of doing business. Underlying this process is a disciplined way of thinking that guides the way educators approach their daily work. We call this foundation the ACE Habits of Mind.

We have come to make the ACE Habits a central part of our teaching because we have learned that, for most of us, these habits do not come naturally, and the habits we follow by default can work against our desire to use data effectively.

Shared commitment to **action**, **assessment**, and **adjustment** means that all of the work you do—not just the formal action plan for improving instruction that you develop in Step 6—is geared toward doing, not just talking. Every meeting that you have has clear objectives, including coming up with questions, analyses, and decisions that

Shared commitment to **A**ction, assessment, and adjustment

Intentional **C**ollaboration

Relentless focus on **E**vidence

help move the work forward. These action steps become the subject of great scrutiny, because you are always assessing the extent to which your actions are leading you in the direction you want to go—and adjusting your actions when they fall short of the mark. We contrast this habit with two default habits that are easy to slip into. One involves falling into a state of analysis paralysis, in which meeting after meeting is devoted to collecting more information and nothing ever gets done. On the other side of the spectrum is the habit of forging blindly ahead. In this case the inclination is to stay the course with a plan (usually out of fear that midcourse corrections would be a sign of failure) or to abandon it entirely (which often means that the good ideas are thrown out with the bad). Cultivating a shared commitment to action, assessment, and adjustment helps teams follow the middle path toward real improvement.

Intentional **collaboration** means being extremely deliberate in how and when you engage educators with the work. This involves making conscious decisions about whom to bring to the table for a particular conversation, and structuring that conversation so the collective wisdom of the group is brought to bear. The default habit here assumes that just because you have put people together in the same room, productive interaction will take place. In reality, what often happens is that people skirt the most important conversations in an effort to keep the interaction pleasant. Or people fall back on preestablished patterns of participation that leave some voices out of the dialogue. Throughout this book, we share specific strategies for organizing different kinds of discussions to build trust and allow people to interact with one another with freshness and purpose.

Relentless focus on **evidence** is a habit that often draws a laugh when we first mention it, since it can sound a bit obsessive. But we offer this habit in all seriousness, since time and time again school leaders have told us that the single most important thing they have done to build trust is to establish a culture that makes decisions based on specific and descriptive statements about a wide range of data sources. But they also tell us that reading all kinds of things into the data that aren't actually there is a deeply ingrained habit for most people, so it takes a determined effort to break it.

We have noticed that, instead of making a factual statement about what they see, people tend to make an inference about *why* they see what they do. The statement, "The teacher doesn't know how to let students do their own thinking" leads to a very different conversation from the statement, "Four out of five times the teacher asked a question, she answered it herself." In the first case, there is an inference and a judgment that can put someone on the defensive. In the second, there is a simple statement of fact, something that is much harder to argue with—and much easier to remedy. When interpretations are offered as facts (and when those interpretations vary widely), it is extremely difficult to get consensus about what the problem is, let alone how to solve it. Because we all have become so accustomed to lacing our statements with inferences, cultivating the habit of maintaining a relentless focus on evidence takes work. But it is possible, and when widely practiced can allow the work of improvement to truly take off.

To help you see how these habits connect to the Data Wise Improvement Process, at the end of each chapter we offer concrete ideas for how to weave the ACE Habits of Mind into a particular step. Don't skip these ACE insights! They have been gleaned from our experience with schools around the United States and the world that have found ways to cultivate these habits in their everyday work. By showing you some of the specific practices that other educators have embedded into their daily routines, we hope to help you be more successful as you do this work.

HOW THIS BOOK IS ORGANIZED

The first eight chapters of this book focus on the tasks school leaders face at each step of the Data Wise Improvement Process, offering tools to accomplish these tasks and lessons from schools that have done this work.

To bring these tasks alive, we have woven vignettes from two case study schools throughout the book: Franklin High School, with students in grades 9–12, and Clark K–8 School, with students in kindergarten through grade 8. Both of our case study schools are working to improve student learning, not simply to improve test scores. Clark faces the challenge of how to build a sense of urgency for continuous improvement, rather than to accept as satisfactory the moderately strong performance most of its students show on standardized tests. Franklin High School faces a different, very difficult challenge: how to respond constructively to the enormous pressure to reduce dropout rates and failure rates on the state graduation exam. Each chapter describes the choices and challenges these schools face at each step of their respective journeys and illustrates the "messiness" of applying the improvement process in practice. When we need to provide a broader range of responses than these two cases can offer, we supplement our examples with brief descriptions of approaches taken by other schools with which we have worked.

The last section of the book is devoted to supporting readers in integrating this improvement into their ongoing work. Chapter 9 describes steps that school district central offices can take to support schools' efforts to make constructive use of student assessment results. It is designed to be a resource for school superintendents and other district leaders committed to helping schools become "data wise."

Chapter 10 provides our best thinking about what it looks like when a school allows the process and habits of mind to grow in a sustainable way. We draw upon our experience, which has shown us the distinctive approaches taken by schools that have been able to really run with this work.

The book concludes with a description of the publications and professional development offerings that we have created to support your Data Wise journey. These tools include our website, to which we continue to add resources as they become available.

HOW TO USE THIS BOOK

For leaders relatively new to the process of using data, we recommend skimming the whole book first and then working through the chapters sequentially with a group of committed faculty. In a sense, each chapter can be read as a "to-do list" of the tasks that will help move the work forward. By following the progress of the two case study schools as they work their way around the improvement cycle, your group will see how other schools handle these tasks. By using the protocols, exercises, and templates offered in the chapters, you should find it relatively straightforward to plan effective faculty meetings on each topic.

For school leaders with considerable experience in using data, it may not be necessary to follow the chapter sequence. Each chapter is designed to stand alone, allowing practitioners to focus on learning strategies that deal with the parts of the process that they find most challenging. Alternatively, school leaders can pick up this book at the point in the cycle where they find themselves, knowing they eventually will work their way around the entire circle. Some readers will want to start with chapter 10 first to get the big picture about how this work can be integrated into schools over time.

Professional development providers and university faculty may find this book useful in planning courses that bring together educators from a variety of settings. In our experience, schools learn a lot by working through the material in a particular chapter on their own and then coming together with people from other schools to share their work, discuss their concerns, and receive technical and moral support from instructors. School leaders are often energized by opportunities to show their school's work to colleagues from other schools and relish the chance to borrow good ideas.

For central office personnel and others who want to learn more about how to support school-level improvement, we recommend reading through the first eight chapters to develop an understanding of the challenges school-based educators face in attempting to learn from student assessment results. Then focus on the chapters in the integration section for insights that may be particularly helpful.

Database designers can use the book to help think through the processes that their software needs to support. Test developers can use it as a window into what school-level people need from assessments—especially formative ones— and what they can do with results once they get them. Finally, policy makers at all levels can use this book to help understand how hard the work of using data to improve schools is, how long it takes, and how worthwhile it can be.

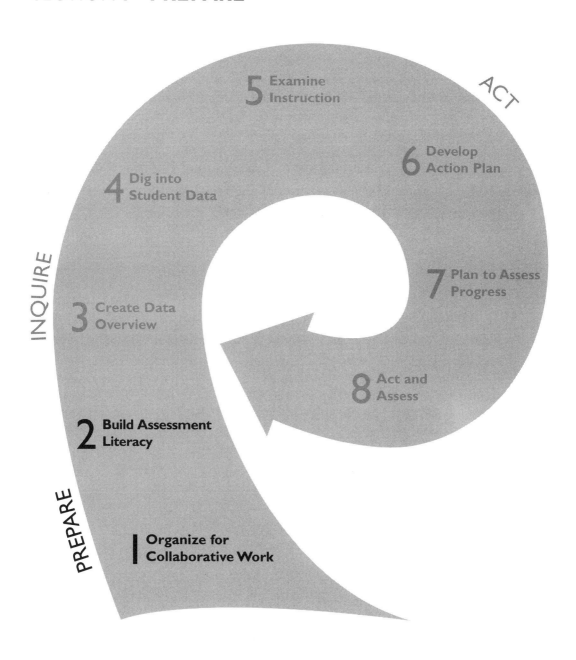

1

ORGANIZING FOR COLLABORATIVE WORK

Kathryn Parker Boudett and Liane Moody

PRINCIPAL SANDY JENKINS'S HEAD WAS SPINNING AS SHE AND THE CLARK K–8 School's assistant principal, Bob Walker, headed back to the school after a three-hour training at the central office. It was the third week of August and the district had unveiled its new approach to whole-school improvement plans. Responding to pressure from the state and federal governments to increase the use of student assessment data, the central office had designed a process that required schools to incorporate increased data analysis into their instructional planning. Sandy was alarmed to learn that to comply with the new policy her school would need to submit a detailed, data-based plan—soon.

"They sure dumped a lot on us," Bob remarked as they walked. "But don't worry . . . it's not as bad as you think. I'm pretty familiar with the software they're asking us to use and I think I can run a bunch of analyses and get that improvement plan drafted before school even starts."

Sandy thought about this. As a first-year principal who was new to the building, she was glad to learn that Bob was willing to take one for the team so early on. It might be efficient in the short run to delegate this task to an eager administrator. Sandy's instinct, though, was that if all this planning was ever going to amount to anything, she would need to involve all of her staff in the process.

Principal Sandy Jenkins is struggling with a question that arises for many school leaders: Is it better to tap a few individuals to become "data experts" and fulfill the reporting requirements alone, or to build a culture where the whole school participates in analyzing data and figuring out the implications for improving instruction? Across the country, school leaders face tough decisions about whether to take the relatively easy route of using data merely to meet external accountability demands or the more challenging path of using data to help educators become accountable to one another and their students for student learning.

Choosing the more challenging path increases the chances that your school will use data to inspire teachers rather than burden them and to illuminate deep issues rather than amplify superficial ones. It means committing to making rich conversations around data part of the everyday work of being a teacher. But it takes effort to make sure these conversations are productive. The central message of this chapter is that there are specific steps school leaders can take to lay the foundation on which to build a collaborative learning process for school improvement.

There are a variety of ways schools can organize to effectively support ongoing conversations about student data. Deciding which approach is most appropriate for your school will require you to think creatively about how you can organize your school's time, people, and other resources in ways that permit teachers and administrators to engage regularly in meaningful discussions about student data. School leaders who make this happen have often described themselves to us as being committed to building a "data culture" or "culture of inquiry" within their schools. We have found that three kinds of foundational tasks can support this kind of school culture: establishing structures, setting the tone, and taking stock. This chapter offers practical advice for engaging in these activities as you take your first steps on the challenging but rewarding path of using data wisely.

ESTABLISHING STRUCTURES

The first set of tasks provides the frame for your collaborative foundation. These include adopting an improvement process, building a strong system of teams, and making time for collaborative work.

Adopt an Improvement Process

An explicit process for improving teaching and learning is the bedrock on which you will build your foundation. As discussed in the introduction, this book is organized around the Data Wise Improvement Process, an inquiry cycle that we developed over the course of years of working with schools. We have consistently found that this cyclical approach helps educators get traction in what can at first feel like unfamiliar terrain. By breaking the work into discrete steps, the process makes an overwhelming prospect feel manageable. By emphasizing the repetition involved, the process shows educators that their investment in learning the steps will be repaid many times over.

When we work with schools, we make it clear that, in practice, educators generally do not work through a complete cycle in order, but instead revisit various parts of the process as reality demands. However, choosing a clear improvement process and locating data discussions within that process can be a great way to show your faculty how the work of improvement affects both whole-school, long-range planning as well as the everyday practice in classrooms.

One exercise we've developed to demonstrate the iterative nature of improvement work involves inviting participants to design their own improvement process, based on the steps we provide (see the Constructing the Improvement Process Protocol, available under Selected Protocols at the end of this book and on the Data Wise Project website).[1] When it is time for groups to share their designs, there is always great variety. One group may make a kind of staircase, while another creates a wheel-like design with data analysis at the center. Almost all groups will have arrows going in many directions among the various steps of the process. In the discussion that accompanies their work on the project, educators explore the importance of each step in the cycle. When the groups see the variation in the posters created, they recognize that although no one way of describing this process is the "right" way, it is helpful to agree on some order of events to guide the work.

Data Wise is an improvement process with its own particular language, actions, and concepts, and many educators have told us that it helps organize their work. However, Data Wise is simply one of several problem-solving, data-based improvement cycles with a strong emphasis on collaboration and looking deeply at instructional practice. Regardless of what you call it or how you help your school make sense of it, what's most important is that you choose and commit to *an* improvement process and allow it to permeate your organization.

Build a Strong System of Teams

In our work with schools, we have seen that many already have an instructional leadership team whose responsibility it is to lead schoolwide improvement in learning and teaching. This team typically consists of the principal and other instructionally oriented administrators and coaches, as well as teachers representing a wide range of grade levels or departments. If your school already has such a team, the first message to get out is that the work of this team is going to become more important than ever, and that work will be increasingly focused on evidence. If you do not have a core group of educators charged with supporting your school in achieving continuous improvement, the time has come to establish one. And although the instructional leadership team will be essential in guiding and modeling the work of improvement, it is important to understand from the start that real change will take place only when the coordinated efforts of all the school teams—leadership and teacher teams—bring improved learning and teaching practices into all classrooms.

> **Principal Sandy Jenkins resisted** the temptation to respond to the district's emphasis on data by creating a separate "data team" that would be responsible for keeping track of test scores. Instead, she decided to use data to help ground the ongoing work of her instructional leadership team, which included herself, assistant principal Bob Walker, and teachers from several grade levels. She knew that the decisions this team made could be readily shared with the school's four well-established teacher-led teams: one for kindergarten, first, and second grade; one for third and fourth grade; one for fifth and sixth; and one for seventh and eighth.
>
> Sandy also planned to revitalize a school-and-community team, a group formed to keep parents and other community members involved in the work of the school. This team had never quite found its purpose, and she hoped that involving this group in rich dialogue about student data would allow it to play a more meaningful role than it had in the past. She summarized the relationships among the teams in a simple diagram (Exhibit 1.1) that conveyed a two-way flow of information between groups within the school.

Creating diagrams like this one can help clarify the teams that will be sharing responsibility for improvement and how the information learned from their conversations will be shared. Paying close attention to the connections between teams is necessary to ensure that everyone is involved in school improvement work. A key to creating a system of interlocking teams is to have every teacher be a member of at least one instructionally oriented team (such as a grade-level or departmental team), and then to have each team send at least one representative to the instructional leadership team, a schoolwide group that makes decisions about learning and teaching.

Exhibit 1.1

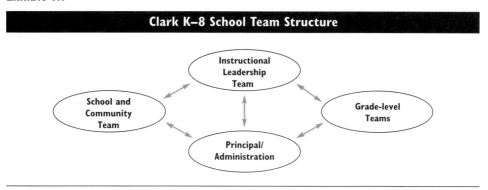

So that these teams can focus most of their work on using data to improve in-struction, it can be very important to allocate responsibility for the technical work of collecting and managing data to a smaller group of people. Many schools tap one or more members of the instructional leadership team to serve as data managers. People who do this work use a variety of skills: organizational skills for overseeing the coordination of multiple assessments; software skills for making the best use of technology; and people skills for interacting effectively with school staff and dis-trict personnel. Data managers need to have a clear understanding of teaching so that they know what kinds of charts and templates teachers will find most useful. And they must want to do this work and be given the time, resources, and support they need to do it well.

The Franklin High School instructional leadership team realized at its August retreat that managing data for the school's 1,520 students was a task too daunting to assign to any one individual. Several Franklin educators volunteered to serve as data managers responsible for overseeing all of the assessments administered in the building. Like many educators we have worked with, they were willing to take on this position because they could see that the school was finally committing to making constructive use of assessment data, and they wanted to play a role in this important transition. Principal Roger Bolton expressed his understanding of the time commit-ment they would be making by exempting data managers from other administrative responsibilities, such as supervising study halls and afterschool activities.

At Clark K–8 School, which serves 450 students in kindergarten through eighth grade, principal Sandy Jenkins asked her assistant principal, Bob Walker, to assume the role of data manager. Bob had a strong interest and aptitude in the technical aspects of using data, and after some discussion agreed to focus his skills not on completing the work quickly but rather on building the capacity of Clark's teachers to use technology to analyze student assessment results. He agreed to work closely with two teacher-leaders over the school year, one from the elementary grades and one from the middle school grades, to ensure that data expertise was not limited to school administration.

Our experience working with schools has shown us that unless school leaders—principals in particular—are willing to champion the cause of analyzing data regularly and using the results to make decisions for the school, data work will not become a meaningful part of schoolwide reform. As a school leader, the best way to keep in touch with the teams is by regularly sitting in on the various team meetings. By making yourself part of the conversation, you send the message that this work is central to your leadership mission and part of the decision-making process for the entire school. However, you may want to carefully consider what role to take in data discussions. Because the purpose of such discussions is to allow your faculty to interpret and construct their own meaning from school data, you will want to take care not to allow your own views to silence the group.

However, you can use other strategies to stay informed even when you can't be there. For example, if you read the notes from a sampling of the meetings that occur in a particular week, you can stay abreast of the conversations that are going on, make sure that information is flowing freely between those teams and the school leadership, and note when teaching teams need assistance. When the principal in one school we've worked with reviewed the notes from the weekly second-grade team meeting, she learned that the teachers were struggling to schedule an author's breakfast at which their students would display their work to their parents and the rest of the school. This information enabled the principal to step in and help the teaching team find a time that worked with the schoolwide calendar. The team's effort to share rich evidence of student learning with families benefited from timely assistance from the principal. Subsequently, they were able to devote their team meeting time to discussing instructional, instead of logistical, issues.

Finally, you can make sure that something happens as a result of all this talk. Once your faculty starts to see that the questions they investigate and insights they gain from looking at data are used to help make decisions about how school resources are allocated and what gets done, you may find that the shift toward a "culture of inquiry" becomes easier and easier to acheive.

Make Time for Collaborative Work

Time is perhaps the scarcest resource in schools. And the only thing more difficult than finding time for an individual to concentrate on a particular task is finding time for groups of people to work together! The team structure you employ for carrying out the work of improvement will determine in large part how time will be used for this work. Fortunately, in recent years many schools have reorganized their schedules to allow for common planning time so that teams of teachers (often called communities of practice or professional learning communities) can meet together. We have found that meeting at least twice a month for collaborative planning seems to work well for schools. If your school has already set aside this time, then your task will involve making sure that the work that takes place during these meetings is tethered to your improvement process and grounded in action, collaboration, and evidence.

If your current schedule does not allow for all teachers to meet at least twice a month on a team dedicated to working collaboratively to improve learning and teaching, you may have to wait until the next semester or grading period to reorganize. In the meantime, you can try to repurpose some of the time you have already set aside. While the work of improvement should occur all year long, it is particularly helpful to have time for concentrated data work at certain points. For example, some schools find data analysis most useful at either the end or the beginning of the school year, when conversations can meaningfully inform long-term instructional planning. Schools might also concentrate heavily on data analysis and discussion in January or February, when teachers can think about midyear adjustments. Some schools find that scheduling full- or half-day retreats with all or part of the faculty is an effective way to engage the staff in intensive data work.

School leaders must make time in the yearly schedule for collaborative meetings. But how can you "make" time? We have seen a number of schools design creative schedules that allow groups of teachers to work together during the school day by being very deliberate in deciding when teachers will not have classroom responsibilities. One middle school designed a schedule in which teachers could meet during the school day by grade level on Mondays, Wednesdays, or Fridays, and by content area on Tuesdays or Thursdays. Teachers decided which day of the week to meet, and then met weekly with their grade-level and content-area teams. At another school, the principal decided that teachers would participate in data discussions during paid afterschool professional development time with their departmental teams. A third school scheduled a 90-minute block every Friday morning for teachers to work together. Many other schools use early-release or late-start days for this work.

SETTING THE TONE

With the framing structures in place, you can turn to setting the tone for *how* people will work together. Three concrete things you can do to support this are to set expectations for effective meetings, set norms for collaborative work, and acknowledge the work style preferences of team members.

Set Expectations for Effective Meetings

Just because you've set aside time for collaborative work doesn't necessarily mean that time will be used effectively. A powerful strategy for making sure that your precious time is used well is to establish a schoolwide format for meeting agendas. One school we worked with documented their strategy for structuring effective teacher-led meetings.[2] In our work in a variety of settings, we have come to appreciate that strong agendas have clearly stated objectives, strategies for making sure all voices are heard, and dedicated time for capturing next steps and discussing how to make the next meeting even better. Good agendas also offer clear stop and start times and distinct roles—such as facilitator, timekeeper and notetaker—that involve many participants in making sure the meeting runs smoothly.

Good agendas often include explicit strategies for helping groups work together. Throughout this book we refer to these strategies as "protocols," a term we learned from a terrific book called *The Power of Protocols: An Educator's Guide to Better Practice.* In this book, Joseph McDonald and his colleagues describe a protocol as a way of organizing interactions among group members. They then offer brief descriptions of more than 20 protocols that educators can use to make their discussions more effective. Some of the protocols we mention in these pages are ones that we learned from this book, some we learned from other educators, and quite a few we designed ourselves. Our hope is that one day we will be hearing from *you* about the powerful protocols that help you work collaboratively with peers.

While some people initially dislike both the "touchy-feely" and rule-bound aspects of protocols, in our experience most educators ultimately embrace them once they see how protocols can make groups function more smoothly. By providing structure, protocols lead to conversations that often deal with much deeper issues while maintaining a nonthreatening atmosphere. Throughout this book, we will show how Clark K–8 School and Franklin High School use protocols to help with the various tasks involved in using data well.

At Franklin High School, Roger and team leader Inés Romero knew that if they were going to get teachers on board with the new focus on using data, the first faculty meeting of the year would be a great time to give the staff a positive, hands-on data experience. So they planned carefully how they would structure the meeting. They wanted to have everyone involved in looking at real data but didn't want to overwhelm them. They wanted to plan an activity that was manageable for the time available and would generate thoughtful discussion.

Inés and Roger agreed that at the first all-school meeting of the year, they would share a handful of easy-to-read charts summarizing Franklin High School's performance on the state test. Then they would organize the faculty into small, cross-grade groups for the first half hour of the meeting to talk about what they saw in the data. Each group would share its major findings and record them on chart paper. In the last half hour they would have teachers follow a structured protocol for formulating questions about why the data looked the way they did. They hoped that if everything went according to plan, at the end of the meeting the faculty would have arrived at some consensus about the most pressing questions that Franklin High would need to address in the coming year.

In our experience, the most effective meetings are as carefully planned as any good classroom lesson. For the schoolwide meeting described above, Inés and Roger planned ahead to ensure the faculty would work on an engaging task. For teacher team meetings, it is equally important that the person facilitating the meeting come prepared with a reasonable agenda, with handouts containing helpful data summaries, and with specific tasks that teachers are expected to complete before the end of the meeting. The structure provided by these "lesson plans" helps teachers stay focused on manageable tasks that may push the boundaries of their experience, but also give the group a powerful sense of accomplishment. When these accomplishments are captured by the meeting's recorder in readily available notes, the meeting becomes a documented component of an ongoing improvement process.

Set Norms for Collaborative Work

When Inés Romero opened the first meeting of the year of the Franklin High School instructional leadership team, her colleagues were surprised to see her writing the word "norms" on a big piece of poster paper. As director of instruction, Inés had been leading meetings at the school for years. Was she suddenly going to try to change the way they did business?

"We're all used to having our test scores turned on us as a weapon," Inés began. "The press does it. The superintendent does it. Parents do it. But that's not how it's going to be inside these four walls. If we're really going to learn from our data, we are going to have to work together in ways we never have before. So I'd like us to start by agreeing on the kind of atmosphere we want to create for ourselves in our meetings.

"To get us started, I'd like to see us adopt a group norm of 'no blame,'" she continued. "When we look at the numbers, let's not use them to point fingers at each other. But I don't want to just stand here making rules; I'd like to hear from everyone." Inés passed out little pads of sticky notes and asked the teachers to each write down three norms they would like to see the group live by. By having teachers express their views on paper, she freed them to make suggestions they might not have been comfortable making out loud. Then she asked team members to group the responses on the poster paper and opened a discussion about which of the recommendations teachers felt ready to adopt.

Looking at data in groups can be an intimidating process for teachers who perhaps don't know how to look at data or who may worry that data will be used to blame them for weaknesses in their students' performance. Inés was beginning the important work of creating a productive environment for collaborative discussions of data by encouraging her team to set ground rules for how members would participate in discussions. Agreeing on norms like "no blame" is an essential first step in creating an atmosphere that supports productive data discussions. It is important to emphasize from the beginning that data will not be used to punish teachers, but to help them figure out how to teach their students more effectively.[3]

Another reason for setting norms is that many teachers have very little experience looking at data and may lack confidence in their ability to understand the numbers. They may resist participating in data discussions out of fear that they do not know how to analyze data the "right way." To deal with this issue, some schools we have worked with establish a norm that all team members approach their work in the role of learner. Understanding that discussions of data are opportunities to explore and learn can make teachers feel more comfortable. One principal we know emphasized the importance of understanding his teachers' individual learning needs with regard to data use. He provided one-on-one help to teachers who needed it, and strove to find leadership roles for those with significant knowledge.

This differentiated support helped lower the barriers for teachers and emphasized the principal's willingness to make the process less intimidating.

There are myriad protocols for setting norms, many of which can be found on the Data Wise Project website. Some involve starting with a blank slate and allowing norms to evolve from the group. Other protocols call for proposing a set of norms, then allowing a group to discuss them. In some settings, we have found it helpful to offer the following three norms, which have been particularly effective in supporting teams as they use the Data Wise Improvement Process and cultivate the ACE Habits of Mind:

- Assume positive intentions

- Take an inquiry stance

- Ground statements in evidence

We start by clarifying what we mean by each norm and then discussing what it would look like if it were followed. For example, we explain that the first norm asks us to start by assuming everyone in the group is acting out of a desire to work toward our shared goal of helping all students learn. Much as the law of "innocent until proven guilty" supports our society, the norm of believing colleagues are "of good will unless proven otherwise" can support openness to diverse viewpoints. This norm is more internal than the other two; when followed it is experienced as a silent reminder to oneself: *this person wants to do well by children too.*

We explain that the second norm challenges individuals to ask questions that allow insight into a colleague's point of view. To put this norm into practice, we often recommend that team members use sentence starters such as, "What led you to conclude . . . ?" "I'm hearing you say . . . is that correct?" and the simple but often effective, "I'm wondering what you mean by . . . ?" At first these words can feel forced. But in time they can become such a natural part of the way the group communicates that people hardly realize they are using them.

The norm of sticking to evidence means making a conscious effort to cite data and offer a rationale when explaining one's point of view. Sentence starters such as, "I see . . . ," "I noticed that . . . ," and "I saw evidence of . . . " can make it more likely that statements are not laced with adjectives and proclamations. We often point out that this norm can be hard to follow, and encourage participants to support one another in using it by feeling free to ask, "Where's your evidence?"

Once we have laid out these norms and allowed for some discussion, we typically ask the group if someone cannot live with any one of these norms, or cannot live without a norm not on this list. Sometimes this leads to further discussion and modification of the list. Other times, no one speaks up and we move on by telling people that we will go forward with these norms and will regularly check in about the extent to which we are following them.

Acknowledge Work Style Preferences

We have made the case that the work of improvement needs to happen in teams. But we have seen that individuals' ideas about what it means to be a productive member of a team can be quite varied. One protocol we have used to get at this variance is called the Compass Points Protocol.[4] This protocol provides an excellent opportunity for members of a group to get to know one another while learning important information about their preferred working styles. In this protocol, individuals choose one of four characterizations that best describes their orientation when working on a team. People who identify as "North" like to jump into action right away. "West" corresponds with wanting to pay attention to details before acting, while "East" is for people who need the big picture before acting and "South" is for people who like to know that everyone's perspectives have been taken into consideration before acting. People with similar preferences work together to create a chart that summarizes—among other things—the strengths and limitations of their style. When these groups report to the whole group, there are always many insights and many laughs. We find that in addition to breaking the ice, the protocol helps a group of people get to know each other (even groups that have worked together before) and build tolerance for differences that might cause tensions in collaborative work—but are also essential for doing good work.

Perhaps the most valuable thing about this protocol is that it provides you and your colleagues with a language to talk about the different ways you approach group work and an impetus to probe these deeper. It also helps you see which work style preferences are most prevalent and where there might be a need to bring on someone to fulfill a role that is lacking in the current group, or where the existing group may need to work to bring in a perspective that they would otherwise miss.

TAKING STOCK

The last set of foundational tasks involves taking stock of where you are; after all, school improvement does not happen in a vacuum. There are three dimensions to consider: What data do we already have? What initiatives are we already implementing? What is our current approach to improvement?

These questions are important to ask because, as we mentioned in the introduction to this book, the Data Wise Improvement Process is not a "program" to "implement" but rather a means of organizing and bringing coherence to the work of improvement that you already do. Most educators are weary of being bombarded with new programs. If you engage your colleagues in describing the current environment, you can help to show that wise data practices are not "one more thing" but *the* thing that unifies your collective efforts.

Create a Data Inventory

When principal Sandy Jenkins announced at her first faculty meeting that this year's school improvement planning process would focus on learning from data, nobody clapped.

"Spending so much time on the state test just feels like such a waste," began a fourth-grade teacher. "Our school has one of the highest passing rates in the district; I don't understand what all the fuss is about."

"They may be passing all right," responded a seventh- and eighth-grade English language arts teacher, "but they're not exactly knocking the socks off the test either. But that is not what bothers me. The problem is that the test gives such an incomplete picture of who our students are. It tells us essentially nothing about a lot of the things we all know really matter: how often they come to school, how they behave when they're here, what specific skills they're struggling with if they are new to learning English, whether they can write a decent term paper, whether they are curious, independent learners. We're not going to be able to figure out how to get our kids beyond simply passing if we don't take these things into account."

"Well then, let's broaden our definition of data," Sandy replied. "Somehow, I bet someone in our school has collected data on all of the things you just mentioned. From what you've all told me, it seems there is an assessment of some kind being made nearly every week around here. I think part of the problem is that, as a school, we are not even sure what kinds of data are available to us."

Ask any teacher if she feels that her students are tested enough, or any school secretary if her school keeps track of enough types of student information. Enough? Most educators are likely to laugh! However, although a great deal of time is spent collecting data, most schools lack a big-picture view of exactly what data they have. A simple but powerful way of seeing this big picture is to create a data inventory like the one the Clark K–8 School instructional leadership team created in Exhibits 1.2a and 1.2b.

Exhibit 1.2a

				Clark K–8 School Data Inventory: External Assessments		
DATA SOURCE	**CONTENT AREA**	**DATES OF COLLECTION**	**STUDENTS ASSESSED**	**ACCESSIBILITY**	**CURRENT DATA USE**	**MORE EFFECTIVE USE**
STATE SKILL MASTERY ASSESSMENT	Reading; English language arts; Math	May (results in October)	Grades 3, 4, 5, 6, 7, 8	Intranet; principal	Instructional leadership team analyzes data, looks for discrepancies and trends, and considers current curriculum and instructional practice with grade-level teams and curriculum coaches	Get all data on one sheet per child, including nonacademic data (student attendance, health issues, etc.)
OBSERVATION SURVEY	Reading	October January May	Grade K	Intranet; teacher	Student benchmarking and retention decisions	Inform instruction
DEVELOPMENTAL READING ASSESSMENT (DRA)	Reading	September January May; each trimester until at benchmark	Grades 1, 2, 3	Intranet; teacher	Student benchmarking and retention decisions	Inform instruction
STANFORD 9	Reading; Math	September	Grades 3, 4, 5	District	Gifted/talented eligibility determinations	Item analysis
ENGLISH PROFICIENCY ASSESSMENTS	English	September; student entry	Grades K–8	Teacher; principal	Student placement and accommodations	Track scores to find out time to proficiency
DISTRICT MATH ASSESSMENT	Math	January May	Grades K–8	District; principal	Student benchmarking determinations	Discuss scores with students

A data inventory provides a summary of all the types of data that are available in your school. If you regularly update your inventory and make it available electronically, you can ensure that it becomes a living document. You may find that putting this information together in one place helps your school develop a comprehensive picture of data resources and needs, which may jumpstart your thinking about the kinds of questions that data can be used to answer.

It is helpful for a data inventory to include information about three types of data sources: external assessments, internal assessments, and other student-level information. External assessments are those required by outside agents, such as district, state, and federal education agencies. Perhaps the most obvious example of an external data source is your state-mandated educational assessment, such as the State Skill Mastery Assessment listed at the beginning of Clark K–8 School's table, or nationally developed and district-mandated tests, such as benchmark or interim assessments. High schools may include the Scholastic Aptitude Test (SAT) and Advanced Placement (AP) exams, among other assessments, in their

Exhibit 1.2b

Clark K–8 School Data Inventory: Internal Assessments						
DATA SOURCE	**CONTENT AREA**	**DATES OF COLLECTION**	**STUDENTS ASSESSED**	**ACCESSIBILITY**	**CURRENT DATA USE**	**MORE EFFECTIVE USE**
READING CHECKLISTS	Reading	January May	Grades K–1	Intranet; teacher	Student benchmarking and retention decisions	Coached discussion about how results inform instruction
RUNNING RECORDS	Reading	January May	Grades 1–3	Teacher	Student benchmarking determinations	Grade-level analysis and conversation
WRITING SAMPLES	Writing	Formally in October and January; in school, about once a month	Grades K–8	Teacher	Looking at student work sessions between coaches and grade-level teachers; mini-lesson strategy development	Track rubric scores over time; create standard grade-level rubric
UNIT ASSESSMENTS	Math	Periodic when units are complete	Grades K–8	Teacher summary sheets	Teachers use to identify student math difficulties	Track data over time to ensure children gain necessary skills
OTHER STUDENT-LEVEL INFORMATION						
• Race/ethnicity • English proficiency		• Disability • Retention		• Attendance • Socioeconomic status (reduced-priced lunch)		
Data Wish List						
• Date entered school		• Number of years in U.S.		• Measures of 21st century skills		

inventories. Internal assessments are instruments developed at your school, such as all-school writing prompts, science fair project assessments, and end-of-unit tests. These assessments are often designed, collected, and scored by individual teachers or groups of teachers. Other useful student-level information includes demographic and background data, such as that listed at the bottom of the Clark K–8 School inventory. Schools also often find it helpful to include a category for types of data they wish they had but do not currently collect. For example, teachers may want to know how well their students demonstrate twenty-first century skills, such as expert thinking or complex communication. Inviting teachers to contribute to a "data wish list" can encourage them to think creatively about what kinds of data could help them get a better picture of their students.

Once you've decided which data sources to include, you must also decide what descriptive information you should list about each source. The column headings of the Clark K–8 School inventory show types of descriptive information that can be particularly helpful. In addition to naming the data source, the inventory shows the content area of the source, dates of collection, and students assessed. Deciding how to fill in the final three columns—which identify who is allowed to see the data, what they are currently used for, and how they might be used more effectively—can get your faculty thinking critically about whether you are making the most of the information you have.

You may find that the process of putting together a data inventory leads your data team to create an assessment calendar. Such a calendar specifies in advance dates on which assessment administration, data collection, and data dissemination will take place and indicates who is responsible for recording, collecting, and compiling the data from each assessment. When you have a good handle on the kinds of information that will become available throughout the year and when, you may find it easier to begin planning how to use your data effectively.

Create an Inventory of Instructional Initiatives

It is important to acknowledge what is already happening instructionally in your school before planning any improvements. Instructional initiatives are programs that the school has consciously put in place to meet an instructional need. These initiatives can be implemented by the teachers of a particular grade or department or can be targeted at a particular student group. Sometimes the initiative pertains to the whole school. The inventory for Franklin High School presented in Exhibit 1.3 shows one way to capture this information in an easy-to-understand format.

As Franklin's inventory shows, this document can be used to capture several types of information. Many schools we have worked with are surprised to see how many programs they have, and by listing them all in one place they have discovered that some initiatives are redundant or contradictory. When the Franklin instructional leadership team created this table, it was surprised to find many schoolwide initiatives devoted to literacy instruction, few to math, and none at all to improving instruction for students with strong academic skills.

Take Stock of Where You Are with Improvement

Once you have selected a process to use schoolwide, you will want to introduce it to staff members and give them a chance to connect it to their experience. To do this, develop a strategy for actively engaging staff members in learning the eight steps of the Data Wise Improvement Process (see the Stoplight Protocol on the Data Wise Project website). In this protocol, individuals independently evaluate the extent to which they believe the school is currently carrying out each step and then discuss how perceptions of the school's approach differ across individuals. This gets people

Exhibit 1.3

Franklin High School Inventory of Instructional Initiatives					
NAME OF INSTRUCTIONAL INITIATIVE	INTENDED TO BE IMPLEMENTED BY	FRACTION OF THE RELEVANT TEACHERS WHO ARE IMPLEMENTING 4=All (100%) 3=Most (>75%) 2=Some (25–75%) 1=Few (<25%)	AMONG IMPLEMENTING FACULTY, EXTENT OF IMPLEMENTATION 4=Completely 3=Mostly 2=Partially 1=Just beginning	EVIDENCE OF IMPLEMENTATION	OTHER EVIDENCE THAT WOULD BE HELPFUL TO COLLECT
COLLABORATIVE COACHING AND CLASSROOM VISITS	All teachers	3	4	Conversations with instructional coaches	Survey of teachers; classroom visits
FOCUS ON WRITING	All English language arts teachers	4	3	Whole school writing prompt	Student focus groups
WORKSHOP MODEL	All English language arts teachers	3	2	Teacher survey	Classroom visits; evaluations
DAILY JOURNALING	Homeroom teachers	Don't know	Don't know	Don't know	Class visits; student journals; student focus groups
RESPECT PROGRAM	Social studies teachers	2	Don't know	Informal conversations	Classroom visits; student projects
TEST PREP FOR STATE EXAM	15 teachers	4	4	Informal conversations	Classroom visits; curriculum overview

talking about their current approach to improvement and where they want to be. This conversation is often a powerful motivator for people to want to learn more about how their various efforts can be more deliberate and coordinated.

It also can be helpful to name the specific data practices that are already ongoing at your school and see how they map to the steps of the Data Wise Improvement Process. The Coherence Protocol is a strategy for helping teams appreciate in a very visual way that the Data Wise Improvement Process can help integrate the work of the school into a coherent whole. (The Coherence Protocol is available in Selected Protocols and on the Data Wise website.) We typically use it immediately after the Stoplight Protocol, and we encourage participants to apply what they learned from the Stoplight to inform their thinking. In this protocol, staff members write each of the school's data practices on a separate sticky note. Practices could include "data walls in every corridor," "bimonthly meetings to discuss interim assessment results," and "the school action plan template." The next steps are to put up a large poster of the Data Wise Improvement Process and have team members place each sticky note near the step(s) of the cycle where they think it belongs (see Exhibit 1.4 for an example from Clark K–8 School). Seeing how existing practices fit into the process as a whole then leads into a conversation about areas of redundant or contradictory effort, as well as parts of the Data Wise Improvement Process that may not be addressed at all by your current practices. It also shows staff members how much they might already be doing with data or school improvement, and this honors their previous efforts and current work. Allowing this conversation to take place can be an important step in ensuring that integration is the goal that everyone is shooting for.

Exhibit 1.4

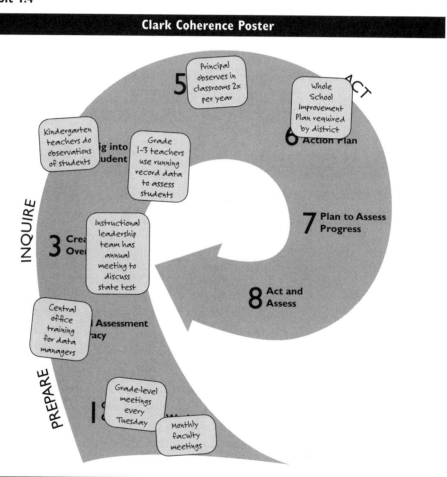

Integrating the ACE Habits of Mind into Step 1: Organizing for Collaborative Work

As we described in the introduction to this book, our work with schools over the past decade has shown us that using data to improve instruction involves much more than checking off the eight steps of the Data Wise Improvement Process. As a backdrop to these steps, it is essential that you cultivate three habits of mind that allow the real transformative work to occur. Below we offer some ideas for weaving the ACE Habits of Mind into this first step.

SHARED COMMITMENT TO ACTION, ASSESSMENT, AND ADJUSTMENT

This step may look like it involves mostly behind-the-scenes housekeeping, but it entails plenty of action items. A data inventory, a map of your school's team structure, and a standard agenda format are all artifacts you'll have produced after going through Step 1. You probably don't want to laminate any of these, however. Until you actually use the tools you create, you won't be able to assess their effectiveness and make the adjustments needed so that they really support your work. For example, the Data Wise Project team found that our initial meeting agenda template left out one important piece that we didn't appreciate until we tried having several meetings without it: our agenda didn't allow any time for us to check in with one another to see how each of us was doing on that particular day. Hurtling into the objectives without first recognizing one another as people—one of whom may have had an emotional encounter with a student, another who's bursting with the news about her child who just got into college, and a third whose allergies kept him up all night—was actually keeping us from doing our best work. Acting, assessing, and adjusting allowed us to fine-tune the way we organized ourselves, and now we begin all our meetings with a five-minute check-in.

INTENTIONAL COLLABORATION

On the Data Wise Improvement Process, Step 1 is located in the wide base area of the arrow. When the arrow curves in on itself, it appears to skip over the Prepare tasks for subsequent trips around the cycle. However, it is important to keep in mind that no matter where you are in the process, you are always revisiting and refreshing the foundational work you did to organize for improvement.

This is particularly true of group norms. When you begin collaborating, it is essential to set aside time to establish the ways in which you will work together. But this conversation is only the starting point, and it is wasted if you do not continually refer back to the norms as your work evolves. We have seen schools use several strategies for making sure that their norms are a living document and their collaboration is always intentional. One approach involves starting every second or third meeting by revisiting norms and asking the group to offer concrete evidence that a particular norm has or has not been followed. This often presses the question of, "What do we do when we break our own norms?" If the answer is "nothing," then the norms are not worth the chart paper they are written on. If the answer is "we figure out why we are not upholding a norm and we brainstorm how we will address it," then the group is on its way to becoming increasingly more intentional in its collaborative work.

In groups that have established a level of trust, individuals can solicit the help of the group in upholding norms that they find particularly challenging. We saw one facilitator begin a norms conversation by giving a minute of reflection time in which she asked individuals to select one of the group norms that they personally would like to get better at following. She then had people write that norm on an oversized index card and fold the card so it would stand up in front of where they were sitting. Making the challenges public in this way led to lots of laughter as team members called one another out: "Hey Mike, how's that sharing airtime norm going?"

RELENTLESS FOCUS ON EVIDENCE

Even when there are no assessments on the table, teams that embody this habit of mind find ways to practice using evidence to ground all of their conversations. Believe it or not, you can start building this habit on the very first day you assemble a group! The Inquiring Introductions Protocol is designed to allow people get to know one another while at the same time helping them to practice the skill of asking questions and offering illuminating answers.[5] The steps are simple: the "introducer" gives his or her name and answers a prompt, such as, "How did you get involved in education?" The person to the introducer's left replies by asking a question directly related to what he or she heard, and the introducer answers this question. Then a third person asks a new question directly related to the response just heard. In their questions, people are encouraged to use sentence starters that help keep conversations grounded, such as "Can you give me an example of what you mean?" and "What led you to that conclusion?" These questions build the muscle of maintaining a relentless focus on evidence as well as using that evidence for further inquiry.

Participants have told us that they are amazed at how carefully this protocol makes them listen. They have also remarked on how deeply they come to understand someone else's experience when permission to ask for evidence is explicitly granted. Questions like, "Can you give me an example of a science lesson in which you really connected with your students?" or "What led you to decide that you were more interested in teaching younger children?" provide windows into someone's experience that the typical get-to-know-you protocol does not offer.

2

BUILDING ASSESSMENT LITERACY

Jennifer Price and Daniel M. Koretz

"WELL, IF WE'RE GOING TO GET SERIOUS ABOUT DATA," CLARK K–8 SCHOOL PRINCIPAL Sandy Jenkins thought to herself, "I'm going to need to get serious about understanding all these reports I get." She started poring over the assessment results. Within minutes, frustration set in.

"Apparent differences in scaled scores may not be statistically or educationally significant," one manual read.[1] She then turned to another and was told that these results should not be used "to decide which instructional objectives should be taught at a certain grade level."[2] A third explained that "the results are most useful when they are considered in combination with other information about the student population and the educational system, such as trends in instruction, changes in the school-age population, funding levels, and societal demands and expectations."[3]

With all this fine print, Sandy wondered how she would be able to guide her teachers in understanding what test scores mean and how they could be used appropriately. She knew there were plenty of assessment experts out there, but she didn't have the time or interest to become one herself. "If only someone would just tell me in plain English the key concepts that I need to know," Sandy mused, "then I could get on with finding out what these test results have to tell me about our kids."

When you look through the assessment reports for your school, it can sometimes feel as if they are written in a different language. So many terms, so many caveats, so many footnotes! As a school leader, how can you help your faculty begin to make sense of it all? Our experience is that if you develop a working knowledge of the key concepts described in this chapter, you will be in a good position to help your faculty develop assessment literacy.

A STYLIZED EXAMPLE

Assume that you confront the following challenge. As head of the English language arts department at your high school, you have been asked to select a senior to send to a national tournament that tests participants' vocabulary skills. Because the prizes include large college scholarships, many students in your school would like to be selected. Of course, you want to select a student who has a particularly strong vocabulary to maximize the chance that the student you choose will win the tournament. You decide to use several different indicators to select the contestant, one of which will be students' scores on a vocabulary test. Designing an exhaustive test would be difficult because even a typical high school graduate has a vocabulary of more than 10,000 root words.[4] The only practical option would be to test the students on a small sample of words that they might know.

Let's assume that you have to construct the test and assume that you will need 40 words. You are given three lists from which to choose words. The first three words from each list are the following:

A	B	C
siliculose	bath	feckless
vilipend	travel	disparage
epimysium	carpet	minuscule

For each list, the words not shown are roughly similar in difficulty to those you see. It is obvious that one would learn nothing useful about an applicant's vocabulary skills from a test using the words in lists A or B. List A contains highly unusual, specialized words that few if any of the applicants are likely to know. Because all of the applicants would do extremely poorly on such a test, one would learn essentially nothing about the relative strength of their vocabularies. Conversely, list B is made up of extremely easy words that all high school seniors would know, which means that a test based on list B would similarly provide no useful information. Consequently, you would choose list C, which consists of words that are of middling difficulty. Some students would know any given word, while others would not. Only the use of list C would allow you to differentiate between the applicants with stronger and weaker vocabularies.

For the sake of this exercise, and for reasons we explain below, assume you decide to replace one word in list C, being careful to select another word that is on average as difficult as the original. For example, say you substitute "parsimonious" for "feckless." You quickly realize that this substitution may alter the ranking of applicants, even though the new word is no harder or easier than the old. One person might know "feckless" but not "parsimonious," while another applicant with a comparable vocabulary might know "parsimonious" but not "feckless."

PRINCIPLES FOR INTERPRETING ASSESSMENT RESULTS

This brief exercise illustrates a number of fundamental principles that are essential for the appropriate interpretation of students' test scores.

Sampling Principle of Testing

The first and most fundamental of these principles could be called the sampling principle of testing. Most achievement testing is aimed at reaching conclusions about students' proficiency in a broad domain of achievement. In our example, the domain is vocabulary; it might be any other common subject area, such as sixth-grade reading or eighth-grade mathematics. You cannot possibly measure proficiency in such domains exhaustively because they are so large. You must instead create a small sample of the domain and measure each student's proficiency on that sample.

Because a test is not a direct measure of a student's degree of mastery of an entire domain, any conclusion you reach about proficiency in that domain is based on an inference from proficiency on the smaller sample. The quality of that inference—that is, the degree to which the inference is supported by performance on the test—is what is meant by validity. This is why measurement experts say that validity is an attribute of an inference based on test scores, not an attribute of the test itself. Even a test that provides good support for one inference may provide weak support for another. For example, an end-of-course algebra test may provide a solid basis for inferences about mastery of basic algebra, but it would not provide a valid basis for inferences about mastery of all of high school mathematics.

Discrimination

The choice of word lists illustrates a second principle, the importance of test items that discriminate. In the parlance of testing, "discriminate" means "differentiate" and has no negative implications. An item that discriminates is simply more likely to be answered correctly by students with a higher level of proficiency in the domain of interest—in this case, students with larger working vocabularies—than by those with lower proficiency. When you want to draw inferences about relative levels of proficiency, you need items that discriminate. There are other types of inferences for which discrimination is not important. For example, if one wants to know how many students have mastered a specific, discrete skill, an item that most students will answer either correctly or incorrectly and that therefore cannot discriminate may be acceptable. For inferences about variations in proficiency, however, one typically wants items that discriminate. Furthermore, one usually needs discriminating items in order to obtain accurate information about whether a student has successfully reached a performance standard. Using discriminating items does not create differences in proficiency, as some critics argue. Rather, discriminating items are used to reveal differences that already exist. Whether that is good or bad depends on the inference the test is used to support. For example, if you simply want to know whether a class has mastered a list of new terms for a chemistry class, you may not be concerned about ranking students and you may want to include items that all or nearly all of the students can answer correctly. However, in the vocabulary example, and in all cases where scores are used to shed light on differences in students' performance, discriminating items are essential.

Measurement Error

The substitution of "parsimonious" for "feckless," as in the example earlier, demonstrates a third principle: measurement error. Measurement error refers to inconsistencies in scores across various "instances of measurement," such as multiple examinations. One source of measurement error, illustrated by our vocabulary example, is inconsistencies that arise when various forms of a test employ different samples of items. Another source of measurement error is inconsistencies in people's behavior over time. For example, a student might be better rested one day than another, or less distracted, or even ill. When students take a test such as the SAT more than once, their scores will typically vary as a result of both of these types of measurement error. When tests require scoring by people, a third source of measurement error is the inconsistencies between individual scorers or by a single scorer over time. Clearly, measurement error can cause scores to be inconsistent.

Reliability

The flip side of measurement error is our fourth principle: reliability. Reliability refers to the degree of consistency of measurement. A reliable measure is one that gives you nearly the same answer time after time, while an unreliable measure is inconsistent. If you have a cheap bathroom scale, for example, the chances are that it is not terribly reliable. You might appear to be two pounds under your target one time and at your target 30 seconds later, when you try again.

In our example, the substitution of "parsimonious" for "feckless" is analogous to your stepping on the scale twice: the two tests are two different "instances of measurement" that are intended to measure the same thing. Yet, the scores and ranking of candidates probably differ. If you asked the candidates to take 100 different tests with similarly difficult words, this difference would wash out over time. The test score is not systematically biased; it is simply variable from time to time. As a result of this variability, however, the score on one particular test is not necessarily a reliable measure of the candidate's true abilities. The key to understanding reliability is that the greater the measurement error, the lower the reliability. Clearly, you would want to design a vocabulary test that was quite reliable if applicants' scores were to play a large role in deciding who was chosen to send to the national competition.

Score Inflation

Up to this point, this hypothetical example mirrors "low-stakes" testing—that is, testing without serious consequences for students or teachers, as is the case with much diagnostic testing. When testing has high stakes, however, we also have to consider how people respond to this pressure and what effect that has on the use of scores. As an extreme example, suppose that someone intercepted each of the applicants on the way to your testing session and taught them all of the words on your vocabulary test. This example brings you face to face with the final principle: score inflation—that is, increases in scores that do not indicate a commensurate increase in actual proficiency. If someone taught the applicants the specific words in the tested sample, their scores would no longer tell you anything about the relative vocabularies of the applicants. Most applicants would get very high scores, regardless of their actual vocabularies. Real-world score inflation is often less extreme than this hypothetical case—which many people would consider simple cheating—but the principle is the same.

A FEW KEY ASSESSMENT ISSUES

In the rest of this chapter, we use "score" to mean a test score—that is, any form of score that describes a student's or a group's performance on a test, such as a percentage correct or an SAT score of 625. Test results are sometimes reported with scores for portions of the test (often called subtests) as well. For example, some achievement tests provide an overall math score as well as scores for several subtests, such as math concepts or computation. Sometimes people use the term "item score" to refer to performance on a single test item. To avoid confusion, however, we will never use "score" to refer to performance on a single item.

Accounting for Sampling Error and Measurement Error

To varying degrees, all assessment results exhibit measurement error, as already discussed, and they may contain sampling error as well. You are likely to encounter the concept of measurement error in test score reports, although it is not always labeled as such. For example, the Massachusetts Department of Education has reported scores from its Massachusetts Comprehensive Assessment System (MCAS) as shown in Exhibit 2.1.

Exhibit 2.1

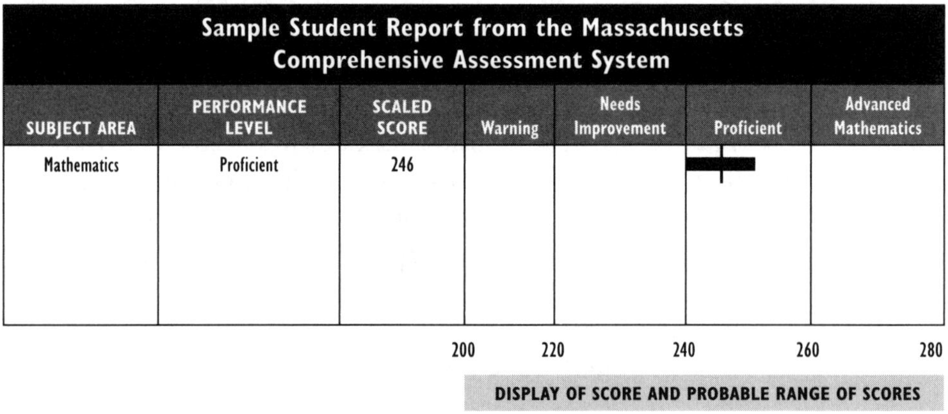

Sample Student Report from the Massachusetts Comprehensive Assessment System						
SUBJECT AREA	**PERFORMANCE LEVEL**	**SCALED SCORE**	**Warning**	**Needs Improvement**	**Proficient**	**Advanced Mathematics**
Mathematics	Proficient	246			┼	

	200	220	240	260	280

DISPLAY OF SCORE AND PROBABLE RANGE OF SCORES

The actual scale score (see explanation on page 43) this student received was a 246, which fell into the "Proficient" category. This scaled score is represented by the vertical line. The horizontal line (from 240 to 252) represents, in the words of the parents' test report guide, "the range of scores your child might receive if the tests were taken many times."[5] Because of measurement error, it would be a mistake to conclude that the student's score is precisely 246; perhaps it was too high this time, or too low. Therefore, the Massachusetts Department of Education has chosen to present a range of scores to illustrate the results one would get with repeated testing because of measurement error. In theory, the range could be of any width. If the range were made very wide, then the student's score would almost always fall within it. If the range were made very narrow— say from 244 to 248—the student, if tested over and over again, would often obtain a score outside of that range. Conventionally, for mathematical reasons, the range is most often wide enough so that if the student were tested repeatedly, 95 percent of the scores would fall within it; occasionally, however, you will find a narrower range that would encompass only about two-thirds of the scores the student would obtain.

Most people are more familiar with another kind of error that is analogous to measurement error: sampling error. While measurement error refers to inconsistency among multiple measures of a single person (or school, etc.), sampling error refers to inconsistency that arises from choosing the particular people (or schools) from whom to take measurements. For example, before every presidential election, we encounter polls showing that x percent of likely voters support a particular candidate, followed by a caveat such as, "These results have a margin of error of plus or minus three percentage points." If one conducted the poll repeatedly, using a different sample of likely voters each time, the results would vary from one sample to the next just by chance because one sample might happen to include a few extra conservatives and another might include a few extra liberals. The margin of error is simply a way to quantify how much the results would vary from one sample to the next. Just as in the example of measurement error above, the "margin of error" is often the percentage point range that would include the results of 95 percent of polls taken from different samples.

Sampling error is an important consideration when considering aggregate scores from classrooms or schools, such as average scores or the percentage of students who reach the "proficient" standard established by federal and state regulations. The cohort of students in any one year is often very different from those in previous years, and these differences among student cohorts cause scores to fluctuate substantially from one year to the next, even if the effectiveness of the school remains unchanged. This inconsistency tends to be particularly large when the performance of classrooms or small schools is described.

Keeping Test Scores in Perspective

In the vocabulary example, an applicant's score was based on a small sample of words that represented a much larger domain. In many cases, the sample included in a test is not only small, but also incomplete in systematic ways. There are many important outcomes of education that are difficult to test. Therefore, while a well-designed test can provide valuable information, there are many questions it cannot answer. How well does a person persevere in solving problems that take a long time and involve many false starts? To what extent has a student developed the dispositions we want—for example, a willingness to try applying what she has learned in math class to problems outside of school? How well does the student write long and complex papers requiring repeated revision? People demonstrate growth and proficiency in many ways that would not show up on any single test.

For more than half a century, many measurement experts have warned educators and others to be wary of the limitations in using scores. These warnings are not an argument against testing but a reminder to use tests sensibly. In fact, some of the clearest warnings about these limitations were written by the authors of widely used tests. Scores from a single standardized test provide a specialized form of information that is very useful. For example, a score on a standardized test is comparable from one school to another because any given score has the same meaning regardless of the school a student attends. This is not true of course grades, or even grades on teachers' own tests. For this reason alone, scores on standardized tests are valuable, but they must be viewed as complements to other information about students' performance. Indeed, it is an explicit axiom in the testing profession that significant decisions about a student should not be made on the basis of a single score. The importance of examining multiple sources of information about students' performance is a theme that will be repeated in different ways, not only in this chapter but throughout this book.

DIFFERENT WAYS OF REPORTING PERFORMANCE

Performance on tests is reported in many ways, and the various forms of reporting sometimes seem to offer different pictures of student achievement. Each way of reporting also has its own advantages and disadvantages. Therefore, understanding some of the most common ways of reporting is critical to learning useful lessons from student test scores.

The simplest way to report performance is with a raw score, which is simply a count or percentage of credits achieved on a test. This is the most common way to report internal assessments; all students are familiar with classroom tests that are graded in terms of the percentage of possible credit. Raw scores seem simple, but they are difficult to compare and interpret because they depend on the difficulty of the particular set of items included on the test. In other words, students with any given level of proficiency will get a higher raw score—number or percentage correct—if the test contains easy items, and a lower raw score if harder items are used. This is a common issue for teachers in schools in which the percentage correct is traditionally a cut score for a letter grade—for example, 90 percent or better gets an A. Teachers who grade this way can easily make some B students into A students (or vice versa) by changing the difficulty of their classroom tests. The same issue arises with external tests. Even if the developer tries to keep the difficulty of items consistent, they are likely to vary from test to test, causing misleading differences in raw scores.

Because raw scores are difficult to interpret without knowledge of the difficulty of the specific items on a test, performance on standardized tests is usually reported in terms of one or more types of scale scores, which we describe in more detail below. Even though the results of any test can be reported using many different types of scales, the scales emphasized in reporting performance should be related to the purposes of the test. We will next describe the main types of tests that are now in widespread use and then describe the types of scale scores often used to report results from those types of test.

Norm-Referenced Tests

Of the tests we consider here, the oldest type comprises major, commercially prepared national achievement tests such as the Iowa Tests of Basic Skills (ITBS), Stanford 9, and the Terra Nova. These tests are all norm-referenced tests (NRTs), which are tests that are designed to describe performance—often the performance of individual students, but in some cases that of schools, districts, states, or even countries—in terms of a distribution of performance. With an NRT, each person's (or school's) performance is reported in comparison to others. For example, the performance of a student would be reported in terms of how that student's performance compares to the distribution of performance of a sample of students nationwide. The group to which an individual is compared is called the norm group.

The simplest norm-referenced scale is the percentile rank, often abbreviated PR, which is simply the percentage of students in the norm group performing below a particular student's score. Thinking back to our vocabulary example, suppose a norm group took the test before you administered it to the candidates. Imagine further that 75 percent of the norm group answered fewer than 24 of the 40 questions correctly. All students who answer 24 items correctly (60% correct as a raw score) would be assigned a percentile rank of 75. Note that the percentile rank is not tied to the percentage correct. The percentile rank tells you where a student stands, but only relative to a specific comparison group taking a specific test. In our hypothetical example, the norm group includes all students taking the test, but it usually would be a nationally representative group or some other group chosen as a reasonable standard for comparison. When the comparison group is a nationally representative group of students, the percentile rank is often called the national percentile rank and is often abbreviated NPR.

For example, the first line of the ITBS report in Exhibit 2.2 indicates that first-grade students of the hypothetical Dalen County scored on average at the 59th percentile rank (NPR) on the ITBS vocabulary test. This result means that the average first grader in Dalen County scored higher than 59 percent of the students who comprised the nationally representative norm group.

The main advantages of the percentile rank are that it is familiar and easy to explain. The main drawback is less obvious: any given amount of improvement in performance can translate into varying changes in percentile ranks. Typically, most students have scores near the average, and a much smaller percentage have very high or very low scores. Therefore, a student near the average who makes a given amount of progress—for example, answering an additional three items correctly—will "pass by" many students, simply because many students have scores similar to hers. As a result, her percentile rank will increase substantially. In contrast, a student with a very high or very low score who answers an additional three items correctly will "pass by" fewer students because there are fewer in that range of scores. Consequently, her percentile rank will increase less.

Criterion-Referenced Tests

A second type of test is a criterion-referenced test (CRT). A CRT is meant to determine whether a student has mastered a defined set of skills or knowledge. In

Exhibit 2.2

An Iowa Tests of Basic Skills (ITBS) System Profile

		Grade:	1
		Level:	7
System:	DALEN COMMUNITY	Form:	K
Norms:	SPRING 1992	Test Date:	03/93
Order No.:	000-A33-76044-00-001	Page:	91

SS=Avg Scale Score
GE=Grade Equivalent of Avg SS
NCE=Avg Normal Curve Equivalent
NPR=PR of Avg SS: Nat'l Student Norms ( )

Avg N Att = Average Number Attempted
Avg %C = Average Percent Correct

TESTS N Tested = 255	SCORES					NATIONAL PERCENTILE RANKS
	N	SS	GE	NCE	NPR	Low Average High 1 10 20 30 40 50 60 70
Vocabulary	247	153.8	2.0	53.6	59	
Reading Comprehension	247	153.6	2.0	52.6	59	
Reading Total	247	153.7	2.0	52.8	58	
Listening	247	152.7	1.9	53.5	58	
Language	247	158.7	2.3	57.7	70	
Language Total	247	155.7	2.1	56.0	64	
Math Concepts	247	153.0	2.0	54.7	59	
Math Problems	247	151.0	1.9	50.7	53	
Math Total	247	152.0	2.0	52.6	55	
Core Total	247	153.8	2.0	53.6	58	
Social Studies	246	151.4	1.9	50.7	54	
Science	246	149.5	1.8	49.9	49	
Sources of Information	246	158.2	2.2	62.6	74	
Composite	246	153.5	1.9	54.1	60	
Word Analysis	247	155.8	2.2	54.3	62	
Math Computation	247	150.0	1.8	50.1	50	

Source: H. D. Hoover et al., *Iowa Tests of Basic Skills Interpretive Guide for School Administrators* (Chicago: Riverside, 1994): p. 102, Forms L and K, Levels 5–15.

the most common usage, CRT refers to a test that measures whether a student has reached a preestablished passing level, often called a cut score. For an example of a CRT, think back again to our vocabulary example. If the English language arts department chair decides that she will only consider students who score 35 or above on the test, it is no longer important whether a candidate scores 40 or 35. In either case, the candidate has passed. In this instance, the vocabulary test does not rank students and serves only to differentiate those who passed from those who failed. The most important examples of CRTs are the minimum-competency tests that many states and districts have imposed as graduation or promotion requirements.

Standards-Referenced Tests

The newest type of standardized assessment is most often called a standards-referenced or standards-based test (SRT). SRTs are developed by specifying content standards (what students should know and be able to do) and performance standards (how much of this content they are expected to know and be able to do). In terms of reporting, SRTs are very much like CRTs, except that in most instances three or four different performance levels are specified. (Many federal and state accountability statutes specify several performance levels, but in most cases, the target to meet the standard is called "proficient.") Some assessments set three performance standards and establish four ranges of performance: "Warning or Failing," "Needs Improvement," "Proficient," and "Advanced." The primary forms of reporting for these tests (although not necessarily the only ones) are reports that show the performance range into which an individual student falls and those that show the percentage of students who exceed one of the performance standards. For example, the parent receiving the report in Exhibit 2.1 is told that her child scores in the "Proficient" range. (The federal government requires that schools and states report performance in terms of the percentages of students reaching or exceeding the proficient standard.)

With a standards-based scale, information about performance within the ranges is not reported. For example, a student who improved from near the bottom of the "needs improvement" range to near the top of that range—a very large difference in many cases—would show no improvement. On the other hand, a student who progressed a very small amount but crossed a performance standard would be shown as having improved. Some states respond to this problem by reporting performance in an additional form. For example, some states use a scale score such as the one reported in Exhibit 2.1. However, to the extent that educators, the press, and policy makers rely on the standards-based scale itself—a common practice today—information about differences in performance between any two standards is obscured.

Standards-based scales have other limitations. The levels at which the standards are set depend on many factors, including the judgment of the panels assembled to set them, the particular method used to set them (there are many), and sometimes the characteristics of the test, such as the difficulty of items and the mix of item formats.

Key Observations on Reporting Standards

In practice, performance on any one of the types of tests described in Exhibit 2.3 may be reported in several ways, and the reporting is not entirely predictable from the type of test. For example, some commercial test companies have added performance standards to their NRTs, giving their customers the option of receiving both standards-referenced and norm-referenced reporting from a single NRT. In many cases, states construct scales for their SRTs that are very similar to those used with NRTs, and these scales are sometimes reported.

It is important to keep in mind that some of the scales that are used to report student scores are necessarily arbitrary. For example, there is no particular reason

Exhibit 2.3

Test Type Comparison		
TYPE OF TEST	**DEFINITION**	**EXAMPLES**
NORM-REFERENCED TEST (NRT)	A test that describes performance of one unit (student, school, etc.) in terms of its relationship to a representative distribution of performance (norm group)	ITBS, Stanford 9, Terra Nova
CRITERION-REFERENCED TEST (CRT)	A test that is designed to determine if a student has mastered a defined set of skills/knowledge	Minimum competency tests
STANDARDS-REFERENCED OR STANDARDS-BASED TEST (SRT)	A test designed to measure a student's level of performance on predetermined content standards	Most current state-mandated testing programs

why the top score is 36 on the ACT and 2400 on the SAT I. The test companies could have chosen any other numbers. There are two important implications of this arbitrariness, however. First, a given score does not necessarily have the same meaning across different tests or even among the different subjects of a single test. Clearly, a 36 does not have the same meaning on the ACT as on the SAT (for which the scale does not even go that low). Typically, however, the scale is fixed so that a given score in one subject on a single test has a similar meaning from one year to the next.

Something is required to give meaning to arbitrary scale scores. In some cases, experience is enough. For example, teachers in high schools know that an SAT I score of 2250 is very high because experience has shown that these scores are rare, and anyone who has experience with college admissions knows that this is a score that would make a student competitive at the most selective colleges.

In most cases, test authors don't rely only on experience, but instead take other steps to address the arbitrariness of scales. One common approach is to rely on norm-referenced reporting. If a student's scale score on an NRT puts her at the 95th percentile rank nationally, then we know her performance has been very good. Similarly, how does one know whether Minnesota's mean scale score of 288 in eighth-grade mathematics on the National Assessment of Educational Progress, or the finding that 40 percent of its students scored at the "Proficient" level or better, is good? One indication is state norms: Minnesota scored at the top of the distribution of all states participating in that assessment that year.[6]

Developmental Scales

Educators and parents often want to trace a student's development as he or she progresses through school. Scales for this purpose are called, logically enough, developmental scales or "vertical" scales. An example of a developmental scale is grade equivalents (GEs), which are developmental scores that report the performance of a student by comparing the student to the median at a specific stage. For instance, a 3.7 grade equivalent represents the median performance of a student in the seventh month of third grade, so a third grader scoring 3.7 is typical, while a third grader scoring 4.3 is more than half a year above average. (There are ten academic months in a year on this scale.) Thus, the 2.0 GE reported as the average vocabulary score for the Dalen County first graders on the spring ITBS in Exhibit 2.2 means that the average first grader in Dalen County is scoring at the median level of a second grader in the first month of school. Given that the ITBS is administered in the spring, this score would be considered to be slightly above the typical score. It is important to note that because the rate of growth changes with age, a difference of any given size—say, one GE—does not necessarily represent the same growth at different grade levels. For example, the difference between 3.7 and 4.7 does not represent the same performance difference as between 6.7 and 7.7. Unfortunately, even though GEs are relatively easy to interpret and explain, they have become unpopular and are rarely used.

A more common type of developmental scale, sometimes called a developmental standard score or a developmental scale score, reports performance on an arbitrary numerical scale. A fifth grader and a sixth grader who both scored 286 on a developmental scale on one test would be considered to have roughly the same level of proficiency, despite their being in different grades. For example, the average developmental scale score (SS) for Dalen County on the ITBS for the first-grade vocabulary test was 153.8 (Exhibit 2.2). This score does not tell you much unless you also know the median performance for a particular grade. In this case, the median performance for first graders is 150, so a score of 153.8 is slightly above what is considered typical. These scales are designed so that a given increase in performance (e.g., 50 points) has the same meaning at any level of the scale or grade level. Unfortunately, it is not clear that this goal is actually met, particularly for grades that are not adjacent.

When interpreting the results of a single test, it is often useful to obtain performance data from more than one scale. For example, a standards-referenced report of school performance is essential information under some federal and state requirements, but reporting only in terms of standards has numerous limitations, such as the lack of information such reports provide about progress within a performance range. Therefore, it is often useful to supplement this standards-referenced information with other types of reporting. Unfortunately, not all schools will have the same information available to them. Some states provide scale scores along with types of benchmarks—in some cases, normative information—that help school leaders interpret the scale scores. Some states provide percentile ranks as well. Because different states provide different information, educators need to explore the options that are available to them. Exhibit 2.4 provides a comparison of different types of scores provided on assessment reports.

Exhibit 2.4

Score Type Comparison		
TYPE OF SCORE	**DEFINITION**	**EXAMPLE**
RAW SCORE	A simple count or percentage of the credits achieved on the test	Classroom tests scored as percentage correct
PERCENTILE RANK	The percentage of students given student outscores	SAT mathematics—a score of 700 = 95th PR
CUT SCORE	The score needed to reach a predetermined passing level	Raw score required to pass a minimum-competency test
PERFORMANCE LEVELS	A number of levels that demonstrate a range of performance	MCAS—Warning or Failing, Needs Improvement, Proficient, Advanced
GRADE EQUIVALENTS	Developmental scores that report the performance of a student by comparing the student to the median at a specific stage	ITBS—a GE of 3.7 represents the median performance of a student in the seventh month of third grade
DEVELOPMENTAL SCALE SCORE	Developmental scores that report the performance of students in different grades on a single numerical scale	ITBS Form K—176 is the developmental scale score corresponding to a GE of 3.2 in reading

Sources: SAT Program Handbook: 2004-2005 (New York: College Board, 2004).
H. D. Hoover et al., *Iowa Tests of Basic Skills Interpretive Guide for School Administrators* (Chicago: Riverside, 1994): p. 74.

TRADING OFF DETAIL FOR RELIABILITY

Typically, performance on external tests is reported at many levels of detail. At one extreme is the total score for the whole test. Performance at this level can be reported in terms of any of the scales noted above. At the other extreme, some tests report performance on individual test items. In between there may be several intermediate levels of detail such as subtest scores. Each subtest typically comprises many test items, and performance on the subtests is often presented in terms of the scales noted above. At a finer-grained level of detail, some tests will report results on small clusters of items that depend on similar knowledge or skills, as shown on the ITBS report in Exhibit 2.5. Most often, as on the ITBS report, performance on these small clusters is not reported in terms of scale scores because there is too little information to create a reasonable scale. It is reported instead in terms of simple statistics, such as the percentage of items in the cluster answered correctly.

For purposes of diagnosis and instructional improvement, most educators want more detail rather than less. Knowing that a class does poorly in math, or even in "math computation," provides limited guidance about how to improve its performance. On the other hand, knowing that many of the students in the class have difficulty with the concept of place value provides a clear starting point for planning improvement.

So why not just use the most fine-grained detail available from a test? As in many aspects of assessment, there are trade-offs—in this case, between detail and reliability. Although finer-grained levels of detail are instructionally more useful, because fewer items are used in reporting performance the results will also be less reliable. For example, looking at an ITBS report similar to the one in Exhibit 2.5, a school leader would be more confident that the test reliably assessed students' performance on "Number Systems and Numeration" (based on nine questions) than their performance on "Estimation" (based on one question). When you opt for a finer level of detail in order to obtain more useful diagnostic information, you simultaneously opt for a measure that is less consistent and has a higher probability of being misleading because of measurement error. As we discuss below, one way to deal with the limitations of information from a single test is to combine it with other information about performance. The finer-grained the information you take from the test and the fewer items it reflects, the more important such additional information becomes.

At the extreme, some states encourage teachers to examine performance on individual items. A single item is a risky basis for inferring what students can and cannot do. To clarify this, it is necessary to distinguish between using a single item to learn about an individual student and relying on it to help describe the performance of a class, school, or other group.

There are two basic reasons why it is risky and often seriously misleading to rely on a single item to draw conclusions about a single student. One reason is the measurement error already discussed—that is, students' performance often varies markedly from one item to another, even when the items are intended to measure the same thing. A second reason is that more than one skill is needed to answer many items correctly, particularly on some modern assessments that deliberately aim for more realistic, and therefore often more complicated, items. When a student answers one item incorrectly, it is often not clear whether she would answer another similar item incorrectly, or which of several skills she has not learned.

When looking at the performance of a class or another group, the problem of measurement error is lessened, but the second problem remains because there are often several possible explanations for poor performance on the item. Therefore, the best way to use information about poor performance on a single item is to understand that such performance suggests possible weaknesses in students'

Exhibit 2.5

Item No.	MATH CONCEPTS	Item Count	Class Avg %C N=21	Building Avg %C N=139	System Avg %C N=247	Nat'l Avg %C	Diff (Class Minus Nat'l)	Difference (Class Minus Nat'l) -20 0 20
	NUMBER SYSTEMS & NUMERATION	9	76	68	68	65	+11	
1	Compare & order		95	89	91	86	+9	
5	Compare & order		90	83	80	72	+18	
7	Compare & order		86	72	75	74	+12	
12	Place value		90	90	89	88	+2	
15	Compare & order		76	68	67	67	+9	
17	Place value		90	83	84	71	+19	
22	Compare & order		38	31	30	30	+8	
26	Properties		48	35	34	32	+16	
29	Compare & order		67	65	62	62	+5	
	WHOLE NUMBERS	3	84	85	83	82	+2	
2	Reading and writing		81	82	64	95	-4	
6	Reading and writing		100	93	89	93	+7	
11	Relative values		71	79	75	68	+3	
	GEOMETRY	4	82	86	84	80	+2	
3	Geometric figures		90	93	92	91	-1	
14	Properties, patterns and relationships		76	82	78	72	+4	
19	Geometric figures		67	74	73	67	0	
25	Properties, patterns and relationships		95	95	93	89	+6	
	MEASUREMENT	4	88	88	88	82	+6	
9	Appropriate units		100	98	97	95	+5	
13	Estimate measurements		81	80	81	72	+9	
16	Length, distance, temp, wt, vol		95	97	95	81	+14	
21	Estimate measurements		76	76	78	79	-3	
	FRACTIONS & MONEY	4	79	63	63	57	+22	
10	Representation		90	71	72	68	+22	
23	Representation		38	24	27	22	+16	
24	Representation		95	82	79	85	+10	
27	Relative values		90	76	74	54	+36	
	NUMBER SENTENCES	4	75	71	67	67	+8	
4	Solving sentences		95	86	84	79	+16	
8	Symbols		86	89	88	91	-5	
18	Variables		57	51	47	48	+9	
20	Variables		62	58	49	51	+11	
	ESTIMATION	1	29	46	49	47	-18	
28	Standard rounding in context		29	46	49	47	-18	

Source: H. D. Hoover et al., *Iowa Tests of Basic Skills Interpretive Guide for School Administrators* (Chicago: Riverside, 1994): p. 88.

knowledge and skills. Measurement experts would generally advise testing these possible explanations by looking at clusters of items that share the skill in question but differ in other respects. In many instances, however, you may find yourself without additional items you can use in this way. When you don't have additional items to rely on, you should take any conclusions based on a single item with a large grain of salt and look for additional evidence to test your hypothesis about the reasons for incorrect answers.

HOW DO YOU MEASURE IMPROVEMENT?

Schools and policy makers follow two very different approaches for using test scores to measure progress over time. The most common model is called a cohort-to-cohort change model. In this approach, schools test a given grade (e.g., fourth grade) every year. To gauge progress, each year's scores for students in that grade are compared to the scores of the previous year's students in that grade. This approach compares one cohort of fourth graders to the previous cohort of fourth graders—hence the name given to the approach. This approach is shown for a hypothetical state in Exhibit 2.6. Average scores for each cohort of fourth graders are presented on a hypothetical developmental (or "vertical" scale). Exhibit 2.6 shows a typical pattern: rapid gains over the first few years of the testing program, followed by slower gains after several years.

An alternative approach measures the gains shown by a given cohort of students as it progresses through school. This approach goes by various names, including "value-added assessment" and "longitudinal assessment." The value-added approach is illustrated for the same hypothetical state in Exhibit 2.7, using the same developmental scale. In Exhibit 2.7, a single cohort of students, those who were tested in the fourth grade in Year 2, are followed as they progress through school. The same graph illustrates the scores of this cohort as its members were tested in fifth grade in Year 3, sixth grade in Year 4, and so on.

Each of these approaches has advantages and drawbacks. The cohort-to-cohort approach is simple to implement and allows schools to use grade-specific tests without worrying about grade-to-grade overlap or vertical scaling. It is designed to measure improvement in the performance of the school's students over time—from one cohort to the next—not its effectiveness in teaching any one cohort of students. On the other hand, the cohort-to-cohort approach has a "perpetual motion machine" flavor because it rests on the assumption that schools can just keep

Exhibit 2.6

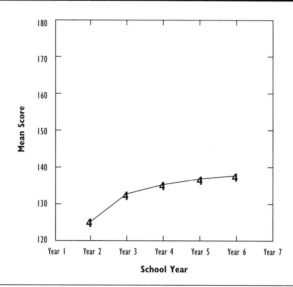

Exhibit 2.7

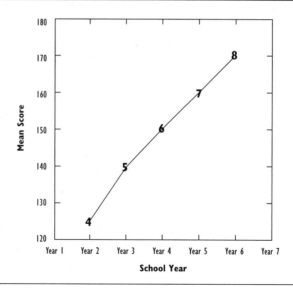

improving without limit. The problem with this assumption is clear if you consider a highly effective school in which students learn a great deal and in which that rate of learning is stable over time. Such a school would show up in a cohort-to-cohort gain system as showing no improvement over time.

The cohort-to-cohort approach is also susceptible to biases caused by changes in the composition of the student population. For example, a school that is improving may show up as making no progress if it is faced with an influx of lower-scoring students, such as students with limited proficiency in English. Estimates of change in a cohort-to-cohort change system are also highly susceptible to meaningless fluctuations that arise from differences among the cohorts entering school in different years. This issue is particularly true of smaller schools.

In contrast, the value-added approach is designed to measure directly what students learn while in school, which makes it an appealing option for many educators and policy makers. However, it too has its disadvantages. One is that comparing a student's performance across grades requires tests that can be placed on a vertical scale. This is possible only when the curriculum is cumulative across grades—as is the case with reading, but not high school science. Because the curriculum changes from grade to grade, these estimates of growth become increasingly questionable as the span of grades increases. These estimates are also highly susceptible to measurement error. For example, research suggests that value-added assessments can reliably distinguish classrooms in which gains are exceptionally large or small but do not reliably distinguish among most classrooms.[7]

STRATEGIES FOR INTERPRETING DATA

Interpreting Single Test Scores

As discussed above, measurement error is one reason not to evaluate a student on the basis of only a score on a single test, but it is not the only reason to avoid using a single score in isolation. We all have had the experience as a student of a test not measuring our true competence in a particular subject area. As educators, we know that a student's situation is sometimes important to understand when viewing test results. Does the student have a learning disability? Does the student suffer from test anxiety that depresses her performance on tests? Does the student show either much stronger or much weaker performance on other types of work than on tests? These are not examples of measurement error because repeated testing would not give you an average score that would be a more accurate indicator of the student's performance. However, they are factors that might cause a score, if taken alone, to be a biased indicator of the student's proficiency.

We suggest three complementary strategies for interpreting scores on a particular assessment, all of which involve use of additional information. First, look beyond one year's assessment results by applying the cohort-to-cohort change or value-added assessment approaches as explained above. While the two approaches provide different information, both are valuable in making sense of the most recent assessment results.

Second, compare your students' results with those of relevant students in the district or the state. For example, a principal might be concerned to see that only 64 percent of the tenth-grade students at her school scored at the proficient or the advanced level on the state English language arts test. However, discovering that the comparable percentages for tenth graders in the district and the state were 62 and 61 percent, respectively, would cause her to reassess her school's performance. Of course, such comparisons raise the question of "how good is good enough?" We will return to this question when we discuss setting goals in chapter 7.

Third, compare your students' results on the most recent assessment with their performance on other assessments. Following the advice in chapter 1 to conduct a data inventory for your school provides the critical information about what other data on student performance are available.

Determining Whether Differences Are Meaningful

Given that many assessments have important consequences for students, educators, and schools, educators, parents, and policy makers are looking for meaning in even the smallest differences. Yet some of these differences may not represent any real change in student performance.

There are three reasons why small differences should not be given credence. As we have discussed, the first is sampling error. This error even affects large groups, such as the samples of roughly 2,500 students that were tested at the state level for the NAEP until recently. If you look at the comparisons among states, you will find that many states with similar scores were rated not statistically significantly different. This result means that if different samples of students were chosen to take the test, the states could score the same as each other or the rank order might even change. The uncertainty resulting from sampling error is, of course, much greater in the case of individual schools, particularly small ones. The second reason, measurement error, is analogous, but it stems not from the sampling of people, but rather from the sampling of items on the test.

A third reason to be wary of small differences is that any given set of content standards could lead to a variety of different blueprints for a test. Different people may reach different conclusions about what specific content should be included and which formats should be used. Therefore, different tests generally provide a somewhat different view of performance. Individuals, schools, and even states and countries will show somewhat different performance on two tests that are designed to measure the same domain.

Although fully addressing these sources of uncertainty requires substantial knowledge of statistics, measurement, and the specific test, there are things you can do to guide your interpretation of assessment results. First, you will sometimes be able to find information about the types and extent of error. For example, score reports for individual students often provide some information about measurement error. Reports of group data often have information about which comparisons are statistically significant—that is, big enough that they would not likely arise from sampling or measurement error, and therefore worth accepting with confidence. Even if such information is not reported, it is worth finding out if it is available.

Second, even in the absence of this information, you should be wary of small differences, including differences between groups or changes in performance over time. Differences that are sizable or that persist for some time should be taken seriously. Small differences, or differences that have appeared only in one time period (say, when comparing this year to last), should be taken with a grain of salt and, if small, should be ignored until more data are available to confirm them.

Understanding "Gaming the System"

Some school leaders respond to the introduction of high-stakes assessments by figuring out how to game the system. Test-preparation firms have developed a profitable business by trying to teach people to succeed on specific tests, and some of their techniques rely on gaming the system rather than on building student mastery. In addition, numerous studies have found that when the pressure to raise scores is high, some teachers will engage in questionable practices to increase student test scores. For example, Exhibit 2.8 provides a summary of responses by teachers in Kentucky and Maryland to surveys investigating their responses to state testing programs.[8]

Exhibit 2.8

Percentage of Teachers Reporting Questionable Test-Administration Practices in Their Schools		
TEACHER PRACTICE	**KY**	**MD**
Questions rephrased	36	27
Questions about content answered	21	13
Revisions recommended	21	14
Hints given or correct answer given	17	6
Answers changed	9	2
Helpful materials or posters in view	na	42

Source: D. Koretz, "Preparing Students for the MSPAP Assessments," in *Assessment-Based Educational Reform: A Look at Two State Programs, Part 2,* symposium presented at the annual meeting of the American Educational Research Association (Jessie Pollack, chair), New York, April 1996.

Another practice that many educators employ to inflate scores is reallocation, which refers to shifts in instructional resources among the various parts of a content area. Research has shown that when scores on a test are important to teachers, some will reallocate their instructional time to focus more on the material emphasized by the test and less on the material that either is omitted from the test—for example, all the words not included in our vocabulary test—or is emphasized less by it.[9] Just as reallocation transfers time among parts of the content area, so does it shift achievement among them. Whether this reallocation inflates scores depends on which material gets more emphasis and which receives less. If teachers deemphasize material that is important for the inferences you and others base on the scores—that is, if they are an important part of the curricular domain (the 10,000 words) the test is supposed to represent—then scores will become inflated. This is true even if the material gaining emphasis is important. Scores will go up, but mastery of the domain will not. This is why having "a test worth teaching to," while desirable for many reasons, is not sufficient to protect against score inflation.

Research has shown that reallocation also occurs between subjects as a result of high-stakes testing.[10] Schools and districts feel the pressure to demonstrate improvement in tested subject areas, and some consequently reallocate instructional resources and time away from untested areas. As Exhibit 2.9 demonstrates, this often leads to a deemphasis on subjects such as science, social studies, arts, and health and fitness. When this occurs, a subsequent increase in math scores, for

Exhibit 2.9

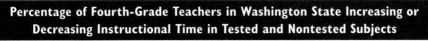

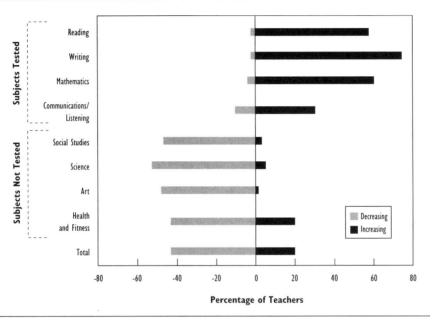

Percentage of Fourth-Grade Teachers in Washington State Increasing or Decreasing Instructional Time in Tested and Nontested Subjects

Source: B. M. Stecher, S. I. Barron, T. Chun, and K. Ross, *The Effects of the Washington State Education Reform on Schools and Classrooms*, CSE Technical Report No. 525 (Los Angeles: National Center for Research on Evaluation, Standards, and Student Testing, 2000).

example, may truly demonstrate increased mastery of math material. Yet, this increase most likely comes at the price of decreased mastery of science and/or social studies material.

Several studies have shown that educators' responses to tests with high stakes result in substantial grade inflation. One relevant study examined performance in a large, predominantly minority, high-poverty district that by today's standard had a "moderate-stakes" testing program—although it carried no formal rewards or sanctions, the administration put a great deal of pressure on educators to raise scores. Through 1986, the district had used one standardized achievement test and had seen test scores rise. Specifically, in the spring of that year, the average third grader scored at a grade equivalent of 4.3 (4 years, 3 months)—fully half an academic year above average. This is shown by the first diamond in Exhibit 2.10.[11] The district then

Exhibit 2.10

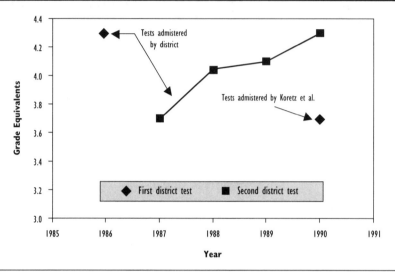

Score Inflation in a Moderate-Stakes System, Third-Grade Mathematics

Source: Adapted from D. Koretz, R. L. Linn, S. B. Dunbar, and L.A. Shepard, "The Effects of High-Stakes Testing: Preliminary Evidence About Generalization Across Tests," in *The Effects of High-Stakes Testing*, symposium presented at the annual meetings of the American Educational Research Association and the National Council on Measurement in Education (R. L. Linn, chair), Chicago, April 1991.

purchased a new, quite similar test, shown by the squares in Exhibit 2.10, and performance dropped to an average level. Four years later, the district's performance on the new test was again half an academic year above average. The researchers then administered to a random sample of classrooms exactly the same test that had been administered previously. They found that while performance on the new test had increased by half an academic year, performance on the old test had declined by the same amount, as shown by the diamond on the right in Exhibit 2.10.

Thus, regardless of the test used, students scored a half-grade equivalent lower on a test that was unexpected than on a test for which teachers had time to prepare. It does not appear that the gains in scores on the second test represent clear improvements in learning—as might occur if the second test were harder or if students learned new material on the new test without losing ground elsewhere. If that had been true, performance on the first test would not have declined. Rather, it appears that students and teachers substituted mastery of material emphasized on the second test for mastery of material emphasized on the first test. Achievement was transferred among material sampled from the domain for the two tests. Unless one could argue that the material from the first test that was deemphasized was unimportant to the conclusions parents and teachers drew about mathematics proficiency, this represents score inflation.

Similar patterns have been shown by a number of other studies.[12] Typically, gains on high-stakes tests have been three to five times as large as gains on other tests with low (or lower) stakes. In numerous cases, large gains on high-stakes tests have been accompanied by no gains whatever on lower-stakes tests.

To understand whether improved student scores are meaningful, educators need to determine whether teaching has been focused on increasing mastery rather than on changing scores. What does it mean to do this? There is no simple answer, but the general rule is to focus on the skills students should know rather than on specific details of the test. Students are not in school to learn how to score well on a specific test required by their state's department of education; they are there to learn the skills they need to be successful in subsequent schooling, in their later work, and as citizens. The criterion to apply as you prepare students for such a test is whether you believe the preparation will create general improvement or merely improve performance on the specific test. Teaching test-taking tricks (e.g., plugging in a formula rather than solving a math problem) fails to meet this standard. So does focusing on details of the particular test. For example, one secondary school teacher told us that she no longer bothers to teach her students about irregular polygons because her state's test includes only regular polygons. This is a shortcut that will generate higher scores but not a truly higher level of competence. If students are gaining mastery, then the improvement will show up in many different places—on other tests they take or in the quality of their later academic work—not just in their scores on their own state's test.

This book focuses on how to use assessment results to change practice in ways that make a long-term, meaningful difference for students. In some cases, school leaders will need to create cultural changes in their schools, provide new forms of professional development, and combat incentives to focus on the test rather than on the broader domains of skills and knowledge. We understand that often this means going against the tide by resisting the pressure to do whatever it takes to raise scores. During this process, it is necessary to monitor not only impediments to raising scores, but also practices that result in score inflation rather than meaningful improvement. As you will see in the following chapters, this work can be challenging and messy.

Integrating the ACE Habits of Mind into Step 2: Building Assessment Literacy

SHARED COMMITMENT TO ACTION, ASSESSMENT, AND ADJUSTMENT

When the Data Wise Project team teaches assessment literacy, a key point we emphasize is this: don't take action on the basis of a single measure. Any time you are tempted to act on one score, ask yourself: What other evidence or information can I gather to paint a more complete picture of what is going on? For example, when deciding whether students are qualified to enroll in Algebra I, one school considered the results of seven common assessments administered over the course of a year. The team did not want to deny students opportunity to take this important gateway course based on their performance on a single test. This principle is helpful to consider for smaller decisions as well. For example, a teacher team might notice that students did poorly on the handful of poetry questions on the state test. Before deciding if and how this data would inform their practice in the coming year, they might ask themselves: What skills did those particular test items assess? How did students perform on the poetry assessments we designed as a team? If performance was different, why was it different?

INTENTIONAL COLLABORATION

It helps to bring many people together around looking at assessments, rather than have that knowledge reside in a few "data experts" at the school. For one thing, a more diverse group of people will all bring different points of view and levels of expertise to looking at the data. Subject-matter experts can provide information about whether a particular set of items covers a small or large part of a domain, such as chemistry within science. Grade-level teachers can provide information about other factors that might affect how a group of students might have performed on the test—for example, there might be measurement error because the eighth grade took that test the Monday after they came back from the weekend class trip. Finally, specialists and special educators have other knowledge to contribute to discussions about data, such as how to be cautious about making inferences about a test for students with learning disabilities, because the lack of spacing between paragraphs or tightly clustered responses might confuse students who have trouble processing information visually. Gathering such a diverse group of people together to discuss assessment results can allow each person to be both expert and learner—sharing their specific knowledge about assessment and learning from the diversity around the table.

RELENTLESS FOCUS ON EVIDENCE

One easy way to build assessment literacy is to give people time to regularly practice reading and interpreting the evidence and data they gather in the form of charts and reports. Take a few minutes at the beginning of every team meeting for teachers to simply look at the charts and reports that are in front of them. Practice looking for key elements like the date range of the assessment results, the sample size, the comparison group, and the domain being tested. Ask questions such as, How are results reported? Are we looking at raw scores or scaled scores? If the scores are scaled, how was the scaling done? Remember that you will continue to build assessment literacy with your faculty all along the Data Wise Improvement Process. From our own experience as teachers and learners, we now believe that the topic of assessment literacy cannot be taught for its own sake or in isolation. Educators will learn this material more deeply and enthusiastically if they learn it in the context of something that matters to them, such as reading their benchmark assessment results, and also when it is related to something they need to know or do in their regular practice, such as creating a chart comparing their students' scores from the previous year to the current year.

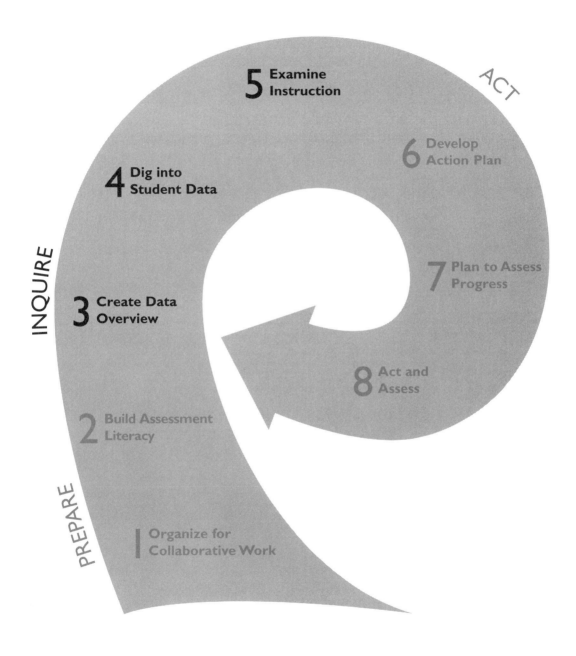

5 Examine Instruction

ACT

6 Develop Action Plan

4 Dig into Student Data

INQUIRE

7 Plan to Assess Progress

3 Create Data Overview

8 Act and Assess

2 Build Assessment Literacy

PREPARE

1 Organize for Collaborative Work

3

CREATING A DATA OVERVIEW

Shannon T. Hodge and John B. Willett

TEAM LEADER INÉS ROMERO AND PRINCIPAL ROGER BOLTON HAD AGREED THAT Franklin High School's first faculty meeting of the year would focus on the newly released results from the state assessment. They hoped to engage the faculty in a spirited conversation about what they saw in the data. However, when they got right down to it, deciding what data to present didn't seem so easy.

"I can tell you right now," Inés remarked as Roger held up a table packed with numbers, "we'll lose them right away if we throw something like that up on the screen."

"I know," responded Roger. "But what do we show them? How do we turn all these data into a story that people can follow?"

This chapter provides advice about how to construct graphic displays that highlight important patterns in assessment results, which can then be used to engage school faculties in constructive conversations about the meaning of those results. The primary challenge in constructing such displays is to direct the audience's attention to important patterns while respecting the limitations of assessment results as described in chapter 2. Other important considerations include deciding which of the many pieces of assessment data to display, how to display those data clearly and effectively, and how to start conversations around these displays.

This chapter has four major sections, each of which is organized around the tasks an instructional leadership team would do to prepare for a faculty meeting on assessment results. The first section explains that the team should begin by choosing a focus area for its inquiry. The second section emphasizes that the team should prepare its displays by using a "simpler is usually better" approach. The third section explains that one good approach for stimulating faculty debate is to seek out and display interesting comparisons—for example, comparisons among student subgroups across yearly cohorts, or over time. The final section describes ways school leaders can use these displays to stimulate constructive conversations among faculty members.

CHOOSE A FOCUS AREA

An important task for the instructional leadership team is to help narrow the scope of inquiry by identifying a focus area for the work.[1] When choosing a focus area, it helps to decide whether this inquiry will take place at the whole school or team level. The area should be directly related to instruction and broad enough so that all staff members engaged in the conversation see themselves playing a role in addressing it. For example, one high school we know decided to focus on how prepared students were for college. Some leadership teams choose to focus on a particular content area, such as English language arts or mathematics, while others decide to work on something that cuts across several disciplines, such as critical reading or problem solving. We also know of schools that pursue a somewhat more abstract focus area, such as the level of instructional rigor demanded of students.

Although it is important for the work of improvement to be a collaborative effort, it is typical for a core group to choose the focus area. Indeed, sometimes schools find that the focus area is handed down from on high as a central office or district initiative. If your superintendent has told you that your first priority this year is to improve literacy across the system, by all means choose literacy as your focus area! The key is to integrate improvement into the core work of the school, not to layer it on as an afterthought. Your data overview will provide an opportunity for you to share evidence of what you already know about student performance within the focus area.

At Franklin High School, student performance in mathematics had been particularly low for several years. Hoping to take advantage of a recent districtwide investment in mathematics coaches, Roger and his team chose mathematics as the focus area for the upcoming year.

ANALYZE THE DATA AND FIND THE STORY

Administrators like Roger Bolton often get their first glimpse of their schools' student assessment results in test-score reports, such as those displayed in the three panels of Exhibit 3.1. These reports present aggregate results of tenth graders at Franklin High School on the State Comprehensive Assessment. They show how Franklin students were distributed across state-defined proficiency levels in the content areas of English language arts and mathematics. The form of these reports is very similar to the test-score reports used by many states and testing companies.

Panel A displays the percentages of tenth-grade students at Franklin High School who fall into the four state-defined proficiency categories ("Advanced," "Proficient,"

Exhibit 3.1

Distribution of Scores of Franklin High School Tenth-Grade Students Across Proficiency Levels on the State Comprehensive Assessment in English Language Arts and Mathematics

Panel A: Percentage of Students at Each Proficiency Level, by Subject and Cohort (Academic Years 1–4)

GRADE 10	ENGLISH LANGUAGE ARTS				MATHEMATICS			
	Year 1	Year 2	Year 3	Year 4	Year 1	Year 2	Year 3	Year 4
Advanced	1	1	2	1	2	6	5	2
Proficient	7	6	5	19	10	9	10	7
Needs Improvement	28	38	42	43	13	12	19	41
Failing	64	55	51	37	75	73	66	50
Total Students	414	425	417	423	417	430	422	425

Panel B: Number and Percentage of Students at Each Proficiency Level for School, District, and State, by Subject Specialty, Academic Year 4

GRADE 10	ENGLISH LANGUAGE ARTS						MATHEMATICS					
	School		District		State		School		District		State	
	#	%	#	%	#	%	#	%	#	%	#	%
Advanced	3	1	355	10	12,877	19	7	2	856	22	20,619	29
Proficient	82	19	1,123	30	30,208	43	29	7	819	21	19,286	28
Needs Improvement	183	43	1,399	37	18,584	27	176	41	1,175	31	19,913	28
Failing	155	37	865	23	7,935	11	213	50	987	26	10,313	15
Total Students	423	100	3,742	100	69,604	100	425	100	3,837	100	70,131	100

"Needs Improvement," and "Failing"). These four categories and the total number of students define the rows in the panel. Across the top of the panel, columns first distinguish the content area ("English Language Arts" and "Mathematics") and then academic year ("Year 1" through "Year 4"). By examining the entries in the fifth column, for example, you can see that only 1 percent of tenth-grade Franklin High School students were assessed at the "Advanced" level in English language arts in Year 4, whereas 37 percent were judged to be "Failing." By comparing the lists of percentages, column by column across the panel, you can examine how the proficiency distribution differed across cohorts of Franklin High School tenth graders in Years 1–4.

Panel B of Exhibit 3.1 presents similar information, but adds student frequencies (numbers of students) to the percentages shown in Panel A. Instead of the cross-cohort comparison in the first panel, however, Panel B provides a comparison between Franklin High School students' proficiency distribution in Year 4 and the performance distributions of tenth graders in the school district and the state for the same year. Notice that the "School" percentage of students at each proficiency level in Panel B is identical to the "Year 4" distributions in Panel A.

By reading this panel, Roger Bolton could see, for instance, that Franklin's tenth-grade students' mathematics proficiency was disappointing when compared to the district and state averages, because disproportionately more of Franklin's tenth graders fell into the "Failing" and "Needs Improvement" categories. However, it is difficult to select the proper columns and remember the numbers while trying to reach a conclusion about the educational significance of the differences. These difficulties suggest the value of capturing the key elements of the comparison graphically.

Panel C of the table gives mathematics proficiency for student subgroups.

Panel C: Total Number of Students and Percentage at Each Proficiency Level, by Selected Student Background Characteristics, Academic Year 4

| | MATHEMATICS | | | | | |
| | All Students | | English-Language Learners (n=81) | | Students with Disabilities (n=85) | |
	#	%	#	%	#	%
Advanced	7	2	0	0	1	1
Proficient	29	7	2	2	5	6
Needs Improvement	176	41	10	13	33	39
Failing	213	50	69	85	46	54
Total	425	100	81	100	85	100

As with Panel B, it is not easy to remember the numbers that are needed for any complex comparison among groups. There is simply too much information in the table for someone seeing it for the first time to grasp key patterns quickly. And, more importantly, there is so much information in the table that it could be used to address many different questions simultaneously.

DISPLAY THE DATA

"Well, they say a picture's worth a thousand words," Roger Bolton said to his instructional leadership team, "but I'm still stuck on what that picture is supposed to look like. There are so many types of graphs we could make . . . What would be best? How much detail do we want to provide?"

Roger recognized that the most interesting and compelling themes in the state assessment results were obscured by its complicated, detailed, and generic tabular formatting. The challenge that he and his instructional leadership team faced was to find sensible ways to redisplay aggregate student assessment data so that the underlying educational stories and themes would be transparent. Graphic displays are key tools for meeting this challenge. The content, organization, labeling, and formatting of effective displays should reflect the presenter's overall objectives for displaying the data and be tailored to the audience that will be examining the display.

Once it has identified the focus area, the instructional leadership team should develop a list of specific questions to have in mind as it examines the data and chooses or creates graphic data displays. Many substantive questions can be informed by the student assessment results that are provided to schools. One effective way to present data and stimulate successful discussions among the faculty is to plan graphic displays that address a logical and interconnected sequence of these substantive questions. These questions will determine the story that is communicated through the data overview.

The underlying questions should also drive every aspect of the presentation of the assessment data and provide a rationale for why it is important to present the data one way rather than another. For example, the questions you are trying to answer should help you make the following decisions about your data presentation: Do you want to emphasize time trends? Are you interested in cohort comparisons? Is it important to analyze student performance by group? Do you want to focus the discussion on the students who fall into the lowest proficiencies or those who occupy the highest? Do you want to focus teachers' attention on the performance of your school's students relative to the average performance of students in the district or the state?

The questions your instructional leadership team identifies provide the organizing themes the data manager should use to set the order and orientation of rows and columns in a table, or the order of bars and lines on a graph. These questions help you decide which features of the display to emphasize so that your audience will take note of them immediately. Your questions suggest how to orient the axes of a plot so that important comparisons can be made. They determine the proper scales so that comparisons among the quantities displayed are informative and not misleading, and they suggest ways of wording the captions to focus the attention of the audience.

Remember that a good picture is worth a thousand words. Each compelling graph your team creates from the statistics provided by assessment reports will enable you to communicate a story to your audience. Good graphs can create a sense of urgency and stimulate conversations about possible explanations for the striking patterns they illustrate.

At Franklin High School, Roger and the instructional leadership team wanted to provide the faculty with overview data in the focus area of mathematics. As a first step, the data manager entered the aggregate data from Panel A of Exhibit 3.1 into spreadsheet software and created the vertical bar chart shown in Exhibit 3.2.

Notice that the proficiency categories are arrayed along the horizontal axis of the chart, with the percentage of students in each proficiency category measured on a scale along the vertical axis. Each bar provides summary information for a different proficiency level, with the height of the bar representing the percentage of students scoring at that level. The percentage of students scoring at each level has also been included above the corresponding bar to ease reading of the graph and to provide information the faculty may refer to in discussing the graph. Unlike the dense tabular representation of the mathematics data shown in Exhibit 3.1, vertical bar charts like this one naturally draw an audience's eyes toward a comparison of the percentage of students in each proficiency category.

There are many other kinds of charts that the team could have chosen to display the performance distribution for Franklin High School's students on the state math test; the team used the vertical bar chart because it is one of the simplest, most easily understood data displays.

Exhibit 3.2

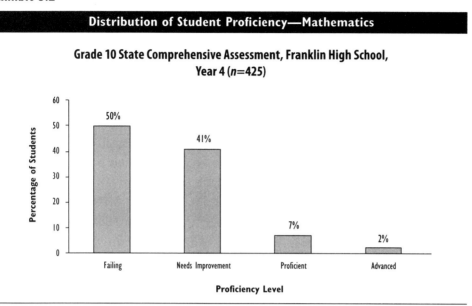

Distribution of Student Proficiency—Mathematics

Grade 10 State Comprehensive Assessment, Franklin High School, Year 4 (*n*=425)

Notice that the team followed the standard practice of locating the conceptual "outcome" of the analysis (in this case, the percentage of the student body in each proficiency category) on the vertical axis and the conceptual "predictor" (here, the proficiency category itself) on the horizontal axis. It also followed standard practice by arraying the "values" of the outcome and predictor along each axis so that they run from a conceptually low value to a conceptually high value. Thus, on the vertical axis, the student percentages run from 0 percent at the bottom of the axis to 60 percent at the top. On the horizontal axis, proficiency begins on the left with the "Failing" category and ends with "Advanced" on the right. In fact, in defining the horizontal axis of the vertical bar chart, the team had to reverse the order of the proficiency categories in the state-provided table (in Exhibit 3.1 the categories start with "Advanced" and end with "Failing").

The team chose not to extend the metric of the vertical axis to include a 100 percent value. Instead, it ended with the 60 percent value because there were no data values that exceeded 60 percent. By limiting the range of values represented on the axis in this way, the team could "stretch out" the vertical bars and take advantage of the space available on the plot. The effect of such stretching is to magnify differences between the percentages of students in each category; modifying the scale of the vertical axis makes sense only if you think these differences are substantively important.

Draw Attention to Critical Comparisons

The Franklin instructional leadership team decided to focus additional faculty discussion on the issue of math performance by asking, "How does our mathematics performance compare to the average performance of students in the state?" To address this question, the team again created a vertical bar chart based on summary statistics from Exhibit 3.1, but this time it superimposed the state proficiency percentages on the plot. To distinguish the school's performance from the state averages, the team used a slightly different way of displaying the comparison data. The vertical bar chart for the state comparison is presented in Exhibit 3.3. Note that the mathematics proficiency profile for Franklin High tenth graders appears as it did in Exhibit 3.2. However, the team superimposed a set of connected line segments

Exhibit 3.3

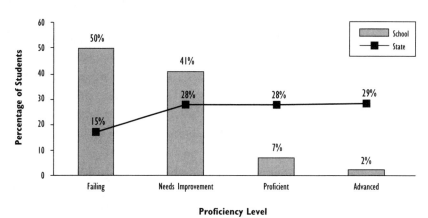

Distribution of School and State Student Proficiency—Mathematics

to represent the average state performance across the four proficiencies. The team's use of the two strategies of display—vertical bars for Franklin High School, squares and line segments for the state—helps the viewer to simultaneously (and distinctly) see the stories of school and state performance.

Understanding how students outside your school perform on the same assessment can provide benchmarks against which to compare the performance of your school's students. By contrasting the Franklin High School and the state average profiles, Roger and his instructional leadership team hoped to create a sense of urgency among their faculty colleagues. From the graph they produced, it was clear that Franklin's 50 percent failure rate in tenth-grade mathematics is more than three times the state failure rate of 15 percent. The display also emphasizes immediately that the percentages of Franklin High students scoring in the "Advanced" and "Proficient" categories are far below the state's percentages. Roger hoped that drawing attention to these patterns would motivate his mathematics faculty to brainstorm possible explanations.

It is important to note that the team used caution in describing the percentage of Franklin High School's tenth graders who scored at the advanced level in mathematics, because the 2 percent figure represents only eight students. If the test were administered again, it is quite possible that the number of Franklin tenth graders scoring in the advanced range would change by three or four students. This would change the percentage figure markedly. In other words, the 2 percent figure may be quite an imprecise estimate of the percentage of Franklin tenth graders with advanced math skills.

Compare the Performances of Groups

It can be helpful to compare the performance distributions of student subgroups. Exhibit 3.4a shows how the percent of Franklin tenth graders scoring in the four proficiency categories in mathematics differs by whether or not a student is an English-language learner (ELL).

In this clustered column chart, it is easy for faculty members to see that failure rates for ELL students are substantially higher than they are for other students. However, when displaying subgroup data, it is important to make sure that faculty members are aware of the size of subgroups so that they understand the extent to which a subgroup's performance may be contributing to the overall findings. For

Exhibit 3.4a

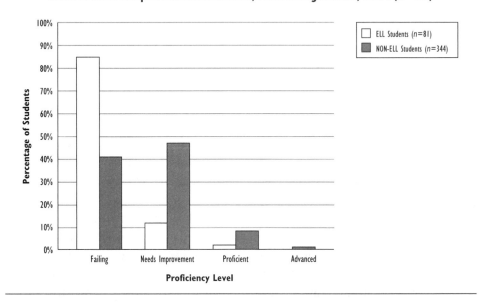

Mathematics: Percentage of Students at Each Proficiency Level, by ELL Status

Grade 10 State Comprehensive Assessment, Franklin High School, Year 4 (*n*=425)

Exhibit 3.4b

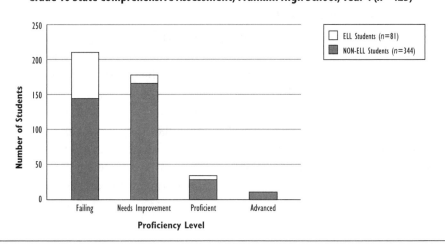

Mathematics: Number of Students at Each Proficiency Level, by ELL Status

Grade 10 State Comprehensive Assessment, Franklin High School, Year 4 (*n*=425)

example, because ELL students account for only 81 of the 425 tenth graders, it would be inappropriate to conclude from this data that a focus on mathematics instruction for ELL students would solve Franklin's performance problems. Because the instructional leadership team wanted to ensure that faculty members would not reach that conclusion, they paired Exhibit 3.4a with Exhibit 3.4b, which shows the *number* of students in each proficiency category instead of the percentages. This stacked column chart makes it clear that most of the students who are failing the mathematics assessment are not English-language learners. This visual representation helps set the stage for a conversation about what the school is going to do to improve mathematics performance *for everyone*.

Display Performance Trends

Principal Sandy Jenkins of Clark K–8 School was glad to see that her school had achieved adequate yearly progress, with more than 75 percent of the students meeting the target. She knew that the school's target would be substantially higher the following year. "As well it should be," Sandy thought to herself. There were a handful of schools in the area where nearly all of the students were performing in the proficient and advanced categories. Why shouldn't Clark be one of them? To get a conversation started with her faculty, Sandy asked the instructional leadership team to produce some charts showing how student performance on the state test had changed over the last several years.

"When you say that you want us to display kids' average reading comprehension scores over time, what exactly do you mean?" asked Elvira Brown, a veteran teacher and member of the instructional leadership team. "Are you looking for graphs of how the third grade did this year, as compared to last year's third grade and the one the year before, or are you asking us to follow the scores of the same group of kids over time, say from third grade through fifth grade?"

Exhibit 3.5 contains state-provided statistics summarizing the reading comprehension skills of students in the third through eighth grades at the Clark School. The figure lists the average reading comprehension score in each grade level for Years 2–5. Fortunately, the state reading comprehension test had been vertically linked so that scores on the test could be compared across children of different ages, and from grade to grade. This vertical linking meant that trends in average reading comprehension could be followed over time.

To address their questions about changes over time, the Clark instructional leadership team used the data in Exhibit 3.5 to create two kinds of plots, each providing

Exhibit 3.5

Average Reading Comprehension Scores of Students in Grades 3–8 at Clark K–8 School			
	ACADEMIC YEAR		
	YEAR 2	YEAR 3	YEAR 4
GRADE 3	249	250	245
GRADE 4	253	252	255
GRADE 5	259	257	256
GRADE 6	260	261	259
GRADE 7	258	263	264
GRADE 8	264	262	265

different insight into trends in the average reading comprehension of Clark students. Exhibit 3.6 contains a clustered vertical bar chart that displays overall differences in average reading comprehension by grade and by academic year. Exhibit 3.7 contains a trend-line plot that illustrates the average developmental trajectories of children in each cohort as they grew older.

Exhibit 3.6 displays the average reading scores in each grade within each academic year cohort. Each bar represents the average reading score (vertical axis) for students in a particular grade for that academic year, as recorded on the horizontal axis. The complete set of scores across the three years is represented by the three separate groups of vertical bars. Each bar is shaded slightly differently to distinguish between the various grades.

From this chart, the Clark team could discern several interesting trends and idiosyncrasies in the reading comprehension data. First, notice that in any one academic year (a grouping of columns), children in the later grades are generally achieving higher reading comprehension scores than children in the earlier grades. A slight deviation from this trend occurred in Year 2, however, when the average performance of the seventh grade fell below that of both the fifth and sixth grades, and in Year 3, when this group (who were now eighth graders) also had relatively low scores. Sandy recognized that there were many possible explanations for this pattern, one of which could be weaknesses in the seventh-grade teaching team. However, she was relieved to see that the average performance of Clark's seventh-grade students in Year 3 and Year 4 was greater than the average performance of

Exhibit 3.6

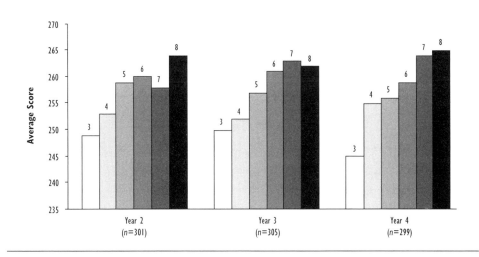

sixth-grade students in these years, and higher than the average performance of the seventh-grade students in Year 2. These were all comparisons Sandy could make quickly using the graph in Exhibit 3.6.

Another possible explanation for the relatively poor performance of Clark seventh graders in Year 2 was that this cohort contained an unusually large group of children new to the school who had not had the benefit of the solid teaching at Clark in the early grades. An important follow-up question for Sandy was whether the group of Clark seventh graders in Year 2 made real progress over the next year— their last in the school. Exhibit 3.7 provides an alternative display of the information in Exhibit 3.5, with an orientation that helped Sandy answer her question.

The display in Exhibit 3.7 recognizes that the group of children who entered seventh grade in Year 2 became the eighth-grade group in Year 3. Of course, it may be that not all the children are the same; some may have left the school and new children may have entered. However, if the instructional leadership team assumes that most of the children who started out in the seventh grade in Year 2 did indeed

Exhibit 3.7

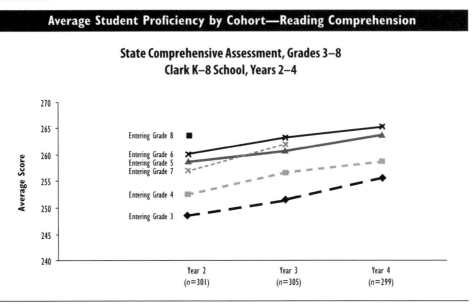

Average Student Proficiency by Cohort—Reading Comprehension

State Comprehensive Assessment, Grades 3–8
Clark K–8 School, Years 2–4

go on to eighth grade at the Clark School the next year, it can attach a developmental interpretation to the average trajectories in Exhibit 3.7.

Each line in Exhibit 3.7 plots the average achievement trajectory for a group of children over time. The label beside each line indicates the grade that group was in during Year 2. Notice, due to limitations in the dataset itself, that there are only two data points for the children who were in the seventh grade in Year 2, and only one data point for the children who were in the eighth grade in Year 2.

A quick look at Exhibit 3.7 shows that the seventh graders in Year 2 improved their average reading performance markedly during the next school year, alleviating somewhat the concern about the academic performance of this group.

Although the graphs in Exhibits 3.6 and 3.7 are based on the same data, the emphases are different. If there is little student mobility in and out of Clark, Exhibit 3.7 illustrates the longitudinal progress of the "same" group of children over time. Note that children entering Clark in the third grade in Year 2, whose scores are represented by the lowest trajectory on the plot, have the lowest reading comprehension scores of any group in the dataset. Of course, this is to be expected, since in any school year they are the youngest children represented. Also notice that the average rate of growth over the three-year period for this group essentially mirrors that of the children in the other entering grades.

The longitudinal display of the reading comprehension scores highlights a pattern that is more difficult to discern in Exhibit 3.6. In Exhibit 3.7, the entire average developmental trajectory of the third graders who entered in Year 2 lies entirely beneath the trajectory for the entering fourth graders, which itself lies entirely below the trajectory for entering fifth graders, and so on. The ranking of the elevations of these several trajectories by entering grade makes sense, given the expected dependence of reading comprehension on children's grade and age. An exception to this pattern, noted above, is the relatively low performance of the group entering seventh grade in Year 2. However, the graph shows the progress this group made over the subsequent school year.

In deciding which display to present at the upcoming faculty meeting, the Clark instructional leadership team recognized that Exhibits 3.6 and 3.7, while based on identical information, were designed for very different purposes. If the team wants to emphasize the pattern of average scores from cohort to cohort of students in grades 3–8 in order to draw attention to noticeable—and substantial—deviations from expected patterns, the simultaneous vertical bar chart in Exhibit 3.6 is preferable. This chart draws attention to the low average performance of the Year 2 seventh graders relative to students in other grades in the same year and to the seventh-grade groups in the subsequent two school years. However, if the team wants to focus attention on how the skills of a group of students develop over time, the connected line segments in Exhibit 3.7 are preferable as they present this information clearly and simply.

In labeling and explaining graphs showing student performance in different school years, it is important to be clear about whether the display illustrates trends in achievement for the same group of students over time, or whether it illustrates cohort-to-cohort differences over a number of years in the performance of students at the same grade level. Exhibits like 3.6 that display only cohort-to-cohort differences are not helpful in tracking true progress or "growth" over time. Exhibits like 3.7 do display progress over time if there is little or no student mobility. Chapter 9, which discusses the district role in supporting data work in schools, explains how a good data-tracking system is invaluable in supporting the work of school-based teams. For example, a good data-tracking system would allow a team to construct a graph showing the progress of students who had been at Clark for at least three years—long enough to benefit from high-quality instruction.

Components of Good Displays

With the endless possibilities available in computer software programs and online tools, it is easy to become enamored of extremely fancy, complicated graphs. However, the main goal of any display is to convey complicated information in a simple, clear manner so that questions of educational significance can be understood, debated, and resolved (see Exhibit 3.8). For each chart you create, ask yourself: Will the audience be able to understand the key takeaways from this chart right away? The following are suggestions for creating data displays that school teams we have worked with have found useful:

- Make an explicit and informative title for every figure in which you indicate critical elements of the chart, such as who was assessed, the number of students whose performance is summarized in the figure, what subject specialty, and when.

- Make clear labels for each axis in a plot, or each row and column in a table.

- Use the available space sensibly, making the dimensions, axes, and themes that are most important for the educational discussion the most dominant in the display.

- Keep plots uncluttered and free of unnecessary detail, extraneous features, and gratuitous cross-hatching and patterns.

- When labeling and explaining graphs showing student performance in different school years, be clear about whether the display illustrates trends in achievement for the same group of students over time, as in Exhibit 3.7, or whether it is illustrating differences in performance from one cohort of students to another at the same grade level over a period of years, as in Exhibit 3.6.

Exhibit 3.8

Tips for Creating Effective Data Displays	
PROVIDE COMPLETE TITLE	**MAKE CHART SIMPLE AND EASY TO READ**
• Assessment name and subject • Grade level tested • School name • Date of assessment • Number of students tested	• Appropriate choice of chart style • Good use of space and color • Fonts large enough to read easily • Clearly labeled legend and axes • Appropriate y-axis scale • Data-point values, where helpful

ALLOW STAFF MEMBERS TO MAKE SENSE OF THE DATA

Principal Roger Bolton was aware that several teachers were not looking forward to Franklin High's first faculty meeting of the year, which they knew would be devoted entirely to talking about results of the state math exam. He could imagine that they expected two hours of listening to him drone on about student performance in a subject that most of them didn't teach. Moreover, he anticipated that teachers' anxiety about math would prevent many of them from engaging fully in the discussion he hoped to have.

To maximize the effectiveness and power of your instructional leadership team's clear and compelling charts, you must use them to stimulate a conversation among your faculty members, specifically about what they see in the data, what questions the data raise, and how they can go about finding answers to these new questions. School leaders we have worked with who successfully involve teachers in addressing learning problems suggest that it is not enough to put copies of charts of state assessment results in faculty mailboxes or to give a lecture about what the charts show. Instead, they actively involve teachers in the data by giving them an opportunity to make sense of the data for themselves, encouraging them to ask questions, and sometimes offering them a chance to experience and discuss the actual items from the test.

Provide Opportunities for Teachers to Work with the Data

One approach to a data overview discussion is to ask a team member to present the various charts to your faculty while pointing out the highlights and conclusions for each graph. However, most teachers recognize that the best way to encourage learning among their students is to give them an opportunity for hands-on exploration, and the same holds true when school leaders "teach" faculty to learn from data. If teachers puzzle over the data displays for themselves, not only are they likely to learn much more from them, but this process will also build their confidence in and comfort with analyzing data.

One particularly effective way of engaging teachers in data analysis is to distribute a few displays and ask teachers to "pair share," or talk with the person next to them about what they see. This approach gets everyone talking right away—in just seconds the room will be alive with discussion. The charts ensure that these conversations will be highly focused around the questions your instructional leadership team has brought to the focus area you explored. Because a pair share allows teachers to formulate their ideas with a partner before being asked to speak in front of the whole group, when you do open the conversation to the larger group, people will be better prepared to join in and share their observations.

Allow Teachers to Experience and Discuss the Actual Test

After looking at a data overview—or before, which can work equally well—you may want to let your faculty experience actual test questions from the relevant assessment. We have worked with several schools that require all teachers in the building to take the same state assessments as their students, either in full or in part, and occasionally under the exam conditions and administration guidelines that are in place for students. By actually experiencing the test themselves, teachers learn firsthand about the content that is being assessed, the ways it is assessed, and the stamina and mind-set that may be needed to perform well. The most significant benefit to having teachers take the test, however, may be in giving them an opportunity to discuss what they learned from the experience.

Engage Teachers in Identifying a Priority Question

Wanting to capitalize on the group energy that the pair share activity generated, Franklin principal Roger Bolton asked the faculty to huddle into ten groups throughout the library. History teacher Pamela Eddy, who was initially reluctant to become involved in any discussion of data—especially math data—found herself surprisingly interested in continuing to explore math performance at Franklin High School. In her group of eight, Pamela volunteered to be the notetaker, recording the group's progress on the next step of data exploration: brainstorming questions.

Attitudes toward data vary widely in schools. There are plenty of "data skeptics" who believe either that student assessment data cannot tell them anything they do not already know or insist that such data can be manipulated to support whatever story the teller wishes. Typically, there are also some "data advocates" who believe that student assessment results contain the solutions to student learning problems and that finding these answers is just a matter of becoming better at data analysis. In reality, student assessment data are neither this weak nor this powerful. The real value in looking at this kind of data is not that it provides answers, but that it inspires questions.

The outcome of your data overview meeting should be identifying a "priority question" that helps you narrow your focus area further to a specific question that will guide your inquiry through the Data Wise Improvement Process. A priority question should have the following characteristics. First, the question is generated from a collaborative process that engages most if not all of the people who will be working to answer the question. Second, it is focused on educational matters, not on other student-related issues that might be outside of your school's control. Third, it serves to narrow the focus for your inquiry, often to a single learning standard, subgroup of students, or type of work. Finally, it takes into account your school's current resources and taps into something that people feel motivated to investigate. For example, if the focus area is writing, possible priority questions might be: How do students use sentence structure in their writing? How are the school's English-language learners using vocabulary in their writing? What parts of the revision process do students struggle with most?

To encourage questions after looking at overview data, some school leaders find it extremely helpful to use a structured protocol. The Right Question Institute has created a particularly engaging and productive protocol called the Question Formulation Technique that we have adapted for our work (see Selected Protocols at the end of this book). The basic premise of this technique is that for people to take ownership of an issue, they need to participate actively in defining it. The protocol involves asking small groups to generate a wide range of questions about a particular issue. As questions are offered, a notetaker records them, exactly as stated, for the group to see. After a certain point, the facilitator asks the group to identify the most important question on their list. The group then generates a new set of questions about the most important question. From this new set of questions, each group can prioritize what it most wants to know. We have found that this process enables educators to focus deeply on an important issue, encourages them to listen to all voices, and provides a useful brake on the usual impulse to jump to solutions.

Once you have identified a priority question, you can engage staff members in a discussion of what data are necessary to begin answering it. At some schools, the instructional leadership team or the data managers function as a resource for collecting this information. For example, as a result of a data overview discussion, faculty members may determine that to make progress on helping students become better writers, they need to know what classes struggling writers take, whether students who perform poorly on state writing tests also perform poorly in the classroom, and if there are opportunities to adapt the new writing curriculum to students' specific needs. Once the faculty has identified the information it needs, the instructional leadership team can pursue it and report back with new evidence. When faculty see that school leaders are committed to exploring many data sources before acting, data skeptics and data advocates alike may modify their opinions about the role of student assessment results in helping solve problems in student learning.

Integrating the ACE Habits of Mind into Step 3: Creating a Data Overview

SHARED COMMITMENT TO ACTION, ASSESSMENT, AND ADJUSTMENT

Many schools we know begin the new academic year by creating a data overview and presenting it to all staff to generate discussion about schoolwide performance on standardized assessments. Broad, school-level data overviews can provide useful information about how students are doing as a larger group, but in order to understand variation on particular skills or content by class or even by student, it is also helpful for teacher teams to discuss "mini" data overviews throughout the year. The charts used in these mini data overviews may be generated from benchmark assessment software, produced by the school's data manager, or even created by tech-savvy teachers. When putting together a mini data overviews, it helps if you follow the guidelines described in this chapter around choosing a focus area (ideally, related to the schoolwide focus), finding the story, and making effective displays. For example, if your school is interested in how your students summarize the main idea from informational text, the English language arts, math, science, and social studies departments could all discuss mini data overviews showing how students typically perform on tasks related to informational text in their subject areas. These overviews can then become a springboard for teacher teams who are ready to dig even deeper into data.

INTENTIONAL COLLABORATION

After a data overview presentation, the involvement of the whole faculty in choosing the priority question is what actually makes it a "priority." In addition, the question becomes a priority when school leaders and eventually the whole staff publicly commit to addressing it. Inviting many voices to the conversation when you present data and discuss the school's focus area encourages people to share what is most important to them. In addition to using the Question Formulation Technique described earlier, we have used an alternative called the Nominal Group Technique to narrow a school's focus on one priority question.[2] Using this protocol, educators first brainstorm a list of questions the data raise. Each person then gets two or three votes (depending on the initial number of items) and distributes them according to their preferences. The votes are tallied to produce a list of top candidates for the priority question. The facilitator can then lead the group through a conversation about which of these questions is really the top priority for the group, and why.

RELENTLESS FOCUS ON EVIDENCE

One of our favorite tools to help educators stay focused on evidence during data conversations is the "ladder of inference" mental model.[3] Developed by organizational learning scholars Chris Argyris and Peter Senge, the ladder of inference is a way of organizing the progression of thought from simply observing something out in the world to doing something about it. The ladder figuratively sits in the middle of all the possible data you can take in with your senses. At the lowest rung of the ladder, you start by selecting some data to observe and describe. As you climb the ladder, you add interpretations and draw conclusions from the data. At the highest rung of the ladder, you decide to take actions, which are informed by your conclusions and interpretations.

In our own work, team members use the ladder imagery to help develop personal awareness of when we are making judgments or inferences about what we observe. We also use it to signal to others that we have made a conscious choice about what kind of statement we are making. We may follow a rather obvious comment by pointing out "I'm keeping it real here, folks—staying low on the ladder," or admit that something we are compelled to say is "way up the ladder." After years of following a norm of grounding statements in evidence, we feel comfortable calling one another out with a simple "What do you see that makes you say that?" or a more playful "Would you like any help coming down from that top rung?"

Educators have told us that when a group stays low on the ladder when re-sponding to charts, student work, or classroom observations, it helps raise aware-ness of how the choice of what facts to pay attention to differs from person to person. "I didn't even notice that!" can become a common refrain. We also hear people say that taking the time to build a shared understanding of the facts gives a group a strong foundation from which to start climbing into interpretation—and that powerful professional learning can occur in that climb. Statement such as "The kids don't want to work in groups" or "The teacher must have given that worksheet because she believed students couldn't handle a more challenging assignment" are seen for the inferences they contain—and can become rich opportunities to unpack and explore.

4

DIGGING INTO DATA

Ethan Mintz, Sarah E. Fiarman, and Tom Buffett

AT A FRANKLIN HIGH SCHOOL MATH DEPARTMENT MEETING, PRINCIPAL ROGER
Bolton shared a graph (see Exhibit 4.1) that the instructional leadership team had made of
the previous year's state test results. "At the last faculty meeting, you wondered whether
there were particular content areas where students need to improve. Based on the data from
the state test, what do you think?"

"I'd say all of them," replied Adelina Swenson, a precalculus teacher who was new to the
building. Eddie Moss, a veteran geometry teacher, jumped in, "It's very clear from looking at
this graph that our students are just not prepared to do math when they get to high school.
We're teaching the curriculum, but they're not getting it. Look, they're having trouble with
number sense and measurement—they should know those by the time they get here! We
need to go back to the fundamentals and get them ready for high school math."

With test scores in hand, Eddie is ready to address Franklin students' low math performance. He thinks he knows the problem—students' lack of "basic skills"—and
he has a solution: drill those basics. The question for Eddie and other educators at
this point in the improvement cycle is, Do you really know what problem you are
trying to solve?

Before committing to a particular course of action or investing time in developing possible solutions, it is important that you fully understand the learner-centered
problem, which we define as a problem of understanding or skill that underlies

Exhibit 4.1

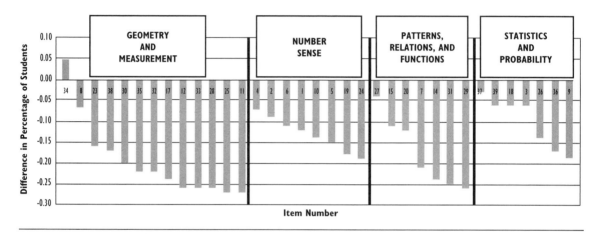

Percentage of Students Answering Each Multiple-Choice Item Correctly

Grade 10 State Comprehensive Assessment—Mathematics
Franklin High School, Year 4 (*n*=425)

students' performance on assessments. "Learner-centered problem" means that the problem is about learning, not that learners are the problem. We know that in reality, no school faces just one learner-centered problem. The goal of this chapter is to help schools identify a learner-centered problem that is common to many students and that, if solved, would help meet the larger goals for students. Educators tend to skip this step, jumping right to developing an action plan and a solution to the problem of low performance. Those educators often find themselves back in the same place the following year, with no improvement to show for their work.

Without an investigation of the data, schools risk misdiagnosing the problem. Poor test scores in geometry and measurement could be a result of weak fundamentals, but they could also be the result of inadequate amounts of homework and independent practice on the topic, students' lack of experience with real-world applications of the topic, the fact that the content is taught long before the test and students aren't retaining what they've learned, or that the content is taught too late for students to use their knowledge on the current year's standardized assessment. Each of these problems requires a different solution; digging into your data helps ensure a more accurate diagnosis of the problem.

Aggregate state test scores, which many principals and teachers are under considerable pressure to improve, can be a good starting point for your conversation, but they don't tell you why students performed the way that they did, and they don't tell you anything about the performance of individual students. To address these important questions, schools have a wide variety of data they can draw on, including test scores, class projects, homework, performances, lab reports, reading journals, teacher observations, and student focus groups. The data inventory you completed in chapter 1 is a good resource for identifying the data available in your school.

The process of using data to identify the learner-centered problem is an iterative process of inquiry. The priority question teachers identified from the data overeiew should lead to further investigation of the data, which inevitably leads to new questions and investigations. Recognizing both the messiness and the richness of this process, this chapter shows how to use data wisely so that you identify the learner-centered problem and avoid the "analysis paralysis" that can come from aimless, endless data analysis. Two complementary approaches can help you identify a learner-centered problem: looking carefully at a single data source and digging into other data sources.

LOOK CAREFULLY AT A SINGLE DATA SOURCE

At Clark K–8 School, the instructional leadership team was trying to figure out what to do next with the faculty. "We generated lots of interesting questions about reading at the last meeting," said principal Sandy Jenkins. "Now we need to figure out how we're going to answer them."

"Well, I think we've milked the state test for all it offers, which is not much," said Vivian Muteba, a fourth-grade teacher. "It's really frustrating that we lose so many days to students taking the tests, and then the tests only tell us that students are a '3' in reading, or have a scale score of 252—what does that mean, anyway?"

"Besides that, we're doing pretty well on the state test, and I don't think a lot of teachers here think the state test reflects all that they're trying to do with kids," said Frank DeLeon, a sixth-grade teacher. "I don't think teachers really want to spend any more time looking at the test."

A useful task in digging into data to identify a learner-centered problem is to look carefully at a single data source. This task begins with choosing a data source based on your data overview and your context. Examining the information from that data source can deepen faculty members' understanding of student thinking and challenge their assumptions about students, which in turn can lead them to hone their definition of the learner-centered problem and to generate new questions. The process of digging into a single data source provides both momentum and direction for further investigation by creating a sense of urgency and curiosity. It can also encourage teachers to refine their initial hunches about the learner-centered problem.

Choosing a Single Data Source as a Starting Place

For many schools, the decision about where to begin data analysis amid the mountains of data available in the school can seem overwhelming. While the data overview generated in chapter 3 provides a good place to begin, the dilemma quickly resurfaces with the questions, concerns, and puzzles that emerge from analysis of the data overview. What next? In our experience, schools too often stay on the surface level of data analysis. Pressed to solve significant problems quickly, many educators take the swift route: look at a table or two, make a judgment based on what they already think is true, and decide to address a problem that they can solve easily and that doesn't require much change on their part. This rapid response often leads to a "stuck point," where schools find themselves either repeating the same pattern by continuing to teach what they've always taught and getting the same results, or by throwing up their hands in frustration and blaming the students for not learning what they are teaching. Teachers may feel that their efforts in the classroom are not reflected in student performance on the "tests that count," and that they are facing the same challenges over and over again. Or, in schools where there is little external pressure to improve what seems to be adequate performance, there may be a different sort of stuck point, where teachers feel that there is not much need for improvement.

Digging into a single data source can help a school move past stuck points like these. Focusing initially on a single data source slows down the common tendency to leap to solutions, makes the data analysis process manageable, and provides an opportunity to move beyond generalizations about the learner-centered problem. Which data source you choose as a starting point will depend on your questions and your context.

The first thing to consider is, What questions do you have about student learning, and what data will help answer those questions? While many schools choose to continue to examine the assessments that provided the initial basis for their inquiry in the data overview, this choice depends in part on what information is available in those assessments. If the assessments include performance by content strand or standards as well as by individual items, schools often can mine the assessments for information that illuminates the learner-centered problem. If the assessment provides little to no information on content strands, standards, or individual items, schools must turn to another data source to continue their inquiry into the problem.

The next consideration is context: What data will be most compelling for the faculty? At a school like Franklin that has been designated by the state as needing improvement because of its poor state assessment results, the faculty often feels a lot of pressure to raise performance on the state test. We have seen many school leaders use the pressure of external accountability as a catalyst for improvement. Teachers are willing to dig more deeply into the state test because they and their students are being judged by the results. At a school like Clark that doesn't face this external pressure, school leaders may choose different data, such as day-to-day student work or writing portfolios, to establish both the need and desire for improvement.

Understanding Student Thinking

At Franklin, the math department continued to look at the state test results. Department head Mallory Golden broke the teachers into groups based on content-area expertise to look at particular strands and to see which skills students struggled with most. The algebra group reported that students had the most difficulty with multistep problems containing variables and equations containing fractions. The geometry group said that students were particularly challenged by anything three-dimensional or requiring proofs, while the statistics/probability group cited student difficulties with interpreting data.

The faculty looked at items from the test in each of those areas. "Do we see any patterns across the different content areas?" asked Mallory.

"I wonder if the problem is language," said Adelina. "Many of these problems require a lot of reading. Maybe kids don't read well, or don't want to read to do math. They seem to do better on problems where they just do math and don't have to read so much."

"I still think the problem is basic skills," said Eddie. "A lot of these problems have a bunch of steps, and if you make a mistake early on, you'll get the problem wrong."

"On the language front, it seems like there's a lot of math vocabulary. I know I taught my students this statistics material, but I didn't call it 'statistics,' and they don't seem to have recognized what they were supposed to do on the test," said intensive math teacher Jean Louis.

Mallory felt that they had moved far beyond thinking that "math" was the problem at Franklin, but she knew they still needed a better understanding of the problem before they could do anything about it.

A student's response on an assessment is just the end product of his or her thinking. In analyzing data to identify a learner-centered problem, it is critical to look not just at the end product of the work, but at the path a student took to get there. Understanding how students arrived at a wrong answer or a poor result is important in knowing how to help them get to the right answer or a good result. Investigating students' thinking processes helps answer questions such as, Do students have any skills and knowledge to build on, or do they need a total reteaching of a particular content area? Do students lack skills and content knowledge, or is the design of the assessment itself giving them difficulty? Working to find answers to these questions will help you identify a meaningful learner-centered problem.

We have seen many schools use item analysis of tests (both state tests and school-based content tests) to understand student thinking. In item analysis, you first look at test items (i.e., questions) in groups by content (such as statistics and probability) or type (such as multiple-choice, short-answer, essay) to see if there were any specific skills or areas of understanding that might have led students to answer the question incorrectly. Then you look for patterns across item groups on the tests. Finally, you look more closely at individual test items to hypothesize why students responded to certain questions in particular ways.

When striving to detect patterns and understand student thinking, it's important for teachers to recognize that students, unless they are guessing wildly at answers, have some logic in how they go about answering questions and doing their work, even if that logic leads them to wrong answers or low-quality work. The teacher's job, in looking closely at the available data, is to try to find that logic pattern. A teacher who understands how a student thinks and approaches school-work will have a clearer sense of what the student needs as a learner. She will also be able to provide instruction that builds on what the student knows and addresses what the student doesn't know. At some schools, teachers take the state assessment themselves, keeping track of their own thinking along the way, so they can begin to understand how students think when they take the assessment.

One of the tensions in using data to improve learning and teaching is the need to figure out the balance between two goals, both of which demand the scarce resource of time. The first goal is having teachers participate in the data analysis process so that they feel ownership of the learner-centered problem, and so that the data analysis is something they do instead of something that is done to them. In other words, teachers are more likely to see the learner-centered problem as a problem that they want to do something about if they've had a major role in identifying it. The second goal, however, is to get to the deeper level of analysis that will help identify the problem. At some schools, data managers or instructional leadership teams do the initial stages of the analysis in order to save time for teachers to focus on the deeper analysis. After a smaller team has done some preliminary analysis (including, but not necessarily limited to, the data overview described in chapter 3), these schools then involve the faculty in a more in-depth analysis to identify the learner-centered problem.

For instance, at one school we know, the data manager makes a chart with each student in a particular grade displayed in a row. Across the top of the chart, he puts each item on the state test. He then highlights each student who scored below proficient, and each item on which fewer than 80 percent of students answered correctly. Before he enlarges the charts to poster size, he blacks out students' names in order to promote collective responsibility and prevent teachers from dismissing the results of particular students. He does this for each subject and each grade that takes the state test. The colorful, highlighted posters become a jumping-off point for discussions with grade-level teams and the whole faculty about the nature of the learner-centered problem. At another school, members of the instructional leadership team show teachers one or two items from the state test or one piece of student writing, and then ask them what they notice about those items and why students may have responded in the ways they did. While they would never draw broad conclusions from any single test item, many school leaders find that getting to the level of a single item or a single student's performance engages teachers and gets them talking about students' thinking and learning in a way that is grounded in evidence.

Challenging Assumptions

At Clark, the instructional leadership team thought that reading journals might provide insight into how students think about and respond to what they read. The team took a random sample of ten third-grade students. After examining and discussing the journals, they chose one representative journal to bring to the faculty.

At the faculty meeting, teachers described what they noticed in the student's journal while another teacher put their comments up on chart paper: "The student summarized the plot of the story he read"; "He described each character in detail"; "He described plot details sequentially, even though the story started in the middle of the action"; "He started each paragraph with a thesis statement."

A seventh-grade teacher commented, "I think we're missing important information about this child's skills as a reader—he lists everything and points out factual information, but what about reading and thinking between the lines?"

"That's a really sophisticated skill." Kristina Wells, a third-grade teacher, jumped in, saying, "You all work on that in the upper grades. Our job is to make sure they know what's happening in the book—and that's plenty hard as it is! Plus, it's hard for kids to decode and read between the lines at the same time."

"I disagree," Lynne Soto, a second-grade teacher, said. "Reading comprehension is much more than factual recall."

Examining student work helps to surface and challenge many assumptions—assumptions about what students can and cannot do, about which students can do what, and about why students are or are not able to do something. Challenging these assumptions is critical for three reasons. First, you want the clearest understanding possible about the learner-centered problem, and assumptions often obscure this understanding by taking the place of evidence. Second, teachers fundamentally have to believe that students are capable of achieving better results. Otherwise, why bother putting any effort into helping students learn? And third, the solutions for the problem will require changes in what faculty members do on a day-to-day basis. Making significant changes in what you do often requires changing what you believe. Opportunities for teachers to share their interpretations of student data allow them to address these fundamental beliefs about learning and teaching.

Starting with data and grounding the conversation in evidence from the data keeps the discussion focused on what we see rather than what we believe. In the Clark example above, the teachers started by noting what they observed in the student's reading journal before they made any judgments of how "good" the work was or what sort of reader the student was. The seventh-grade teacher drew on evidence from the journal to pose her question about "reading between the lines." The third-grade teacher's response, which was not grounded in the student's journal, surfaced an important assumption—that reading between the lines is too sophisticated for third graders.

Data can also be used to challenge assumptions. At one high school, the principal started a fall faculty meeting by presenting two graphs to his faculty (see Exhibit 4.2). He told the faculty that the percentages represented groups of students but didn't say what groups they were. After giving teachers some time to think about whom the numbers might represent, the principal told them group one was

Exhibit 4.2

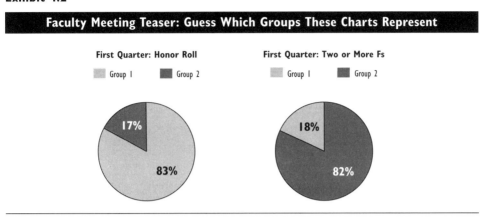

Faculty Meeting Teaser: Guess Which Groups These Charts Represent

First Quarter: Honor Roll

Group 1   Group 2

17%

83%

First Quarter: Two or More Fs

Group 1   Group 2

18%

82%

girls and group two was boys. The first-quarter honor roll was 83 percent girls, while the group of students receiving two or more Fs in the first quarter was 82 percent boys. The data surprised the faculty, who had assumed the poor scores were from other student groups, like students with disabilities or students who qualified for free/reduced-price lunch. The data, and teachers' surprise, led to discussion and exploration of why boys were having less academic success than girls.

It is not uncommon to make assumptions about which students are "low performers" or "high performers." Taking a closer look at student work can often challenge these assumptions, and in so doing, strengthen understanding of what students do and do not know how to do. In one middle school, teachers were analyzing data from a short reading-comprehension assessment for seventh graders. When they began to look closely at student work, a special education teacher pointed to the work of one of her students, Delmar, who got four of the five questions correct, including the short-answer questions, putting him among the best of the seventh graders during this particular assessment. The teachers were stunned. This was a completely unexpected result from Delmar, who had a very difficult time staying focused in class. As teachers talked about Delmar's responses and his work on the assessment, one of the teachers said, "This makes things confusing." This was "confusing" in a good way—the picture of Delmar had changed from one of a student who "spaces out" in class and has little academic strength to a student who merits a closer look and higher teacher expectations. This new picture of Delmar pushed the teachers to look more closely at all of their students' work to find examples of particular strengths. It also reminded them not to make easy—but often false—assumptions about students' skills and capabilities.

DIG INTO MULTIPLE DATA SOURCES

At Clark, the faculty meeting about the third-grade student's reading journal continued.

"I think that reading has to be more than a mechanical process at all grade levels," said a second-grade teacher. "All students need to think about what they read and make inferences from the text. Listing facts is important, but it's only part of what reading is all about."

"I agree with you," said Jae, a third-grade teacher. "But I'm wondering if we're making too big a deal about this—after all, we're looking at only one student's journal. How do we know that this is an issue for more than this student?"

After analyzing a single data source in depth, you will have learned some things to help identify the learner-centered problem on which you will focus your improvement efforts. Undoubtedly, though, the process has raised more questions than can be answered with a single data source. All data sources are limited in the information they provide. Any single test or classroom assignment addresses only a portion of what you want children to learn. No single data source can provide a full picture of students' abilities.

If you rely on one data source to identify a problem, it is unlikely that you will select a problem that is worthy of your ongoing time and attention—in part because you may be identifying a problem with the data source rather than a problem you can address as a faculty. Just as asking friends and checking various consumer reports online will boost your car-buying smarts, so will examining multiple data sources raise your confidence that you will select the right problem to tackle. Furthermore, digging into other sources will help make sure your faculty shares expectations for what students should know and be able to do in a variety of contexts.

We know many schools that look closely at multiple data sources with the purpose of understanding student thinking. These data can include students' projects, classwork, or homework. The process of "looking at student work" (sometimes known by the acronym LASW) can give teachers considerable insight into students' thinking.[1] For example, by examining students' homework on questions that deal with statistics, the math teachers at Franklin might be able to determine whether the students simply didn't know statistical terms, as Jean surmised, or whether they were faltering in their understanding of key statistical concepts. At another school, teachers bring two or three student essay samples to LASW meetings, where they collectively look for evidence of students' ability to write topic sentences, provide evidence for assertions, and so forth. By looking collaboratively at students' everyday work, teachers can deepen their understanding of students' strengths and misconceptions.

Triangulating Data Sources

By "triangulating" your findings from multiple data sources—that is, by analyzing other data to illuminate, confirm, or dispute what you learned through your initial analysis—you will be able to identify your problem with more accuracy and specificity. When triangulating sources, it can be helpful to draw on different types of assessments (such as tests, portfolios, and student conferences) and on assessments taken at different intervals (such as daily, at the end of a curriculum unit, and at the end of a grading period or semester), and to look for both patterns and inconsistencies across student responses to the assessments. Schools that look at state data as their initial data source might next examine classroom tests and homework. Schools that focus initially on daily classroom work might consult annual or quarterly assessments.

At Clark, the discussion of reading journals brought the issue of reading between the lines to the surface. Could it be that the prompts to which students responded in the reading journal encouraged factual responses? Could it be something about the process of writing that interfered with students' ability to show how well they could read? Clark teachers would need to examine other data sources to investigate whether students could read between the lines in other contexts.

A rich source of data is the students themselves. For example, after doing an analysis of the wrong answers students gave on the state test, teachers at one middle school were intrigued by the common mistakes. They decided to conduct focus groups with students to understand why they seemed to be making the same types of errors. Students are an important and underused source of insight, and having focus groups with students to talk about their thinking can help you identify a problem underlying low student performance.

When triangulating data, be prepared to be surprised. It is important to approach the process of digging deeper into other data sources with the idea that you will find something new. When the goal is merely to confirm a hypothesis or assumption, only particular pieces of data tend to be looked at, and the work often stops when the original belief is confirmed. Instead, look for and embrace unexpected trends and leads. School leaders can play an important role by modeling the ideas that it is acceptable to ask questions and that faculty should expect to understand something new about student learning by the end of a meeting. In this context, it's important that school leaders not try to portray themselves as all-knowing experts. Schools should be led by what they discover, which will lead to new questions to investigate as they identify the learner-centered problem.

At Franklin, for example, the math teachers examined unit tests and homework and realized that students correctly answered basic-skills problems when all they had to do was use a single skill. This finding debunked Eddie's assertion that the issue was basic skills and led teachers back to the state test, where they noticed that few problems required only a single skill, and those few were word problems that placed the skill in a real-world context instead of just presenting a numerical problem to solve. When they examined classwork to see if there were differences among students, they were surprised to see that many students with disabilities were solving complex problems more accurately than regular education students. This finding did not match the state test results, where students with disabilities performed worse than regular education students on all problems, including complex ones. When teachers investigated further by talking with students and teachers and looking at the classwork again, they realized that students with disabilities were approaching their classwork differently. With the support of the special education teachers, students were highlighting important words in the problem and breaking the problem into separate pieces. Teachers saw some evidence of students using this approach on unit tests, but the students said they forgot the approach when it came to the state test. After examining multiple data sources, sometimes returning to data sources with new questions, Franklin is closer to identifying a learner-centered problem as having something to do with complex math problems, which few students seem to have a process for solving that they could apply in different contexts.

Developing a Shared Understanding of the Knowledge and Skills Students Need

At Clark K–8 School, the instructional leadership team decided to take a "slice" of student work to investigate what students were doing with reading and what "reading between the lines" looked like in different grade levels and content areas.[2]

The slice was all the classwork and homework that 30 students, chosen randomly from the first, fifth, and eighth grades, had completed from noon one day until noon the next day. The faculty used one of their afternoons together on an early release day to examine the work and discuss it.

"What did you notice about the work students are doing in reading?" asked principal Sandy Jenkins.

"I noticed that students use art to show meaning. The first graders drew pictures to go with the stories they wrote, and the eighth graders made storyboards interpreting scenes from the book they're reading."

"I noticed that there was evidence that fifth-grade students had read at home for home-work—the reading log signed by their parents—but I wasn't sure if students had discussed their reading at home or at school, or had written anything down, or in some way showed their thinking about what they had read."

"I noticed that a lot of the reading students seemed to be doing was pretty factual, so there wasn't much cause to read between the lines. At least in the work we saw, the reading that students were responding to tended to be short, informative pieces, like a section of a history book or science book that students were answering questions about."

"It seems like students are pretty much giving us what we ask for—maybe we're not ask-ing for enough."

While you refine your definition of the learner-centered problem, you also build a common understanding among teachers of the knowledge and skills students need to have—in other words, what you expect students to know and be able to do, and how well they are meeting your expectations. Perhaps you want students to be "proficient" or "advanced" or "good readers" or "complex problem solvers," but what do those words really mean? Do you all agree on what you expect, and at what point do you think it's a problem if students aren't meeting those expectations? As you and your colleagues examine various data sources, you develop a richer understanding of the curriculum and external standards, as well as shared internal standards for high-quality work.

The process of examining and discussing student data can feel threatening to teachers, especially if there is not a norm of collaborative practice at a school. His-torically, teachers have taught in isolation, in the privacy of their classrooms, and only recently have they been expected to share their practice in any concrete form. It is therefore not surprising that teachers often feel exposed when they share the work of their students with peers. Teachers need to know that they are not opening them-selves up to a free-wheeling critique based on their peers' perceptions of their prac-tice. Structuring conversations using protocols assures teachers that they will have the opportunity to be heard and that peers' comments will not be speculative, but will be grounded in the student work in front of them and moderated by a facilitator.

At the same time, teachers need to feel comfortable asking challenging, constructive questions of each other. Collaboratively examining student work often leads to important new insights. Having a built-in expectation and a designated time to ask probing questions supports the constructive practice of talking specifically about student learning. Finally, by agreeing to certain ground rules for examining student work and by using relevant protocols, you can ensure that the conversation includes multiple voices rather than just the usual ones. This leads to greater consistency in defining the problem.

There are a number of strategies for using data to build a shared understanding of content among your faculty members. One common strategy, as noted previously, is for teachers to take, or at least examine, the tests their students take. This practice allows teachers to determine whether standardized tests align with the skills they are teaching. Another strategy is for teachers to photocopy student work on an assignment, grade it individually, and then compare how they evaluated the work with how their peers assessed it. In both strategies, data are used as a springboard for focused conversations about academic content that the faculty believes is important for students to know and understand.

Conversations like these may lead to questions about the breadth or depth of the curriculum. When looking at disappointing test results, we've heard overwhelmed teachers say, "But that's not in the curriculum!" or "I taught it—they just didn't learn it!" or "There isn't time to teach that." This is a good opportunity to investigate how content areas are addressed in the curriculum based on a question or concern that arises from the data. A group of fourth-grade teachers investigating students' poor performance in reading nonfiction mapped their curriculum projects across the school year and realized that the vast majority of their reading and writing assignments were about fiction. Students had little opportunity to read nonfiction, which teachers agreed was a problem not only because it was on the state test, but also because students needed to be able to read nonfiction well to access information and be independent learners.

Careful investigations of student work usually lead to discussions about work quality. If teachers on your team don't agree on what a high or low level of student performance looks like, it will be hard for your team to identify a meaningful learner-centered problem to address throughout your improvement effort. Investigations into the data may result in different conclusions from different teachers. A common way to address this is to use a rubric—a delineation of the skills and knowledge students need to produce high-quality work. Developing and using rubrics ensures that data analysis is based on a common set of criteria. Rubrics help teachers identify discrete areas of student strengths and weaknesses, which can point the way to understanding a meaningful problem that can be addressed through an action plan. As will be explained in chapter 7, rubrics are also a helpful tool in measuring student progress.

Developing Common Language

At the Franklin High School math department meeting, department chair Mallory Golden said, "We keep coming back to complex math questions as posing challenges for kids. We've definitely started to identify the learner-centered problem as one of solving 'multistep math problems,' but I'm not sure I know what we mean by that."

"I think of 'multistep problems' as problems where students need to do more than one mathematical operation to answer the question," answered Eddie.

"Oh, I was thinking of it as problems in which students need to use more than one piece of information to answer the question," said Adelina.

As conversations about student work progress, it's important to develop common language to describe a learner-centered problem worthy of your time and energy. At Franklin, though becoming proficient with multistep questions was both a school and state priority, teachers held very different definitions of what constituted a multistep question. When teachers don't take the time to pinpoint exactly what they mean when discussing their learner-centered problem, their findings and consequent actions will be inconsistent at best, and potentially inaccurate.

Important differences in how teachers think about student learning often remain hidden when discussions remain at an abstract level. Teachers may identify "number sense" as a student weakness in math, but do all teachers mean the same thing when they use that phrase? Teachers leave a meeting with the decision that struggling students need more "scaffolding," but do they share an understanding of why students are struggling? If teachers each have a different understanding of the problem, it is more likely that their responses will be inconsistent because, in fact, they are addressing different problems! To get to the heart of a problem and systematically improve instruction, it's important to make sure teachers clearly understand one another, as well as the nature of the topic they're exploring.

Groups of teachers develop a common language around teaching and learning in different ways. In some schools, teachers use a common rubric to assess student essays to determine whether they share a common definition of "voice" in narrative writing. In other schools, teachers categorize test questions into conceptual areas and compare their categories. At Clark, teachers noted that students were weakest in the area of "interpretation" on the state test, but didn't know exactly what that meant. The data manager pulled sample "interpretation" questions off the state department of education website. Teachers answered the questions and then discussed the skills needed to answer them correctly. In each of these examples, the exchange among teachers is based on work or test items that are in front of them. With this common reference point, the substance of discussions becomes fine-grained, leaves less room for misunderstandings, and offers more opportunities for colleagues to build on one another's insights.

Articulating the Learner-Centered Problem

When teachers thoughtfully examine data, there are always more questions to ask and more leads to follow. Deeper knowledge about the nature of the problem and how to solve it are the building blocks of your school's theory of how to improve learning and teaching. Much like a research project, in which having a good question is the driving force behind a strong research process, identifying a meaningful problem to work on is the driving force behind a strong instructional improvement process.

Data analysis supports a culture of improvement by building the habit of inquiry in which you constantly ask questions and find answers, not in your preconceived judgments of children, but in observable data. The learner-centered problem is:

- Directly related to the priority question

- Based on multiple forms of evidence found when digging into data

- Within the school's control

- A statement about student learning, not a question

- Specific and small

At Clark, the learner-centered problem teachers identified was "Students have trouble drawing text-based inferences when reading." At Franklin, the learner-centered problem was "Students have trouble solving multistep problems independently."

It is critical to invest the time and effort needed to identify a meaningful problem that becomes the focus of the improvement process and supports your larger goals for students. However, waiting too long to act runs the risk of analysis paralysis. Thus, it is important to realize that you can always conduct additional analyses and examine other types of data either later in the improvement cycle that you are currently working on, or the next time you work your way through the eight steps.

■

Integrating the ACE Habits of Mind into Step 4: Digging into Data

SHARED COMMITMENT TO ACTION, ASSESSMENT, AND ADJUSTMENT

The main deliverable that comes from Step 4 is a learner-centered problem that will focus your inquiry and improvement efforts for one cycle through the Data Wise Improvement Process. We are often asked, "We know that students have many needs and don't want to leave anything out. How do we choose the right learner-centered problem?" We understand this concern, but we strongly encourage you to let go of worrying about "leaving anything out." It is not humanly possible to address all problems at once! Choosing a learner-centered problem will help you develop a culture of inquiry by giving you a place to begin. Just to get yourself moving, you might start with a problem that at first appears to scratch the surface of the students' learning needs. Educators at one middle school we have worked with took this route when they decided to address a problem, strongly supported by their data, that students had difficulty following directions. This problem was broad enough that most teachers could get invested in it—teachers across the grade levels could bring examples of student work where students did not follow the directions. The instructional leadership team was then able to engage the faculty in a discussion about the variety in the length, styles, and wording across teachers' sets of directions. Cutting their teeth on this problem gave them fluency with using the Data Wise Improvement Process, supported the faculty in developing a common language around one area of instruction, and allowed them to move on to richer problems. The key is working through the problems systematically—and you may find that starting with one avenue of inquiry will actually address several related issues.

INTENTIONAL COLLABORATION

It is important to involve as many people as possible in collecting data around the priority question that you identified from overview data. For example, one school was interested in the priority question, "Are our students college and career ready?" They focused their initial data overview on examining high school PSAT and SAT data because they used these national standardized exams as one well-recognized indicator of college readiness. The faculty discovered that their tenth-grade students were having trouble with items on the PSAT that asked them to identify the author's argument in expository text and items where students had to compare two different authors' arguments about the same text. This initial inquiry focused on a specific group of students taking one particular test, but they chose to involve their entire instructional leadership team in collecting and analyzing other examples of data to triangulate their hypotheses about student learning needs. The middle and high school English language arts (ELA) teachers all collected samples of student work where they asked students to define and compare multiple authors' arguments, and both the cross-grade ELA team and the instructional leadership team focused their next meetings on triangulating what they saw in the student work with the results of the PSAT. They ultimately decided to formulate their first learner-centered problem as, "Students struggle to identify and compare authors' point of view, especially between multiple rigorous texts." The team discovered that they could gain greater buy-in from the whole faculty because this learner-centered problem involved data from classrooms across the school, and teachers from many grades and subject areas contributed to the analysis.

RELENTLESS FOCUS ON EVIDENCE

When thinking about gathering data to use as evidence for a learner-centered problem, always define "data" broadly. Be creative in what you consider as data: student surveys, teacher surveys, classroom observation notes, student "exit tickets," and student narrative reflections all yield rich and varied forms of evidence. Also consider that some meaningful priority questions might require you to collect forms of data you have never used before. For example, faculty at one school might decide that their priority question is, "How well are our students doing with public speaking and presentation skills?" This priority question does not lend itself well to standardized pen-and-paper or computer-based assessments. However, it is a worthwhile avenue for inquiry and it aligns with the need for students to develop the complex communication skills that they will need to succeed in a knowledge-based economy. Investigating this type of priority question might require your faculty to work together to develop a common understanding and language for what high-quality speaking and presentation skills look and sound like, and what teachers and students could consider evidence of success. Then the faculty could collaboratively design performance-based assessments, such as a series of presentations that all students will give in different grade levels and subjects. Faculty can also create criteria for a common rubric that teachers will use to assess student proficiency in speaking and presentation, and a process for documenting written feedback for students. Discussing, generating, and examining multiple forms of data helps dispel the notion that rich data can only be obtained on a score report.

5

EXAMINING INSTRUCTION

Elizabeth A. City, Melissa Kagle, and Mark B. Teoh

FRANKLIN MATH DEPARTMENT HEAD MALLORY GOLDEN BEGAN THE MEETING BY acknowledging the department's work: "Well, we've made a lot of progress so far. We've decided that our learner-centered problem is that students are not able to solve multistep problems very well. Now, our next step is to understand why they're having so much trouble with multistep problems."

"Are we really going to talk about this for another meeting?" interrupted Eddie. "All we do is talk. Students are going to fail the state test again while we sit around and talk."

"I hear you," replied Mallory. "But my question is, what's happening—or not happening—in our teaching that's leading our students to struggle with multistep problems?"

"Look, it's not as if we haven't taught multistep problems," responded Eddie. "They're in every book I've used, not to mention on the state test. It would help if kids would do their homework and come prepared to class, but I don't see that happening anytime soon, so I'll give them more multistep problems to work on in class."

Educators are constantly solving problems. These problems range from simple (a student doesn't have a pencil) to complex (a student doesn't understand an assignment or two students aren't getting along). To manage the steady stream of problems, we tend to leap to solutions. However, many of the problems we face are too complicated for us to solve quickly on our own.

The learner-centered problem you have articulated by digging into data is a complicated problem—if it were an easy one, you would have solved it by now. To solve it, you need to understand its teaching dimensions as well. While many factors outside of school influence children's learning, these are outside the reach of most teachers. What educators can control is teaching. Teaching, therefore, will be the focus of the action plan. You need a process that allows teachers to take responsibility for solving the problem, instead of backing away from it because they feel it's not their problem, or that they can't do anything about it anyway, or that they're being blamed for it.

To do this, you reframe the learner-centered problem as a "problem of practice" that, if solved, will mean progress toward your larger goals for students.[1] The problem of practice is:

- Directly related to the learner-centered problem
- Based on evidence found when examining instruction
- Within the school's control
- A statement about practice, not a question
- Specific and small

Not only does identifying the problem of practice lay important groundwork for future action, it also saves time. Even though it may feel like one more thing to do, remember that this investment will likely keep you from spending months or years on something that won't work because it doesn't address the actual problem of practice that is at the heart of student learning difficulties.

Four main tasks will help you investigate instruction and articulate a problem of practice:

1. Link learning and teaching: With this particular learner-centered problem, how does instruction have an impact on what students learn?

2. Develop the skill of observing practice: How do we look at instructional data?

3. Develop a shared understanding of effective practice: What does effective instruction for our learner-centered problem look like and what makes it effective?

4. Analyze current practice: What is actually happening in the classroom in terms of the learner-centered problem, and how does it relate to our understanding of effective practice?

Because learning and teaching are so intertwined, you may already have partially completed one or more of these tasks when your school was digging into data. While schools that are new to the improvement process may find it easiest to proceed through these tasks in the sequence above, many schools find that examining instruction involves doing them more or less simultaneously. More important than the order in which the tasks are done is the necessity that they all be addressed.

LINK LEARNING AND TEACHING

Mallory continued the math department meeting by asking teachers to use their experience in the classroom to brainstorm why Franklin students were struggling with multistep problems. Teachers wrote their responses on sticky notes:

Students don't come to high school adequately prepared for complex problems.

Students aren't able to think abstractly.

Students give up when the problem is hard.

The vocabulary on the state math tests is unfamiliar to students.

Students have a math phobia—they think they can't do math.

Students aren't familiar with the format of the state test.

Students have a lot of social and emotional issues.

Students are working after school, and they don't do their homework.

The first step in articulating a problem of practice is to establish a link between learning and teaching. This may sound surprising, since we presumably wouldn't be teachers if we didn't think our efforts mattered for learning. However, in the context of accountability policies and the day-to-day pressures of school, it can be easy to forget that teaching makes a difference in student learning. If teachers don't fundamentally believe this, then it's going to be difficult to convince them to change their teaching.

Linking learning and teaching is also about helping teachers take responsibility for student learning. "Responsibility" doesn't mean "it's my fault"—it means, "I can and will do something about the learner-centered problem." Poor test results and external pressures can lead educators to try to shift responsibility to others through finger-pointing and blame. For school-based educators, however, the primary focus has to be on what we have control over—what happens at school. This is not an easy task. Despite their hard work, teachers don't often see great improvements on state tests, and they don't think it's possible to work any harder. They see lots of big issues that affect student learning that they can't readily fix, like poverty, previous learning experiences, and parental education. The school leader must keep the conversation focused on what teachers can do in the classroom.

What we can do is teach well. To improve the quality of teaching in a school, leaders must push the conversation about the learning problem past the level of what *students* are and aren't doing to look at what *teachers* are and aren't doing. Additionally, school leaders have to help teachers link learning and teaching in a way that doesn't make them defensive but does get them thinking about their own practice. When planning opportunities for teachers to link learning and teaching, consider these points:

- How will you move the conversation from "students" (or "parents" or "community," etc.) to "teachers"?

- How will you frame the work as an opportunity to improve instruction, rather than as a failure (proactive vs. reactive)?

- How will you help teachers have a questioning rather than a defensive stance?

- How will you reinforce a collective conviction that teaching matters for learning?

Many school leaders we have worked with use structured protocols to address these questions and make the conversation both safer and closer to instruction for teachers. At Franklin, Mallory used the Affinity Protocol (see Selected Protocols at the end of the book) to have teachers brainstorm hypotheses about the learner-centered problem. After Mallory saw that most of the sticky notes started with "Students," she encouraged teachers to consider other reasons students might be struggling with multistep problems, and to try starting some ideas with "I" or "Teachers." Teachers' responses included:

There's too much math to teach in a year—no time to spend on long problems.	Parents don't know the math, so they can't help their kids.	Teachers spend most of their time on applying formulas, not on complex problems.	I put multistep problems at the end of assignments, and they are often skipped.
I don't really teach strategies for doing multistep problems.	Teachers spend too much time lecturing at students and doing all the work.	Students don't practice on their own enough.	The math book doesn't have enough multistep problems to practice, and I don't have time to find more.

Although many of their sticky notes still didn't focus specifically on teachers, when they organized all of their notes into categories, they labeled the categories "Curriculum," "Instruction," and "Motivation/Expectations," and added a "Parking Lot" category for things over which they had no control. The process of working through the protocol helped teachers decide that ideas like "Students aren't able to think abstractly" should be in the category of "Instruction," even though they hadn't thought of it that way originally. The categories, which focus on what teachers are doing rather than on students, reflected the faculty's evolving understanding of their role in students' learning. We have seen many schools use the Affinity Protocol with great success because it's anonymous (thus letting participants write down things they might not say out loud), it levels the speaking field (thus addressing the potential for one person to dominate or for everyone to wait to see what the principal says), and it's fun (people appreciate the hands-on experience of using sticky notes and moving them around, rather than sitting and talking).

Other schools use a process of asking "why?" repeatedly to peel away the layers of the learning problem. They start with their learner-centered problem and then ask why they have that problem. For each answer they come up with, they ask why again, and repeat that process several times. One middle school's "why-why-why" diagram about its special education students who were not answering math questions beyond the first step is displayed in Exhibit 5.1.[2]

Exhibit 5.1

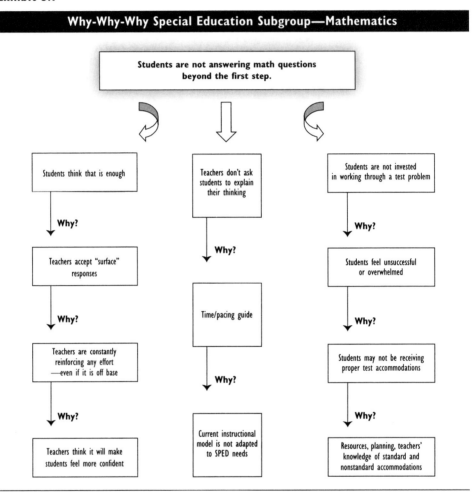

Why-Why-Why Special Education Subgroup—Mathematics

Students are not answering math questions beyond the first step.

Students think that is enough	Teachers don't ask students to explain their thinking	Students are not invested in working through a test problem
Why?	**Why?**	**Why?**
Teachers accept "surface" responses	Time/pacing guide	Students feel unsuccessful or overwhelmed
Why?	**Why?**	**Why?**
Teachers are constantly reinforcing any effort —even if it is off base	Current instructional model is not adapted to SPED needs	Students may not be receiving proper test accommodations
Why?		**Why?**
Teachers think it will make students feel more confident		Resources, planning, teachers' knowledge of standard and nonstandard accommodations

The initial step of linking learning and teaching need not take a long time—most schools we know devote one meeting to it. However, it lays the groundwork for closer examination of practice by focusing attention squarely on the instructional core, which is defined as the interaction between teachers, students, and content.[3] The data used in the protocols above are teachers' own experiences, including their assumptions and beliefs. This is a good place to start because this type of data is easily accessible and influences how teachers approach the problem of practice.

To truly understand the problem of practice, however, you will have to get closer to what actually happens in classrooms.

DEVELOP THE SKILL OF OBSERVING PRACTICE

At Clark, teachers had spent the previous few weeks doing peer observations, with each teacher visiting one colleague. In team meetings, teachers shared what they had seen.

"I enjoyed visiting Anita's classroom. I saw students who were really engaged," began Kristina, a third-grade teacher.

"That was true in Jae's classroom, too," said Vivian, a fourth-grade teacher. "Students were well-behaved, they worked well in groups, and they looked like they were really on task."

"Good," replied Sandy, the principal. "Engagement is important. The next question is, what evidence did you see that students were engaged, and what task were students engaged in?"

Examining instruction is a complex undertaking. There are many potential sources of evidence to explore, ranging from artifacts (such as assignments or assessments), to self-reports (such as surveys or interviews of teachers), to observations (in person or via video). When weighing this evidence, educators need to be able to recognize, understand, and describe what they're seeing. This is not as easy as it sounds, especially when the evidence under consideration is actual classroom practice.

Understanding the Key Elements of Observing Practice

Most teachers have not had much experience with examining teaching, which means they have neither the skills to describe teaching in a fine-grained, evidence-based way, nor the collegial culture in which examining practice feels supportive rather than threatening. If you plunge right into examining instruction without developing skills for doing so, you will find the conversation is awash in compliments and generalities like "students are engaged" and "the lesson was well planned." One principal we know calls this "happy talk"—our tendency as educators to be overly nice to colleagues, especially when we're just beginning to examine practice. Although it is often helpful to point out what is working well, that level of generality and abstraction does little to help us understand how our teaching links to the learning in the classroom.

Developing skills for examining practice takes time, and dogged determination. In response to consistent feedback from educators who find this work particularly challenging, the Data Wise Project team developed *Key Elements of Observing Practice: A Data Wise DVD and Facilitator's Guide.* This resource offers a set of tools for developing teachers' capacity to observe practice, including videos, agendas, protocols, and handouts to support professional development on this topic. The main message is that observation of practice is most effective when embedded in a formal protocol. The specific format of the protocol is less important than that it be designed to support an ongoing conversation, based on evidence, about what practice looks like. In particular, we found that effective protocols contain five key elements, and when the purpose of the observation is to identify a problem of practice, the elements involve the following tasks:

Key Element	Tasks Associated with This Element *(when the purpose of the observation is to identify a problem of practice)*
Focus	Review the learner-centered problem, provide context for the lesson(s) to be observed, discuss how observers will focus their attention during the observation.
Observe	View one or more classrooms, taking notes that capture details about what the teachers and students are saying and doing and what tasks students are asked to complete.
Debrief	Discuss the teaching and learning observed using descriptions (not inferences or judgments) and commit to next steps.
Adjust	Carry out the next steps agreed on during debriefing.
Follow Up	Discuss what was learned during adjustment and plan future work.

When debriefing an observation, it is important that teachers be able to describe what they see using precise, shared vocabulary. For example, a teacher who has not had much practice analyzing instruction might observe a teacher introducing a new math concept and respond with the comment, "I noticed that students seem confused." "Confused," like "engaged," could mean many things to different teachers. In contrast, a more precise observation might be, "I noticed that several students didn't start the assignment immediately. One student was looking at other students. Two students were talking to each other while looking at the assignment, and four students raised their hands after the teacher gave directions for the assignment." Cultivating the habit of maintaining a relentless focus on evidence helps build the precise, shared vocabulary that will allow you to identify a meaningful problem of practice.

Cultivating the habit of intentional collaboration is also essential. It is more powerful to observe and analyze practice collaboratively because each person brings his or her own set of beliefs and assumptions to the observation. Hearing others' responses to the same lesson helps challenge individual assumptions, allows everyone to notice different things and see the same things in a new way, and leads to a better understanding of the practice observed. For collaboration to be productive and safe, your team will need to adhere to the norms you set when organizing for collaborative work (see chapter 1) and perhaps revisit and expand upon those ground rules for discussion so that discussing teaching openly is possible. An important norm that many teams have is confidentiality, meaning that what is discussed about an observation will not be shared outside the group doing the analysis.

Learning to See

To develop the skills of observing practice, you need not jump right into having teachers observe one another. Schools we have worked with often start by having teachers watch videos of teaching from outside the school (such as the videos available in the *Key Elements* DVD mentioned above). Observing and discussing the practice of teachers they don't know gives teachers the opportunity to build the skills necessary for safe and insightful conversations about practice. One principal we know called it "learning to see." She gave teachers time to watch videos and make note of what they saw. She modeled using language like "I noticed that . . . ," "I saw that . . . ," and "I heard that . . ." with examples of what she saw and heard. With her persistent reminders to cite evidence rather than rush to judgments, teachers developed the habit of doing so, and then used this skill to examine their own practice when they observed each other teach.

We have also seen teams develop these skills when one brave soul, such as a teacher or instructional coach, volunteers to have other teachers observe his teaching. Group members then discuss their observations, practicing using evidence, precise vocabulary, and norms. It can be especially compelling when the school leader volunteers to have teachers observe and discuss her teaching, thus opening his or her own practice to faculty for examination.

This step of "learning to see" instruction focuses on description rather than evaluation. The distinction is important because our normative judgments tend to cloud our ability to see what's happening—for example, students look "engaged," which we think is good, but when we look at what they're "engaged" with, we see that they're doing work that's several grade levels below where they should be. There are limits, though, to what describing can do.

DEVELOP A SHARED UNDERSTANDING OF EFFECTIVE PRACTICE

At Clark, a seventh-grade teacher had volunteered to have colleagues observe her teaching the concept of inference. At the next faculty meeting, teachers discussed what they had seen and were thinking about teaching inference.

"The kids were doing inference through drama," said Vivian, a fourth-grade teacher. "First, they were taking lines from everyday interactions, like 'I'm fine' or 'Excuse me,' and they were saying the lines in all different ways, and then the rest of the class was guessing—or inferring—what they were actually thinking when they said it. One student said 'Excuse me' like she was really embarrassed, and another said it like he was really annoyed. Then they moved on to reading lines from A Midsummer Night's Dream, and they worked on saying those lines with meaning that was appropriate, based on the text."

"It was great, but I hope there are other ways to teach inferring—I'm just not the drama type and I can't see using Shakespeare with third graders," Kristina said, referring to her students. "Do we have any other ideas about teaching inference?"

A critical step in articulating a problem of practice is to develop a shared understanding of instruction that will effectively address the learner-centered problem that you have identified. You need a vision for what this effective teaching looks like so you can assess whether what you're doing now fits or doesn't fit that vision. The problem of practice is in the gap between current practice and effective practice for addressing the learner-centered problem. If an understanding of effective practice for addressing the problem already existed among your faculty, you probably wouldn't have the learner-centered problem, as teachers would know how to successfully teach inferring or solving multistep problems, or whatever your learner-centered problem is. Thus, building teacher knowledge is important in articulating the problem of practice. The faculty will continue to develop and refine their understanding of effective practice as they develop the action plan, implement the plan, and assess progress, but it's important to lay the groundwork at this stage. Without a vision of what's possible, we limit our expectations and goals for addressing the learner-centered problem, as well as our ability to examine our own practice with an informed eye.

Drawing on Internal Resources

In developing a shared understanding of effective practice, the essential question is, Based on student and teacher data, what does instruction that addresses the learner-centered problem look like? To answer this question, schools can look internally at instruction in their own buildings and look externally to other practitioners and to research. Looking internally has advantages: it honors the work of teachers in the building, which can build a sense of confidence and competence, and the practice is very specific to the context of the school, thus requiring less translation or adaptation than an external practice might. Looking internally also has potential disadvantages: the scope of ideas may be narrow because we don't have all the answers; singling out particular teachers as examples of "effective practice" may promote a sense of competition or comparison among teachers; and our assumptions about what's possible may be limited. A school that chooses to use examples of effective practice from inside the school can mitigate these pitfalls in several ways. First, introduce a wider range of practices by bringing in outside resources, such as journal articles that address the learner-centered problem. Second, involve the whole staff in identifying effective practice to cut down on feelings of competition. And third, facilitate conversations carefully to get teachers thinking more widely about practice.

When looking internally to develop ideas of effective practice, the key is to ground the discussion in evidence. We know many schools where teachers share instructional strategies that they call "best practices." This is an important way to develop craft knowledge, but is often disconnected from data and from the learner-centered problem. Some schools we work with address this by inviting teachers to share practices related to the learner-centered problem and to support the belief that these are "best" practices with evidence of student learning. In these schools, teachers use the following protocol: "This is a 'best practice' because when I did this, the learning looked like this." They then present their instructional strategy and evidence from student work. Connecting best practices to data serves multiple purposes: it increases the likelihood that the practice is effective rather than simply congenial; it reinforces the discipline of grounding all conversations about teaching and learning in evidence rather than generalities or assumptions; it's more persuasive—teachers are more likely to try something for which there's evidence that it works; and it reinforces the link between learning and teaching.

Drawing on External Resources

At Franklin, Sasha, the math coach, showed the math department videos of algebra lessons from Japan, Germany, and the United States from the TIMSS (Trends in International Math and Science Study).

"Well, sure, it would be great if our lessons looked like the Japanese one, but our classrooms are really different," Eddie said. "First of all, we're dealing with a much more diverse population than those Japanese teachers are. Second, I've tried that approach of putting a problem on the board and having kids try to solve it, and it just doesn't work. Some of them don't even start it, and just talk to their neighbors. Others start it, and then stop as soon as they're stuck. If I'm not helping them through each step of the problem, they just give up."

"What do you see in these videos that relates to the article that I gave you about differences in teaching practice across countries at different performance levels on international math tests?" asked Sasha.

"The article said that countries in the middle of the pack, like the U.S. and Germany, tend to spend lots of class time on reviewing homework and applying formulas. We definitely saw that in the video," said Mallory.

"The article also said that the countries that score higher, like Japan, have students develop some understanding of the theory behind an operation, rather than just applying an algorithm. And there was the piece in the article about breadth versus depth—U.S. textbooks are much fatter than Japanese and Korean textbooks and cover a lot more concepts. We saw some of both of those things. In the U.S. classroom, students were doing many problems that drew on a number of different math concepts, whereas in the Japanese classroom, students did two problems in the class period, both on the same math concepts."

"Okay," said Eddie. "Like I said, I'd love to teach just like those Japanese teachers. But how would this work at Franklin?"

In schools, internal resources often are not adequate for developing a shared understanding of effective practice related to the learner-centered problem. This is when school leaders should use external resources to seed the conversation about effective practice and build teachers' knowledge. You can go to the source, by visiting another school or attending a professional conference, or you can bring it in, by learning from consultants or reviewing research. Looking externally brings its own advantages and disadvantages. Some advantages include bringing in a range of ideas and expertise that is beyond that of your staff, and making it easier to have an "objective" conversation. Many school leaders we know bring in articles and videos to start conversations with their faculty, which helps teachers get perspective on their own practice and talk about effective practice. External resources also can challenge assumptions about what's possible by showing evidence of other practitioners succeeding where we have not; providing access to ideas that have potentially been tested more systematically or for a longer period of time (e.g., research); and helping triangulate teachers' hunches and experiences of good practice with external ideas.

Drawing on outside resources also brings potential disadvantages. For some teachers, external resources challenge their professionalism and suggest that they're not good teachers or don't know what good teaching is. There is also the "But they're different! That wouldn't work here!" problem, as math teacher Eddie exemplified at Franklin. In this view, educators assume that whatever success the external resource had won't hold when applied to their own unique setting. With external resources, it's not always clear which elements are essential and which can be adapted (or how) to another context.

Adopting an inquiry stance, in which any resource—internal or external—is questioned and investigated, addresses these disadvantages. Inquiry is essential in developing a shared understanding of effective practice because you want everyone to understand not only what effective practice for the learner-centered problem looks like but why it is effective. In the Clark example about using Shakespeare to teach inferring, teachers need to move beyond simply deciding that drama is a good tool for teaching inferring to inquire *why* drama seems to be effective. Is it because students have the opportunity to use nontext clues like body language and intonation to interpret text? Or perhaps because the Shakespearean text is so difficult that students have to figure out ways to make sense of it? Or is it because of the kinds of questions the teacher asked? Similarly, in the Franklin example, is the Japanese math teacher's practice effective because he is helping students understand theory instead of applying an algorithm, because he allows students to solve the problem in different ways, or because he is going into more depth and covering less content? As teachers ask and answer these questions, they'll form a vision of effective practice that they can adapt to fit their own setting. This depth of understanding will support both their examination of practice and their implementation of it later in the improvement process.

Some schools form inquiry groups in which teachers frame a question about teaching related to their learner-centered problem and then investigate resources to help them answer the question. At Clark, teachers inquired about Think Alouds, the process of teachers making their own thinking explicit for students as they modeled a strategy or skill, such as inferring.[4] In one high school, teachers wanted to know how to help their students who were several years below grade level in reading catch up. They particularly wanted strategies that were both effective and age-appropriate for their students, and no one on the faculty knew what to do. The teachers formed an inquiry group in which they found, read, and discussed several articles and books on the subject. After a lengthy discussion, they generated a list of effective practices for helping students significantly behind in reading.

It often helps to draw on both internal and external resources. Some people are more persuaded by research, others by a colleague's success, while some people have to see the effectiveness of a practice to both believe and understand it. Very often, we need a combination of research, practices, and experience to develop our understanding of effective practice. At one elementary school, the faculty thought that differentiated instruction might be a good strategy for meeting needs of various learners, but didn't know what it would look like. They read articles, watched videos, listened to their special education teachers describe their practice, and discussed all of the ideas to develop a common understanding of differentiated instruction as it applied in their particular context.

ANALYZE CURRENT PRACTICE

At Franklin, the math teachers had decided to focus their next faculty meeting on exploring two questions generated by both their brainstorm about why students were struggling with multistep problems and their investigation into effective practice: (1) Are we teaching a consistent strategy for solving multistep problems? (2) Do we give students sufficient practice with multistep problems? Now they had to decide how they were going to answer those questions.

Sasha, the math coach, suggested that they observe each other teaching to get a sense of what was being done in different classrooms.

Eddie disagreed. "I'm not giving up my planning period to observe people teaching. I need my planning time."

Mallory countered, "Well, Roger might be able to get subs to cover so we can see each other."

"I don't want to miss teaching a class so that I can go observe other people, either. I'm behind where I need to be with the kids as it is. Besides, do we really need to see each other teach to answer these questions? I think it's safe to say we're not teaching a consistent strategy for solving multistep problems—I have no idea how anyone else teaches them. Do we give students sufficient practice? Well, I don't know what 'sufficient' is, but apparently it's not enough or they'd be doing better. And we tell students they can do the problems if they'll try."

To articulate a problem of practice, faculty must be able to describe what is going on currently in the school, with a shared understanding of effective practice as the referent point. Gathering data about teaching to examine what's happening in classrooms helps move the conversation away from an emotional blame game and toward identifying the teaching dimensions of a problem of practice. Just as we can think students have learned something until we look at their work and see they haven't, as teachers, so can we think we've taught something until we look at our work and see otherwise.

As with any improvement effort, when examining instruction, school leaders face many decisions about what data to look at and how to examine them. These decisions come with trade-offs and depend heavily on the context of particular schools. The data that may help educators at one school understand their teaching practice as it relates to their learner-centered problem may not help another school at all, or may take so long to collect and analyze that the energy for improvement dwindles and no action is ever taken. Consider these three questions when making decisions about how to examine instruction:

- What data will answer your questions about teaching practice in your school?

- What are teachers ready for and willing to do?

- What are your resources, including time?

What Data Will Answer Your Questions About Teaching Practice in Your School?

As discussed in chapter 3, decisions about what data to look at should start with questions. In the case of teaching practice, it's critical to frame what questions you have about what's happening in classrooms in terms of the learner-centered problem. If you don't, you're likely to collect lots of data that don't help you. This can waste precious time, as well as goodwill about engaging in the improvement process, particularly around something as sensitive as teaching practice. The questions should draw on your inquiry up to this point, including your understanding of effective practice. We know one school that approaches describing current practice as an instructional audit. The faculty develops a list of questions related to things they would expect to see in classrooms effectively teaching to the learner-centered problem, and then observe each other teaching, taking notes on the answers to those questions. We have also seen schools use the Question Formulation Technique mentioned in chapter 3, and we have seen schools fill out a simple form, as shown in Exhibit 5.2.

Exhibit 5.2

Exploring the Learner-Centered Problem		
Statement of learner-centered problem: _____		
Why are students having the learner-centered problem?	**What questions do we have?**	**What data will help us answer our questions?**

The questions will determine what the relevant data are. For example, if the prevailing chorus from teachers is, "I'm teaching it—they're just not learning it," a question might be whether teachers are actually teaching whatever "it" is. The data needed to answer this question will most likely involve seeing teachers in action. If the question is what kinds of tasks we ask students to do related to the learner-centered problem, the data involved might be homework and classwork assignments, tests, and other assessments. If the question is about what teachers *think* they're doing, helpful data would come from asking teachers to describe their practice through surveys, focus groups, or interviews.

One elementary school investigating problem solving in math met in cross-grade groups to try to understand their lowest-performing students' experience of a math curriculum that relied heavily on having students construct their own meaning of math concepts. Teachers wondered if more structure was needed in the lessons for the most struggling students. If so, what was the best method, what would it look like, and when should they introduce it? After sharing lesson plans and student work, teachers decided to observe in each other's classrooms to get more data on the classroom performance of this neediest group of students and the instruction in the classrooms. Each teacher arranged to observe a peer before the next meeting. They then shared their observations to determine patterns of response and brainstorm the kinds of support they felt their students needed, based on the observation data they'd collected from their own and their peers' students.

Another school devoted several staff meetings to something called triads. The principal divided the staff into groups of three, mixing up specialists and teachers of different grade levels. Each triad came up with a focused question it wanted to investigate, such as a question about teaching inference in reading. Teachers were then released from team meetings in order to observe their colleagues and collect data in response to the question posed by their colleagues. At the next meeting, faculty met in their triads to share observation data and reflect on what they'd learned.

What Are Teachers Ready for and Willing to Do?

The next step is to figure out what sorts of data teachers are ready and willing to examine about their own practice. Two helpful questions to consider: Are teachers accustomed to being in each other's classrooms, having people watch them teach, and discussing their practice? Is there a culture of inquiry where talking about teaching practice is seen as an opportunity to improve rather than an evaluation? If the answer to these questions is yes, then all data about teaching practice is a possibility, including data that come from directly observing teaching, like video and class visits. If the answer is no, then direct observation may be too threatening to teachers and they may refuse to do it, or be so general in their observations that the data aren't helpful. In this case, data that rely on self-reports from teachers, such as surveys, focus groups, or interviews, can be less threatening, provide information, and begin to get teachers accustomed to the idea of examining their practice. If the answer is somewhere in between, then examining artifacts of teaching such as student or teacher work may be appropriate.

At an elementary school where math scores on the state test were low and teachers weren't comfortable having someone watch them teach, the instructional leadership team designed a survey based on their questions about what was happening with math. The teachers on the team made a special point of distributing and collecting the survey themselves without involvement from the principal, because they hoped teachers would answer more honestly if the questions came from other teachers. The team learned several important things when they analyzed the results from the survey: teachers weren't spending the 60 minutes per day they were supposed to on math, teachers generally didn't use the hands-on materials that were part of the curriculum, and teachers wanted more support in how to teach math well.

In many schools, custom or contract will dictate the extent of and the guidelines for classroom observation. We have found that schools that use questions and data to establish a culture of inquiry in which teachers are participants rather than targets find ways to examine practice. Teachers want to know the answers to the questions they have generated, and thus are more likely to participate in collecting the data and examining their own practice.

What Are Your Resources, Including Time?

Finally, resources—especially time—play a role in determining what data you decide to examine. Again, two questions: How much time do you have to collect and analyze the data about instruction? What other resources are available to you? The answers to these questions influence how many data sources you can examine and which ones you choose. If, like Franklin, you are under intense pressure to take action and you have only a couple of meetings available in which to examine instruction, you might choose to look at artifacts of teaching and hear self-reports through a focus group. If, like Clark, you have less urgency and schedule more regular meetings, you might choose a more lengthy process, such as teacher and administrator observations in classrooms. Other resources will influence your choices as well. Do you have someone who can collect the data and do an initial analysis? If not, you may not want to do a survey, which is quick for teachers to complete but takes time to compile and analyze. Do you have a way to free teachers to visit each other's classrooms? Some schools use combinations of substitute teachers, administrators, and teachers who have a planning period to cover for teachers who are visiting colleagues' classrooms. Other schools have limited resources in terms of time and people, but use technology to support their data efforts. We've seen schools use electronic survey and polling tools to do a survey of their teachers (and their students, too).

If you are a school leader, you are an important resource for examining instruction because you have the distinct advantages of flexibility and time that allow for examination of practice across the whole school. Though it may not seem that you can get into classrooms as much as you would like, you do not have the responsibility of being in a single classroom in fixed periods for most of the day. Thus, you have the opportunity to visit multiple classrooms, attend different grade-level and content-area meetings, and get a sense of the bigger picture of what's happening across classrooms.

Trade-Offs

With all of these decisions there are trade-offs. If you examine instruction more quickly with limited data sources, you will get to designing and implementing solutions faster, but you may sacrifice some accuracy in framing the problem of practice. If you take your time and examine several data sources, you may be more accurate, but you may lose a sense of urgency and momentum for improvement. If you are an administrator, you might have a more flexible schedule but teachers might worry that you will use some of the observation data in their final evaluation. If you tread carefully and don't push too hard on teachers' comfort level about examining practice, you may get willing participants, but not the level of precision and depth you want in the problem of practice. Push too hard, and you may get resistance when you go to implement solutions. If you have a few people do most of the work of examining instruction, it may be done more quickly and at greater depth, but you may not get the level of understanding and buy-in you'll want from the rest of the teachers whose practice you ultimately want to improve. As a leader, you have to balance your questions, your teachers' skills and readiness, and your resources with the goal of answering your questions as thoroughly as possible in the time frame you have.

Articulating the Problem of Practice

Once you have linked learning and teaching, developed the skill of examining practice, developed a shared understanding of effective practice, and analyzed current practice in your school, you can articulate the problem of practice that will be the focus of your improvement efforts. At Clark, the problem of practice is "As teachers, we do not teach inference explicitly, and do not help students make connections between the inferences they make in their lives and the inferences they need to make from texts." At Franklin, the problem of practice is "As teachers, we do not consistently teach a process for solving multistep problems, and we don't give students enough opportunities to work with multistep problems." After articulating your problem of practice, like the teams at Clark and Franklin, your team will be ready to design an action plan to address it.

Integrating the ACE Habits of Mind into Step 5: Examining Instruction

SHARED COMMITMENT TO ACTION, ASSESSMENT, AND ADJUSTMENT

The main deliverable that you produce in Step 5 is your problem of practice statement. For the improvement process to be effective, it is important that you phrase this problem in a way that sets you up for—but does not lock you into—action. One thing that we have found to be effective is encouraging educators to start the problem of practice with the phrase, "As teachers, we . . . ." This helps ensure that the problem is truly focused on teachers, and that teachers are taking ownership of it. Another caveat is to be sure that you haven't snuck a solution into your statement. Doing this can be tempting, but it means you are skipping the important conversation about choosing instructional strategies that is described in chapter 6. When a team tells us that their problem of practice is "As teachers, we do not showcase student work on the bulletin board outside our classrooms," we ask them to pause. Is this really the problem of practice, or is it an idea for how to solve a more fundamental problem? Rephrasing the problem—"As teachers, we do not provide incentives for students to do their best work"—gets at a much deeper issue. And it opens the door for much more creative instructional strategies than the one they jumped to in their original statement.

INTENTIONAL COLLABORATION

Observing and discussing instruction is difficult because it goes against long-standing practices in education in which teachers work behind closed doors, with observers in their classrooms only for evaluative purposes. As mentioned in this chapter, one way to lessen anxiety about observations is to begin by looking at videos of instruction, rather than visiting classrooms directly, so teachers can simply practice taking observation notes and describing what they see. (The Data Wise Project website provides links to publicly available websites containing example videos of instruction.) Practicing with such videos allows educators to develop the necessary skills for observing instruction in a relatively neutral context. We have found that some teachers prefer to start examining instruction at their school by videotaping their own lesson, and then choosing *what part* of the video to show and *how* it is used. A teacher can watch the video alone and pick a five- or ten-minute segment to show others, along with specific questions to ask the group. Another suggestion is to be thoughtful about *who* is doing the videotaping. Encourage teachers to work with another teacher they trust, or to videotape the lesson themselves using a tripod or setting the camera at a good angle to capture the whole room. It is also worth being thoughtful about *what* is recorded. Many discussions after the observation focus on what the students were doing, so ideally the video would capture the students and not be focused exclusively on the teacher. Some teachers may find this helps remove the impression that video puts them personally under the microscope. Intentional collaboration is all about building trust. In our experience, having colleagues give one another rich, descriptive information on their practice can be a more powerful strategy for building trust than any team-building activity done outside the context of teaching.

RELENTLESS FOCUS ON EVIDENCE

There are a few ways to support colleagues in engaging in a productive conversation that is grounded in evidence from the classroom observation. First, ensuring the effectiveness of a conversation *after* observing practice actually begins with thinking about the conversation that occurs *before* entering the classroom. In that conversation (which we refer to as a *focus* meeting in the *Key Elements of Observing Practice DVD and Facilitator's Guide*), the host teacher actively enlists colleagues in naming what evidence to collect from the observation that will help shed light on his or her practice. Then, when it is time for the *debrief* meeting, the objective is for colleagues to share the evidence that they were asked to collect.

Another effective way of sorting through the evidence is to use the four-quadrant diagram shown in Exhibit 5.3 during the Affinity Protocol. We have found that using this diagram and the Affinity Protocol (for example, by sorting each sticky note into the quadrant that best matches the type of evidence on the note) keeps teachers to specific, non-normative statements, "depersonalizes" the observation data, and allows teams to make sense of what they see. The diagram provides guidance about what type of evidence to collect during the observation—as much as possible, evidence should be both descriptive and specific, instead of general and judgmental. It will take practice before most educators are good at writing down specific, descriptive statements from an observation of instruction—but in the end, the practice will pay off when you have rich, detailed data from each observation.

Exhibit 5.3

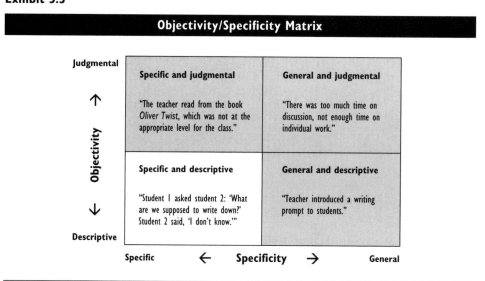

Source: Adapted from Massachusetts Department of Elementary & Secondary Education, *Learning Walkthrough Implementation Guide*, Version 1.2, February 2010.

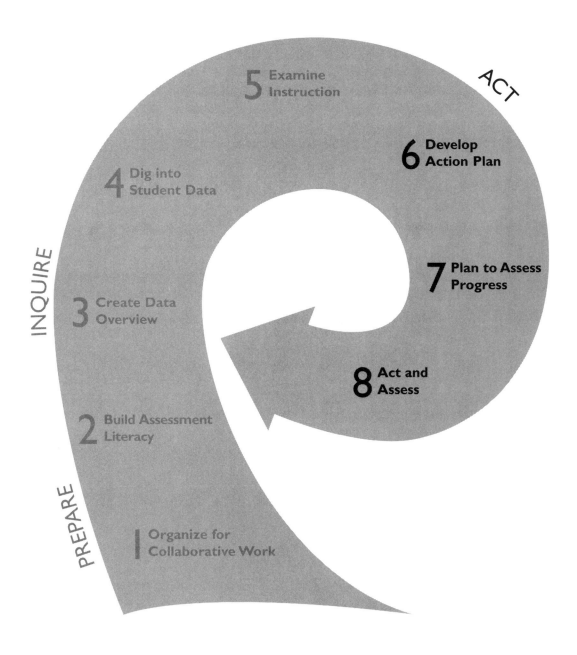

5 Examine Instruction

ACT

6 **Develop Action Plan**

4 Dig into Student Data

INQUIRE

7 **Plan to Assess Progress**

3 Create Data Overview

8 **Act and Assess**

2 Build Assessment Literacy

PREPARE

| Organize for Collaborative Work

6

DEVELOPING AN ACTION PLAN

Tom Buffett, Mark B. Teoh, and Gerardo Martinez

CLARK'S THIRD- AND FOURTH-GRADE TEAM LEADER, ANITA SUAREZ, FOUND IT hard to interrupt her colleagues' animated conversation. "I used that current events activity that we read about last week," Vivian was saying. "The kids loved it. I often have a hard time getting them interested in a nonfiction reading exercise, but this time they were really into it."

"Well, I tried that 'Think Aloud' thing we saw you do in your classroom," Jae told Vivian. "You know, when you projected that poem on the screen and then you walked the kids through what was going on in your head as you read? I don't know how you made it look so easy . . . I could only keep it going for a few minutes before it kind of started feeling like a monologue."

It was encouraging to see the teachers trying out some of the new ideas that had come out of their work together. But so far, the efforts were individualized and uncoordinated. As leader of her team, Anita knew that she would be responsible for helping them come up with a coherent plan for making instructional changes together. But she hadn't led this kind of work before, and she wondered how she could channel her team's energy into getting a formal plan down on paper.

The third- and fourth-grade team at Clark K–8 School has deepened its knowledge about effective reading instruction by observing team members teach, discussing professional literature on this subject, and watching and debriefing a video related to literacy instruction. In the process, the team has identified some promising strategies for helping students learn how to make text-based inferences. Like Anita at Clark K–8 School, you may find that teachers at your school begin to improve their instruction as a result of participating in these kinds of activities.

Nevertheless, explicitly committing to a particular strategy or set of strategies for instructional improvement and writing up a formal action plan is important. Creating an action plan will increase the clarity and transparency of your work. You can use the document for communication within your school as well as between your school and key external constituents such as families, the district office, and partner organizations. By committing your team's thinking to paper, you create a process through which team members can raise and address the different understandings that naturally develop when discussing practice. And perhaps most important, action planning is a way to translate what you learn through analyzing a broad swath of data—from state test scores to current instructional practices—into concrete strategies for improving what is happening in classrooms.

Successful action planning typically includes the following four tasks:

1. *Decide on an instructional strategy* or strategies that will solve the problem of practice you identified through your analysis of student and teacher data. The instructional strategy your team commits to is the heart of the action plan.

2. *Agree on what your plan will look like in classrooms.* Your team can reach a shared understanding of the strategy by carefully describing what team members would expect to see teachers and students doing if the plan were implemented well.

3. *Put the plan in writing.* By documenting team members' roles and responsibilities and specifying the concrete steps that need to occur, you build internal accountability for making the plan work. Identifying the professional development your team will need and including it in your action plan lets teachers know they will be supported throughout the process of instructional improvement.

4. *Decide how you will know if the plan is working.* Before implementing your plan, it is important to determine what type of student outcome data you will need to collect in order to understand whether students are indeed learning more. Because this task represents a substantial undertaking that is often overlooked, we discuss it as the sole topic of chapter 7, "Planning to Assess Progress."

Working together to create an instructional action plan that you will collaboratively implement can help build a professional community at your school. But it isn't easy. This chapter highlights key aspects of each of the first three action-planning tasks listed above and identifies some of the opportunities and tensions that may arise during this phase of the improvement process.

DECIDE ON AN INSTRUCTIONAL STRATEGY

Solutions at last! If you are new to the improvement process recommended by this book, it may seem as though you have had to work through quite a number of steps before turning to the task of deciding what to do about the student learning difficulties you unearthed in data analysis. Now that you have reached this task, however, it is worth the time to deliberately consider possible solutions by first clarifying the scope of your plan, then brainstorming a list of ideas, and, finally, deciding which of the ideas makes the most sense to implement.

Clarify the Scope of Your Plan

The scope of the plan your team develops will depend on the unit of improvement the team seeks to address. The term "unit" in this case refers to the group that is the subject of your proposed improvement, whether that is a content area, a grade level, the whole building, or some other grouping at your school. Which unit you choose depends on the scope of the problem of practice. When the data show that the problem of practice is consistent across the school, a schoolwide solution makes sense. On the other hand, when the data indicate that the problem of practice is particular to a content area, grade level, or group of students and teachers, a more directed solution will be appropriate. Note, however, that if the unit of improvement you select is smaller than the whole school, your action plan must fit within the context of your schoolwide strategy for improvement. In other words, there should be a connection between the smaller unit's action plan and your school's overall approach to improvement so that any success you achieve also serves a larger schoolwide goal.[1]

At Clark K–8 School, the principal asked each grade-level team to create its own action plan that would support the schoolwide goal of improving student reading performance. At Franklin High School, the principal asked the entire math department to work together to develop a plan that would be implemented in all math classes across all grade levels. The instructional leadership team at one school we have worked with identified the problem of practice as the fact that teachers weren't adequately supporting students in becoming critical thinkers and independent learners. Rather than choose schoolwide strategies that would apply across all classrooms, they had the literacy and math teams prepare their own action plans. Each plan was content-specific, yet addressed the schoolwide goal of teaching students to be critical thinkers and independent learners.

School leaders should also consider other factors, such as the availability of resources and faculty capacity, when determining the appropriate scope for their action plans. Some schools choose to do a schoolwide plan because they do not have the resources to support multiple teams, each pursuing a different plan. Other schools conduct a pilot action plan with a single grade-level or content-area team to test the plan before investing in bringing it to the whole school. Still others choose the whole school as the unit of improvement precisely because they want to send a clear signal that they are all responsible for all children, and their collective problem of practice is not just the concern of the willing.

School leaders must weigh all of these considerations. As you think about the scope of action planning in the context of your school, be aware of the potential tension involved in identifying a strategy that is both broad enough to be relevant to teachers who teach different content or students in different grades, and specific enough to ground instructional conversations and improvement efforts in concrete classroom practices.

Brainstorm Solutions to the Problem

Even schools we know that are very skilled at examining data and identifying the problem of practice can get stuck at the point of figuring out how to solve the problem. As one principal said to us, "Now what do I do? We know what the problem is, but if we knew what to do about it, we'd have done it already." Looking for solutions can involve engaging teachers in a conversation about how to address a problem, identifying and making creative use of in-house expertise, and being honest about when it is time to seek guidance from outside sources. It is also an opportunity to give teachers time and space to create something collaboratively that is larger and more powerful than anything they could do individually. Developing a shared understanding of effective practice among your faculty, as described in chapter 5, will help generate ideas about appropriate solutions to your problem of practice.

As with all steps of the improvement process, generating solutions is both an end and a means—it is important to come up with the good solutions for your problem, but how you come up with those solutions matters, too. Some schools choose to spend more time than others in developing solutions in order to help faculty "buy in" to those solutions. After all, teachers are the ones who will be implementing the solutions, so it is essential that they understand them and appreciate their potential to improve student learning.

There are a number of approaches that you can use to identify possible solutions. The simplest approach is to assemble a group and ask people to brainstorm ideas, which you can keep track of on poster paper or projected on a screen. You can also use a variation of the Affinity Protocol discussed in the previous chapter, where individuals use sticky notes to capture their proposed solutions and then work together to group them into logical categories. One school leader we know used a Café Protocol in which faculty discussed possible solutions in small groups at a number of tables in the library.[2] The protocol called for teachers to switch groups twice, each time bringing the solutions from the previous conversation to their new group. At the end of the protocol, the faculty compiled the list of suggestions their conversations had generated. Although the protocol took a full hour, the conversations went much deeper into discussing possible solutions than a brainstorming session would have and allowed faculty to have extended, substantive conversations with one another, a welcome change of pace from their usual focus on protocols with tight time limits.

A few days after the November math department meeting, department chair Mallory Golden met with Sasha Chang, the district math coach assigned to Franklin High School. "So," Mallory explained, "we talked about designing a formal process for solving problems, and teachers got really excited thinking about how we could ask students in all classes to create posters demonstrating their use of this process in solving complex problems. People seemed pretty enthusiastic about teaching a consistent method across classes, and we are going to talk about it more at our next meeting." Mallory paused for a moment. "Frankly," she continued, "I have to say I'm a bit worried we're going to get bogged down in agreeing on the wording of the method and we'll never quite get to using it with the kids."

Like Mallory, many school leaders find that after taking the first important steps toward defining a solution, their faculty may need some guidance about how to implement it.

After hearing Mallory's concern, the math coach showed her a diagram of a process called the Problem-Solving Approach adapted from George Polya's book, *How to Solve It* (see Exhibit 6.1).[3] The coach, Sasha, had used this particular approach

Exhibit 6.1

Problem-Solving Approach

Components of the multistep problem-solving approach that will be evident in all classrooms at Franklin High School

UNDERSTAND
- Use reading strategies to attack the text.
- Take notes on three categories:
  1. What is given?
  2. What is being asked?
  3. What do you know already that will help with this problem?

PLAN
- Identify specific steps you will follow to solve the problem.
- Connect the steps to the information noted in the UNDERSTAND phase of the approach.

LOOK BACK
- Reread your notes on "What is being asked?" in the UNDERSTAND phase of the approach.
- Is your answer reasonable?
- Check computations.
- Label units.

SOLVE
- Accurately execute your plan.

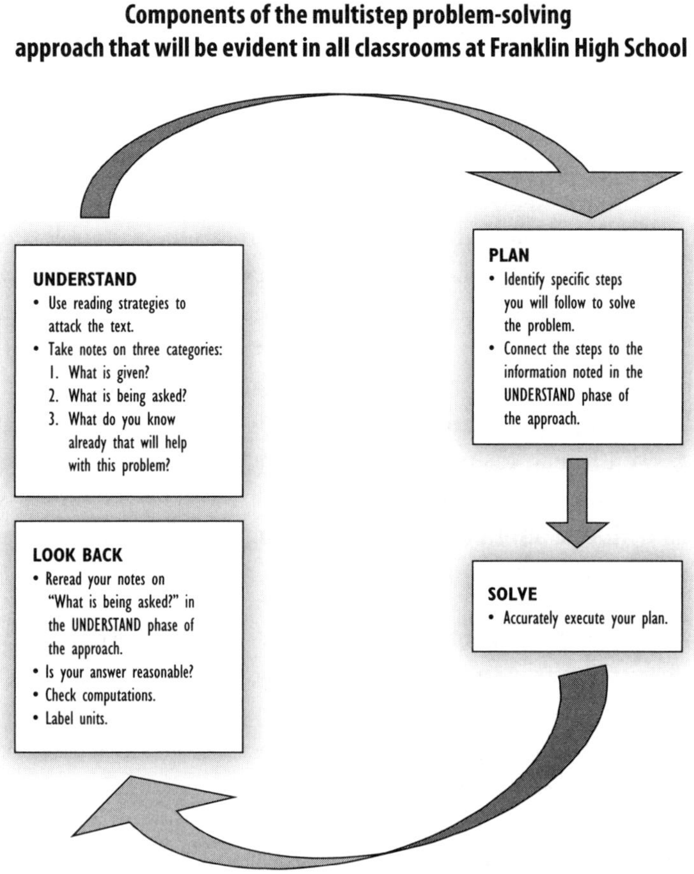

Source: Adapted from G. Polya, *How to Solve It: A New Aspect of Mathematical Method* (Princeton, NJ: Princeton University Press, 2004).

successfully at other schools. Mallory felt it was just what the team needed to make progress on defining their solution, so she asked Sasha to bring her diagram of the Problem-Solving Approach to the next department meeting and talk about how she had used it with other schools. When Sasha did this, the faculty was quite interested in the approach and by the end of the meeting had decided to adopt it instead of spending any more time trying to reinvent the proverbial wheel.

It is doubtful that the teachers at Franklin High would have embraced the Problem-Solving Approach if someone from the district's central office had mandated it at the beginning of the school year. But because the teachers learned about the approach after they had identified the problem of practice and begun to look for solutions, they received the idea enthusiastically. Many school leaders find that a successful search for solutions involves allowing faculty to offer their own suggestions while at the same time planting good ideas from outside sources.

Select a Solution to Implement

Anita posted the list of teaching strategies the Clark third- and fourth-grade team had brainstormed at their previous meeting and told the team they had to decide what solutions they were going to implement. "It looks like a great list to me," said Jae. "I think we should do all of them!" "I don't know about that," Kristina countered. "That list looks overwhelming to me. Why don't we just do one thing well—maybe something straightforward, like working on vocabulary words related to inferring?"

Successful teams are clear about why they select particular strategies. Two important criteria for selecting strategies are the feasibility of implementing the strategy and its likely impact. The feasibility of a particular approach depends on the availability of resources. Commonly required resources for implementing improvement strategies include professional development materials (such as videos relating to specific content areas or instructional techniques), support (including workshops and internal or external people who can teach and provide ongoing guidance about the strategy), and time (which can involve deciding how much of the team's precious collaborative time to devote to this effort). The feasibility of any approach also depends on teachers' existing skills and capacities. The degree of trust that exists among the faculty members is also important. Simply put, some of the most promising strategies for instructional improvement are feasible only if the faculty members trust each other enough to open their classrooms and learn from one another.

Teams can assess the likely impact of potential strategies in a variety of ways, including reviewing academic research and examining student performance data from other places that are already implementing the strategy in question. As a practical matter, however, teams most often rely on their members' professional knowledge and experience. One useful way of thinking about the impact of a particular strategy is to challenge your faculty to identify "high-leverage" solutions. High-leverage solutions are those that, because of their intensity or the sheer number of students they affect, are likely to make the biggest difference in what children learn.

Clark's third- and fourth-grade team assessed both the feasibility and potential impact of their potential solutions on the chart shown in Exhibit 6.2. Though teachers agreed that the new curriculum solution might have the greatest potential impact among all the items on the chart, the team concluded that this option was not feasible because there were not enough funds in the school's budget. Instead, Clark K–8 School selected from among the strategies that were both feasible and likely to have an impact, and they decided to adopt the strategy of using regular Think Alouds as part of their reading instruction.

At schools that have not developed a collaborative orientation toward continuous instructional improvement, teachers will often identify "solutions" that do not involve a change in their instruction. For example, it is common for teachers at schools that lack such a professional community to propose an afterschool program as the key strategy for addressing student weaknesses. While we have seen schools use afterschool programs very effectively as part of their improvement strategy, such programs are effective only in combination with—not in lieu of—instructional improvements during the school day. It is easy to achieve consensus on

Exhibit 6.2

Clark K–8 School Assessment of Inference Strategies		
STRATEGY	IMPACT	FEASIBILITY
Develop students' inference vocabulary	LOW-MEDIUM	HIGH
Adopt new curriculum that we read about	HIGH	LOW
Think aloud about inferring (make our thinking explicit)	MEDIUM-HIGH	HIGH
Draw on ways that students already know how to make inferences to teach them what inference is	MEDIUM	HIGH
Use literature that is relevant and meaningful to students to model the inference process	MEDIUM	MEDIUM
Ask open-ended questions that promote inferring	MEDIUM	HIGH

solutions that do not require teachers to make changes in their day-to-day practice, even when data show that such practices are consistently ineffective. As a school leader, when it comes time to choose a solution from your brainstormed list, you may need to remind teachers that the goal is a solution that changes how students learn in their classrooms. You may find that the more involved teachers are in selecting the solution, the more committed they will be to doing the hard work of implementing it.

A final component of choosing an instructional strategy is for school leaders to determine how much change to tackle in the action plan. While some schools will not take on enough—like schools that decide an afterschool program will solve all their problems—most schools actually attempt too much in their action plans. While such enthusiasm is laudable, it is also dangerous. We have seen too many schools come up with a fine list of strategies in their action plan and then not implement any of them well because they are stretching their resources too thin and pushing beyond teachers' capacity to learn and apply new instructional approaches. Under these conditions, most teachers ultimately retreat to their previous practices, which the data showed were not achieving the desired student learning outcomes. School leaders need to be sure that the strategies selected not only are focused on day-to-day instruction in classrooms and are likely to solve the problem of practice, but also can be reasonably implemented in the action plan's time frame. Listening to both the "we can do it all" teachers (who are always easier to listen to) and the "we can't do this" teachers (who are always more tempting to ignore) is important in gauging what strategies will effectively and manageably accomplish important changes in practice.

AGREE ON WHAT YOUR PLAN WILL LOOK LIKE IN CLASSROOMS

Anita was concerned. After talking informally with a number of third- and fourth-grade teachers, she began to realize that although teachers had expressed a lot of enthusiasm for using Think Alouds in their reading instruction, each individual seemed to have his or her own concept of what this would actually look like in the classroom.

How your team defines an instructional strategy to address weaknesses in students' skills is a critical part of implementing that strategy. A faculty gains much of its understanding about what the strategy is and why it is the focus of the action plan in the process of selecting the strategy. However, even if your team is faced with the challenge of implementing an instructional strategy that was determined unilaterally (perhaps by district mandate), your faculty can still deepen their understanding and appreciation of the strategy by participating in a discussion of what it actually looks like in practice. We have found that it is important for faculty discussions on this topic to accomplish two things: develop a common vision for implementing the strategy and lay out a theory of how the strategy will affect learning.

Develop a Common Vision for Implementation

It is often not enough to select an instructional strategy by name because it is too easy for people to attach different meanings to commonly used names or words. For example, if you select a strategy that calls for peer editing of draft writing assignments, teachers may have a variety of ideas about what this means. After deciding on an improvement strategy, successful teams develop a shared understanding of what effective instruction looks like by establishing implementation indicators. These include descriptions of what teachers will be doing, what students will be doing, and what the classroom environment will look like when the instructional strategy is in place. The process of creating these indicators allows teams to develop the capacity to have increasingly specific instructional conversations. It also facilitates implementation by making the team's expectations clear. After two team meetings at Clark K–8 School, the third- and fourth-grade teachers produced the list of implementation indicators for their Think Aloud strategy shown in Exhibit 6.3.

Exhibit 6.3

Implementation Indicators	
CLARK K–8 SCHOOL Implementing Think Alouds About Inferring: What We Will See in Classrooms	
Teachers	• Model inferring by walking students through their own thought processes as they read a piece of text • Project a text on a screen and mark it up while thinking aloud about inferring • Conference with students, asking them to think aloud while reading • Move throughout room to monitor students' inferring
Students	• Know what the word "infer" means and use it accurately to describe their reading process • Use Think Aloud strategies to infer in whole-class, small-group, and conference discussions of text • Answer questions that show their ability to infer
Classrooms	• Display evidence of students inferring from text • Include class-generated poster of what good readers do when they infer (for students to reference while reading) • Allow flexible arrangement of furniture to enable paired reading, group activities, and sustained independent work
Student Work	• Demonstrates students' ability to infer, predict, connect, and evaluate in their reading journals and other reading assessments

Lay Out the Theory Behind Your Solution

The Franklin High School math department had invited principal Roger Bolton to join their December meeting. They described with enthusiasm the Problem-Solving Approach and how they planned to implement it across all math classes. "You've got yourself a plan here, and it feels like a good one," said Roger. "Now, can you walk me through how teaching this approach is going to lead our students to become stronger mathematical thinkers?"

Roger's question is deceptively powerful. At this stage in the game, it can be very helpful to push your team members to put into words exactly how they believe their plan is going to achieve its desired effect. Chances are, there are a number of ways the plan could produce positive results, and not all teachers agree on the theory behind the solution. For example, do teachers believe that the Problem-Solving Approach will lead students to become more independent problem solvers? Will it increase students' confidence and make them more willing to try problems that they already have the math knowledge to solve but have been too disorganized to tackle? Will it make them pay more attention in math class, thus getting more out of lessons they might ordinarily have tuned out and making them more capable of solving problems themselves? Will it help teachers give students responsibility for deciding what to do rather than guide them through problems step by step? Alternatively, is the real strength of this strategy that students will be able to use the same approach from class to class and from year to year, thus allowing them to build experience with problem solving so that it eventually becomes second nature? When pressing teachers to articulate how they think the plan will work, it is also worth asking them if they can imagine any unintended negative consequences. For example, will requiring students to use the Problem-Solving Approach squelch the creativity of real mathematical thinkers by reducing math to following a recipe?[4]

The answers to these questions are not mutually exclusive—in all likelihood, some students will benefit most from consistent instruction from year to year, while others will find it helpful to have a clear strategy for tackling particular assignments. Answering these questions collaboratively will help your team develop a shared understanding of the theory or theories that drive its approach to improving instruction and student learning. Articulating the theory also helps with implementation, as we will see in chapter 8. If teachers understand and agree how the action plan should address the problem of practice, they are more likely to implement the action plan and be able to adapt it to meet students' needs. For example, if the theory behind Franklin's Problem-Solving Approach is that breaking the process into steps will help make it less overwhelming for students so they are more likely to persevere through each step, then a teacher might adapt the steps for her students. If, on the other hand, the theory is that having a consistent strategy from class to class will help students, she should not adapt the steps, but instead make a point of using the exact terminology laid out in the model.

PUT THE PLAN IN WRITING

Mallory stood up from her desk and took a long stretch. She had offered to convert the scribbles from Franklin High School's last math department meeting into a draft action plan for implementing the Problem-Solving Approach. She was amazed at how many steps there were when she typed it all out. Was she making it more complicated than it needed to be?

After choosing an instructional strategy and agreeing on what it will look like in practice, it is time to identify the specific tasks that need to be completed for successful implementation. This step involves assigning responsibilities and time frames, as well as planning for how your school will support teachers as they carry out this new work.

Franklin High School's action plan (see Exhibit 6.4) shows one way of summarizing this kind of information, but there are many others. Whatever display you choose, it is important to be very clear about what the tasks are, who is going do them, and when they are going to be accomplished. You will find that your action plan contains two different types of tasks. One type is the instructional strategies that teachers will use in their classrooms when working with students. The other type is professional development activities that are designed to support teachers' implementation of the selected strategy or strategies. Since these two kinds of activity are likely to occur simultaneously, it is helpful to capture both in a single action plan.

Assign Responsibilities and Time Frames

Writing down what you and your colleagues agree to accomplish and when is an important step in developing the internal accountability that allows you to hold one another responsible for following through on your actions and creates a shared written history that your school can refer to over time. This document can help teachers think outside their classrooms and consider their larger roles within the school, and it can be an important avenue for strengthening and developing shared expectations among teachers and between teachers and students, parents or administrators.

Exhibit 6.4

Draft Action Plan for Improving Learning and Teaching in Franklin High School Math Classes	
LEARNER-CENTERED PROBLEM:	Students have trouble solving multistep problems independently.
PROBLEM OF PRACTICE:	As teachers, we do not consistently teach a process for solving multistep problems, and we don't give students enough opportunities to work with multistep problems.
INSTRUCTIONAL STRATEGY:	As teachers, we will integrate the Problem-Solving Approach (PSA) into our daily lessons, class assignments, and assessments. We will explain the rubric for evaluating problem-solving to students and will use the rubric regularly in grading assignments.

TASK	WHEN
Math department chair and math coach create materials for professional development (PD), including poster rubric and anchor chart listing steps of the problem-solving process to post in the classroom for student reference	January, week 1
Math coach models teaching PSA in four classes; all math teachers attend at least one modeling session	January, week 2
Math coach leads PD session with math department, debriefs model lessons, offers list of poster problems with a range of difficulty	January 18, dept. meeting
Math teachers work in small teams to design PSA lessons for their classes and choose which problems to use for Poster #1 assignment	January, week 3
Math teachers model PSA in classes, share poster rubric with students, and assign Poster #1	January, week 4
Math teachers integrate PSA into regular lessons; students work on posters (Due Feb. 15)	February, weeks 1 and 2
Math teachers work in small teams to assess student work using rubric	February, weeks 3 and 4
Math coach observes four math teachers (volunteers) integrating PSA into teaching and provides over-the-shoulder coaching	February, weeks 3 and 4
Math coach leads PD session with math department, discussing student work and offering guidance for the next round of teaching and Poster #2	March 7, dept. meeting
Math teachers continue to integrate PSA in classes; students work on Poster #2 (Due April 25)	March and April
Math teachers meet weekly in small groups to discuss student work on Poster #2 and other assignments, and administer district math final exams on June 15	May and June

When assigning responsibilities and creating a timeline for implementation, you'll want to be sensitive to the other demands and duties placed on your teachers, as well as the scope of the plan. The level of detail in the plan will depend on the time frame in which you intend to implement it. If the timeline is relatively short, then you may want your action plan to be very specific and indicate what will happen each week. If the timeline is longer, like Clark K–8 School's plan (see Exhibit 6.5) that is designed to be implemented over an entire school year, then the plan may be a bit more broad.

If the time line takes you across an upcoming academic year, one option is to prepare an action plan that is more specific for the fall semester and less so for the

Exhibit 6.5

Clark Third- and Fourth-Grade Team Reading Action Plan		
LEARNER-CENTERED PROBLEM: Students have trouble drawing text-based inferences when reading.		
PROBLEM OF PRACTICE: As teachers, we do not teach inference explicitly, and we do not help students make connections between the inferences they make in their lives and the inferences they need to make from text.		
INSTRUCTIONAL STRATEGY: Think Alouds		
TASK	**WHO**	**WHEN**
Find literacy consultant with expertise in Think Aloud strategies and teaching inference	Anita	August–September
Participate in half-day PD with literacy consultant focused on Think Aloud strategies for inferring	Grade 3 & 4 team members	September–October
Use Think Aloud strategies to demonstrate inferring	Grade 3 & 4 team members	September–January
Have consultant observe each teacher and provide feedback	Consultant and individual teachers	October–November
Visit one another's classrooms and provide feedback	Grade 3 & 4 team members	November–December
Participate in half-day PD with literacy consultant focused on common challenges in implementing Think Aloud strategies	Grade 3 & 4 team members	January
Continue using Think Aloud strategies to demonstrate inferring, refining based on first-semester feedback	Grade 3 & 4 team members	January–May

spring, with the expectation that the spring portion of the plan will be laid out in more detail once implementation is under way and the team can assess its progress. Short-term plans can be helpful for schools that are just beginning the improvement process because they keep the implementation steps concrete, manageable, and immediate.

Plan How to Support Teachers in Their New Work

What can school leaders do to support the action plan? The first and generally easiest step is to provide the resources teachers need to implement the action plan, which might include books, curriculum materials, chart paper, or instructional technologies. The second and far more challenging step is to help teachers develop the skills and knowledge they need to engage in the heart of the work. The school leaders we know who do the best job of supporting teachers in improving their practice think of themselves as "teachers of teachers" who are committed to supporting adult learning.

Support for teachers is most effective if it is coherent, content focused, and frequent.[5] "Coherent" means that the support should align with the action plan; avoid professional development that doesn't directly support your schoolwide instructional strategy. "Content focused" means that the support should be specifically grounded in what teachers teach, and it may need to provide opportunities for teachers to develop their content knowledge and pedagogy. In one school district we know, elementary teachers took math courses to complement their learning of a new curriculum. The courses were specifically designed to provide the deep level of mathematical knowledge they needed to successfully implement the new curriculum. "Frequent" means that support must be sustained and substantial. Small amounts of time and one-shot workshops will not suffice. The schools we know that are most successful at the work of instructional improvement support teachers at least on a biweekly basis through common planning time or at meetings before and after school. These schools also often dedicate larger blocks of time to significant learning experiences, such as full days during the summer or school year.

Your school culture, which is a reflection of the nature and level of expectations shared among you and your colleagues, will have implications for how best to provide teacher support and how ambitious you can be in your planning efforts. At Clark K–8 School, where teachers have a strong history of collaborative work, the action plan calls for teachers to regularly observe in each other's classrooms and to offer one another feedback for improving instruction. The same support strategy would probably not work as well at Franklin High School, where the math department has a deeply rooted tradition of teacher autonomy and isolation.

Just as strong teachers are expected to differentiate their methods of instruction according to the needs of their students, so should a thoughtful system of support account for teachers' different professional needs. How do you know what your faculty needs to be supported most effectively? As with all learners, sometimes it's best just to ask them. We have found that involving teachers in deciding what kinds of support they will be offered goes a long way toward developing the buy-in necessary for successful implementation. One school we know spent two months on extensive plans for the following year's professional development. The instructional leadership team concluded that involving all the teachers in conversations about their professional development needs was critical. The end product was a detailed plan that mapped out how grade-level meetings, content-area meetings, and afterschool sessions would be used together to support teachers.

In sum, developing an action plan is an opportunity to identify relevant and focused professional development for your teachers. Remember, if teachers already had the skills and knowledge they needed to teach differently, they'd probably be doing it. Like all learners, teachers need explicit, specific support in order to improve their practice. Real improvement in student learning takes real time, real resources, and a real commitment to improve. Planning for how to measure whether student learning is in fact improving is the subject of the next chapter.

Integrating the ACE Habits of Mind into Step 6: Developing an Action Plan

SHARED COMMITMENT TO ACTION, ASSESSMENT, AND ADJUSTMENT

Since we first published *Data Wise*, we've developed a real appreciation for shorter action plans. This chapter's two examples—Franklin High School's six-month plan and Clark K–8 School's yearlong one—took quite a while to enact. But action plans spanning as little as two to six weeks and targeting very sharply defined problems of practice can also be quite effective. This is especially true if the team enacting the plan meets weekly, with regular collaboration allowing for quick midcourse corrections that can lead to rapid progress.

The thing to watch out for when designing shorter plans is a tight connection between a rich problem of practice and your plan for addressing it. With interim assessments becoming widely available, many teachers have frequent updates on student skills and knowledge, usually as measured by multiple-choice tests. It can be quite tempting to look at these results at the end of the unit and then use common planning time to identify the items students struggled with most and create a plan for reteaching the content measured by those items. But is that really the most powerful action that the team can take? Will reteaching truly help teachers to become better at their craft?

One thing you can do to make sure that the action plan serves the purpose of making real and lasting improvements in teaching is to ask yourself whether the plan calls for changing *what* you are teaching or *how* you are teaching it. If the answer is how, you are generally in better shape. Another idea is to design your action plan template so that it forces you to write at the top of the page both the specific learner-centered problem you found in the data and the problem of practice that you believe underlies it. This will keep you from either skipping the step of examining instruction, or from doing that step and then ignoring the problem of practice that you found. Too often, we've seen teams do the hard work of coming up with a nice juicy problem of practice—for example, "As teachers, we give students tasks that reward summarizing more than evaluation"—and then proceed to design an action plan that calls for something that does not address the problem, such as giving students "more practice" with a particular skill. Having the problem of practice statement as a key component of the action plan document can be a helpful reminder to make your actions directly connected to what you learned through inquiry.

INTENTIONAL COLLABORATION

The collective effort that got you through the Prepare and Inquire phases is every bit as important when you hit the Act phase. When designing your action plan, it is essential to get the input of everyone on the team. It is equally important to make sure that everyone has a role in enacting it. Putting names and due dates right on the action plan is a good way of making it clear who is involved and exactly what they are responsible for. Another idea is to suggest that team members say out loud what their personal next steps are—we call this "making commitments." Presenting your commitments in front of others is a public act that builds internal accountability for getting the work done.

When designing your plan, look for opportunities to break the work into small pieces that individuals or pairs can do either between meetings or even during some of the collaborative time that you have set aside. Not everything needs to be done by committee! Sometimes it is more efficient to allow pairs to go off and draft a lesson plan, a rubric, or an assignment description and then bring a draft back to the group for feedback (the Tuning Protocol can be particularly effective for this).[6] The secret is making it clear to all that a draft is only a work in progress, and that the descriptive and specific feedback of everyone at the table is needed to make the plan worthy of your collective effort.

RELENTLESS FOCUS ON EVIDENCE

As discussed earlier this chapter, deciding what to do to address your problem of practice is a critical part of action planning. After brainstorming a number of solutions, what do you use to help you decide which one to implement? Evidence! For each idea on the brainstormed list, you can have each team member provide a piece of evidence supporting the argument that this idea would indeed address your problem of practice. (Team members can provide evidence in favor of an idea whether they first proposed it or not.) You then go around the circle again and have each member provide evidence that might argue against the idea. The advantage of this approach is that it allows you to keep ideas separate from the person who introduced them, and it challenges people to look for evidence on both sides of the argument. Warning: this activity is bound to leave you feeling you need to collect a bit more evidence to support your decision. But hopefully, it gives you a pretty good idea of exactly what evidence you need, and this extra step may save you time in the long run.

7

PLANNING TO ASSESS PROGRESS

Jennifer L. Steele and Jane E. King

ANITA, THE TEAM LEADER, DISTRIBUTED THE AGENDA AT CLARK K–8 SCHOOL'S third- and fourth-grade team meeting. "Are we still planning?" Vivian asked, sounding a bit exasperated. "I thought we finalized the action plan last week. We're doing Think Alouds, right?" She looked around at her colleagues. "When are we supposed to take action with our action plan?"

"I'm glad we're all so excited to get started," Anita replied. "But remember that we haven't yet made a plan for how we're going to measure student progress."

"I think the state and the feds will tell us whether or not we're making progress all right," Jae replied.

"To be worth all of the time and energy we are investing," Kristina responded, "this can't all be just about raising test scores. I didn't become a teacher to spend my days doing test prep. I mean, I'm trying to help my students become avid readers and critical thinkers. These are complex skills . . . no standardized test is going to really capture what my kids can do."

Clark K–8 School is struggling with an essential part of designing a strong action plan: deciding how to measure progress. Public schools annually confront the question of how well students are performing on state assessments. However, systematically measuring students' progress isn't an activity that needs to be put on hold until the state test results arrive. Assessing progress is an integral part of the improvement process, through which educators build their internal accountability to one another and find better ways to meet all students' learning needs. Too often, educators begin implementing action plans without thinking about how they will assess progress. As a result, they aren't likely to know whether they're making progress, and they may not even agree on what making progress means in the context of the plan. Schools engaged in improvement work benefit from setting clear goals for student improvement and proficiency, and from deciding in advance how and when they will measure progress toward those goals. This chapter is a guide to developing an assessment plan as an essential complement to your action plan. Assessment plans address the following questions:

- What assessments will be used to measure progress?

- When will each type of assessment data be collected?

- Who is responsible for collecting and keeping track of the data?

- How will the data be shared among faculty and administrators?

- What are the goals for student improvement and proficiency?

Of these, the two most challenging decisions are identifying the kinds of assessments to use to measure progress and deciding how to set appropriate goals for student progress.

CHOOSE ASSESSMENTS TO MEASURE PROGRESS

Just as teachers at Clark K–8 School and Franklin High School used multiple data sources to identify a learner-centered problem (see chapter 4), so should schools plan to use multiple sources to measure progress in students' learning. We have found it helpful to begin such planning by categorizing the available data sources by three time frames: short term, medium term, and long term. Organizing data sources by time frame encourages the use of multiple data sources and helps make the assessment of progress an ongoing part of the school's professional culture. In general, "short-term data" refers to information that can be collected daily or weekly from students' work and classroom interactions. "Medium-term data" is gathered systematically within a school, grade, or department at periodic intervals during the year. "Long-term data" is gathered annually and includes students' performance on statewide tests. Each type of data can provide important information about what students know and are able to do.

Planning to Use Short-Term Data

Because short-term data are generated continuously within a school, teachers can use them to make assessments of students' progress a regular, embedded part of their practice. Good sources of short-term data that educators can plan to use to measure progress include students' classwork and homework, classroom observations of student performance, and conferences with students about their learning. In answer to the questions of who will collect the data, when to collect it, and how it will be shared, we've found that responsibility for short-term data collection and analysis is often best delegated to individual classroom teachers because they can examine student work, observe students' participation, and confer with their students on a regular basis. Teachers have primary responsibility for keeping track of this information, and schools and districts can support the effort by making available data tracking systems that are easy to use.

Looking at Classwork and Homework

The advantage of using students' classwork and homework to gauge learning is that teachers have access to a constant stream of data. What's more, these data are closely aligned with classroom instruction, so teachers can keep track, in real time, of which students seemed to learn the critical skills of a lesson. Teachers can then use these short-term data to inform their instruction so that it responds to students' learning needs.

In planning to use student work to assess progress, teachers should realize that the task of assessing progress goes far beyond checking completion of classwork and homework. The holistic impressions a teacher can glean from skimming the work of an entire class are helpful to a point, but real use of students' work to measure progress entails systematically gathering concrete data. For example, a teacher may prepare a small number of yes-or-no questions that she would like to answer about students' work on a particular assignment. If she has asked students to mark up a short text to show their inferences, her list might include these questions: Does the student list three or more inferences in the margin of this text? Are at least two of the listed inferences plausible? For an open-response math question, she might ask: Did the student get the question right? Did he begin the question correctly? Did he omit subsequent steps? She could then review each student's work to determine the answers to her questions, which she would record in a spreadsheet where she maintains short-term assessment data.

After collecting the information described above, a teacher should consider its implications for her instruction and look for areas of performance in which groups or individual students continue to struggle. Realistically, teachers would not engage in this level of specific analysis every day. However, the assessment plan should include a strategy for permitting teachers to examine performance in the action plan's priority area (e.g., inferences or multistep problems) at regular intervals.

One advantage of collecting short-term data is that teachers can bring samples of the data to discuss at meetings of their departments or grade-level teams. The assessment plan should include time for teachers to share and discuss the short-term data they've collected in their classrooms. Ideally, the work teachers share with one another includes direct evidence of the skills that are the focus of the action plan. For instance, each of the math teachers at Franklin High School might bring to their department meeting a sample of student work that demonstrates their students' ability to solve multistep mathematics problems. Sharing student work in this manner enables teachers to gain insights from their colleagues about individual students' work, while also encouraging teachers to develop common norms of what high-quality student work should look like.

Observing Students' Participation

Another way schools can plan to measure student learning in the short term is by observing students' participation and demonstrated understanding of a particular concept or skill in the classroom. This kind of observation may be conducted by teachers in their own classrooms or by classroom visitors. Observations can provide rich data on what tasks students are engaged in and how they talk about texts, concepts, and problems they are working on. However, using classroom observations to measure student learning has two limitations. First, it provides more information about the skill levels of the students who participate most vocally than it does about students who are quieter. Second, students may be less willing to take intellectual risks by participating when they are being observed by people other than their teacher. The first limitation is readily addressed by drawing on additional data sources, such as individual conferences or examination of students' written work to develop a more complete picture of student performance. The second limitation can be mitigated by creating a classroom culture in which teachers and administrators frequently observe classes, so that having multiple adults in the room becomes less unusual to students. In our experience, students adjust to observers more readily than teachers do. Talking with students about why visitors are coming can also provide a good opportunity to involve them in discussions about their own learning and the school's efforts to support it.

Asking Students About Their Learning

A third and often overlooked strategy for measuring students' progress in the short term is asking the students themselves to talk about their learning. Insights from students can be gleaned through individual conferences, small focus groups, surveys, or written reflections. Conversations can be conducted by teachers in their own classrooms or by colleagues who are visiting classes.

There are several ways to gather information from students about their learning. One approach is to have students share their thinking about a particular academic problem or question while the interviewer takes notes on a conference sheet, as a Franklin teacher did on a form her team designed (see Exhibit 7.1).

The interviewer can ask students what they're doing, why, and what they're learning. When students talk through problems out loud, it is easy to see where their understanding of a concept is strong and where it falters. This insight can help teachers correct students' misconceptions, either through large-group instruction (when the misconception is common) or through individual instruction (when it is unique to that student).

Another approach to these conversations is to simply ask students to describe how they think about a particular concept in the abstract. For instance, a math teacher at Franklin High School could ask her student what the term "multistep problem" means to him and how he would know when multiple steps are required to solve a problem. She might also ask him about what he learned from particular lessons she had delivered in the past. In situations where classwork and homework show stronger growth for some students than for others, it may be useful to ask students whose learning grew considerably about how they learned the material. At the same time, conversations with struggling learners may provide insights into why these students are not benefiting from the instructional strategies listed in the action plan. The interviewers should share the information gained from these interviews with other teachers so that the faculty can revise the action plan to better meet the needs of all students.

Exhibit 7.1

Franklin High School Individual Student Conference Sheet	
Student's Name:	Michael Serrano
Date:	March 18
Class and Period:	Ms. McGovern's 4th period Intensive Math
Skill to Focus on:	Using the Problem-Solving Approach
Teacher's Questions (Summarize what you ask the student to talk about.)	I asked Michael to talk through a word problem in the text that asked him to solve for the rate given the distance and the time.
Student's Responses (Summarize key points in the student's response.)	Michael seemed uncertain and said he would need to know "how fast the guy was going." Asked if it was supposed to be in miles. I said, "What do you think?" He stalled, and I asked if there was a formula he might apply. Then a lightbulb went on, and he recalled the formula (rate)(time) = (distance). At this point, he plugged in the numbers correctly and solved for the rate.
Student's Understanding (What does the response reveal about the student's understanding of the concept?)	Michael still needs prompting to know when to use a formula he obviously knows how to use. He just doesn't know when to apply the formula. This seems to be a common problem in several conferences I've had with students this week, and it's consistent with the math poster evaluations we did in January.
Implications for Instruction (What does the student's response suggest about future instructional approaches?)	I need to give students more word problems out of context, so they don't rely on the lecture preceding the assignment to determine how to attack the problem. We need to spend more time in class on the "understanding" and "planning" phases of problem-solving, just having kids strategize based on what is given and what is asked for in the problem.

As is the case with all forms of data, having a consistent method for collecting and recording the data from these conversations can support the subsequent analysis because it keeps the data focused and facilitates looking for patterns. In some schools we know, the instructional leadership team generates and provides teachers with templates for recording information from student conferences; in other schools, teacher teams generate the templates to meet their specific needs.

As an alternative to interviewing students individually, some schools have conducted focus groups and online surveys of students about their learning. In many cases, these were conducted following a test administration to detect areas where students felt well prepared for the test as well as areas where they perceived gaps in their own learning. Another useful technique is to ask students to write reflections about their learning on a particular topic. The advantage of focus groups, surveys, and written reflections is that these methods allow teachers to collect information from a large number of students much more rapidly than is possible with individual conferences. The trade-off is that the information may not be as individualized or as detailed as information obtained through conferences.

Planning to Use Medium-Term Data

Almost from the moment the Franklin math department had agreed that they would all teach a consistent approach to problem-solving, they had been talking about how students could demonstrate their understanding of the approach. Someone had thrown out the idea of asking students to create posters that showed the steps they had taken to solve complex problems, and before they knew it, Poster #1 and Poster #2 had been written into the action plan. Math department chair Mallory Golden liked the poster idea and wanted to make it work. But if they really were going to be able to use the posters to measure student progress, there was still a lot they would need to think through.

Unlike short-term data, which the school generates internally through students' regular work and classroom performance, medium-term data are gathered systematically at wider intervals throughout the school year. Medium-term data are helpful for tracking students' progress within a single school year. Sources of medium-term data include commercial tests and assessments developed by a school or district. Some people use the term "benchmark" or "interim" assessments to describe tests that help teachers measure how close students have come to mastery of a particular group of skills.[1] The real power in benchmark assessments lies in administering them several times over the year to track students' progress.

Using Benchmark or Interim Assessments

Some schools use commercially prepared tests to measure students' performance several times a year. These tests are particularly used in the core content areas and are often in a multiple-choice format. Because some commercial tests provide multiple forms of the test for each grade level, it is possible for a school to administer these tests many times a year and track students' progress. Districts often decide on the types of medium-term assessments their schools will use and when the assessments will be administered. Schools without such district requirements, however, can choose which tests they want to administer throughout the year.

In selecting benchmark assessments, leaders must consider the kinds of diagnostic information they want the tests to provide. For instance, some measures of student performance yield rich information about the processes students use to complete tasks and are useful in planning instruction. Also, many assessments are designed so that analyzing which *wrong* answer a student selects can provide useful information. When teachers analyze medium-term data together they can learn a great deal about their students' skills. Later, they can confer with individual students about their responses and about where they encountered difficulty, and thus get an even better sense of how to best help students. When choosing which assessment to use, it is important to keep in mind the amount of effort needed to administer the assessment (some of the most valuable instruments require teachers to sit with students individually), the speed with which results can be obtained, and the richness of the information they provide.

Using In-House Assessments

"Okay," said Mallory as she opened the December math department meeting. "We agreed we would use a rubric to assess the problem-solving posters. Today we are going to figure out what goes in that rubric."

Adelina asked, "How about if we measure how well students complete each of the four steps of the Problem-Solving Approach?"

Will replied, "I think we should start by asking what we want to measure: students' ability to get the right answer, or their ability to use the four-step approach?"

"Well, the PSA is a high-leverage skill that we want them to internalize," said Adelina.

"Um, aren't we then prioritizing the means over the ends?" asked Eddie. "Isn't it most important that they get the question right?"

Developing in-house assessments offers schools tremendous flexibility. Schools can design in-house assessments that are closely aligned to the goals of the action plan, and they can use these assessments to track student progress. As we see at Franklin High School, when you design an open-ended assessment, you will need to agree on how to score it. Taking the time to develop a common rubric is an important part of this process.

We also know of schools that have developed their own schoolwide quarterly writing assessments and created their own rubrics (see Exhibit 7.2 for an example from Franklin) or adapted widely available writing rubrics like the 6+1 Trait Writing model created by the Northwest Regional Educational Laboratory.[2]

The trade-off in creating internal assessments is that these in-house tests face many of the validity and reliability challenges that were discussed in chapter 2. There

Exhibit 7.2

Franklin High School's Problem-Solving Poster Evaluation Rubric					
	LEVEL 1: Needs Improvement (0 points)	**LEVEL 2:** Approaches Standard (1 point)	**LEVEL 3:** Meets Standard (2 points)	**LEVEL 4:** Exceeds Standard (3 points)	**Score for Each Step**
Step 1: Understanding	Student does not correctly state what is given or what is asked in the problem.	Student correctly states what is given or what is asked, but not both.	Student correctly states what is given and what is asked in the problem with up to one minor omission.	Student correctly states what is given and asked in the problem with no errors or omissions.	
Step 2: Planning	Student does not accurately list the steps that can be taken to solve the problem. Student does not accurately list information needed to solve the problem.	Student creates a list of information needed to solve the problem, but with some errors or omissions. Student correctly lists the steps that can be taken to solve the problem, but with some errors or omissions.	Student correctly creates a list of information needed to solve the problem with up to one minor omission. Student correctly lists the steps that can be taken to solve the problem with up to one minor omission.	Student correctly creates a list of information needed to solve the problem with no errors or omissions. Student correctly lists the steps that can be taken to solve the problem with no errors or omissions.	
Step 3: Solving	Student does not attempt to solve the problem or attempts to solve it but makes considerable errors.	Student solves part of the question correctly but makes errors in some portions.	Student correctly obtains an answer, but certain steps in the solution are not clear.	Student clearly and correctly solves each portion of the problem.	
Step 4: Checking	Student does not label the units of the final answer. Student does not indicate that the work was checked.	Student labels the units of the final answer, but with errors. Student writes a sentence about checking the work, but does not state how it was checked.	Student correctly labels the units of the final answer. Student writes a sentence correctly indicating how the work was checked.	Student neatly indicates and labels the answer to each step of the problem and the final answer. Student clearly explains not only how the work was checked but also why the answer is reasonable.	
				OVERALL SCORE FOR POSTER: _____	

are four particular challenges that schools should attempt to address when developing their own assessments. First, each version of the assessment must measure the same skills. If, for instance, Franklin teachers were to give a permutation problem in January that students could solve through trial and error, and a different permutation problem in March that required students to know the permutation formula, then these assessments would measure largely different skills, albeit unintentionally. Schools can minimize the risk of this problem by having teachers who are well versed in their content work together to develop the assessment.

Second, difficulty levels should be consistent from one version of the assessment to the next. If a school administers a literary analysis writing prompt using an F. Scott Fitzgerald passage in September and another using a John Milton passage in December, the scores will not necessarily be comparable because there may be a significant difference in difficulty between the two passages. Again, schools can minimize this problem by developing all prompts in advance and carefully considering the difficulty of each. When schools borrow questions from released versions of standardized tests, they may be able to obtain difficulty ratings for each question. Schools can then use these ratings to ensure that assessments are of comparable difficulty from one version to the next.

Third, tests must be administered under standardized conditions. For example, if some teachers allowed students to converse during one assessment and others did not, the scores would not be comparable between classrooms. Faculty can minimize these problems by deciding collectively on test-administration procedures.

Fourth, a consistent scoring system must be established. If teachers are left to use rubrics in whatever way they see fit when they assess students' math posters, essays, or other work, their scores will not necessarily be comparable. Schools can also minimize variations in scoring approaches by training teachers to calibrate their scoring as a group and by removing students' names from the work to minimize the impact of preexisting assumptions about individual students. In addition, the school can have two teachers score each assessment, and if the two differ considerably in their scoring, a third scorer can help resolve the disagreement.

As with all assessments, schools should do their best to address these concerns and should not rely too heavily on any single measure. Because medium-term assessments allow teachers to track students over the course of a year, they offer an excellent opportunity for teachers to monitor how individuals are progressing and diagnose what each student needs. In addition, these data are valuable for identifying patterns by class, grade level, or other categories.

Planning to Use Long-Term Data

Long-term data such as statewide assessments are data collected on an annual basis and present both challenges and opportunities. Long-term data are often generated by an external accountability system connected to state and federal mandates that relies on statewide tests to measure whether schools are meeting the needs of all students. As a result, long-term data are the data that seem to "count" and that schools are under the most pressure to improve. Although these pressures can create an important urgency for improvement, they can unfortunately lead schools to adopt a tunnel-vision focus on long-term data as the sole measure of success. Like any single measure of performance, long-term data give one slice of information that needs to be compared with other data to create a complete picture. The following assessment plan developed by Clark K–8 School shows how multiple measures of student performance can be incorporated (see Exhibit 7.3).

Long-term data can be very helpful for evaluating progress over a longer time frame, such as several years. When the state test remains consistent and the school's scores are averaged over multiple years and compared over time, end-of-year test data can reveal useful information about a school's performance trajectory. While statewide tests may also be used longitudinally to track the performance of individual students from one year to the next, their usefulness for that purpose depends on having comparable forms across grade levels. Such tests are generally more valuable

Exhibit 7.3

DATA TYPE	MEASUREMENT TASKS	PEOPLE	SCHEDULE FOR GATHERING INFORMATION	SCHEDULE FOR SHARING AND INTERPRETING INFORMATION	GOALS
Short-term data	1. Conduct 1:1 conferences with students in which they draw inferences about written passages.	Grade 3 and 4 classroom teachers	Teachers will confer with five students per week during Sustained Silent Reading and keep records on conference sheets.	Teachers share key findings at one grade-level team meeting in October, December, February, and April.	
Short-term data	2. Observe text-based discussions in grade 3 and 4 classrooms.	Principal Sandy Jenkins, Asst. Principal/Data Manager Bob Walker	Conduct student-focused observations in November and March.	Discuss post-observation findings with teachers immediately after the lesson. Present larger observations about students' inference skills at whole-faculty meetings in early December and early April.	
Medium-term data	3. Assess inferring skills using the district's reading assessment.	Asst. Principal/Data Manager Bob Walker	Administer the test to all students in the second weeks of September, December, and April. In the first weeks of October, January, and May, data manager receives scores, sorts them by classroom or advisory teacher in Excel, and e-mails scores to the appropriate teachers. Classroom teachers add scores to their records and examine individual students' progress.	In the first weeks of October, January, and May, data manager creates data displays to present at whole-faculty meetings. He also creates grade-level–specific displays to facilitate discussion at grade-level team meetings.	
Long-term data	4. Use statewide, end-of-year test results to determine whether the school made AYP.	Principal Sandy Jenkins, Asst. Principal/Data Manager Bob Walker	Gather results from prior year's assessment in late September, and e-mail to appropriate teachers. Administer current year's test in the second week of May.	In late September, data manager prepares displays for whole-faculty meeting, led by Principal Jenkins.	

Clark K–8 School Progress Assessment Plan, Third- and Fourth-Grade Team for examining trends over time than for focusing on individual performance. State tests are also limited in their diagnostic usefulness because in many (but not all) states, the results arrive in the school year after the test is administered.

SET STUDENT LEARNING GOALS

Anita was pleased with the plan that she and her grade-level team at Clark had come up with. She liked the way they would be looking at data throughout the year to see how students' reading skills were coming along. The only problem now was that she had included a "Goals" column on the plan, and it was looking pretty empty. How should the team think about setting goals for student learning? It seemed like any target they would come up with would be, in some sense, arbitrary. What amount of progress was reasonable to expect?

It is important to establish short-term, medium-term, and long-term goals so teachers have targets to aim for and benchmarks by which to assess their students' progress. Setting goals is part of establishing a culture of internal accountability and high expectations, and of envisioning what's possible. While you may not initially know what constitutes reasonable goals, having a candid conversation about how much progress you expect to achieve is essential. Goal setting is a recursive process that becomes more precise as you learn more about your students' learning trajectories.

We often encourage teams to set audacious goals, while reminding them that the improvement process will not necessarily be a steady climb to the summit. School improvement takes a long time, and proceeds in dips, plateaus, and surges as teachers learn new skills and incorporate them into their practice. Schools sometimes even see declines in student performance at the beginning of the improvement process because teachers are struggling to master unfamiliar strategies. However, as teachers become more confident in using new instructional strategies and as students internalize teachers' heightened expectations, setting—and reaching—ambitious goals may become easier and easier.

Improvement Goals and Proficiency Goals

Your goals for short-term, medium-term, and long-term assessments should include goals for both improvement and proficiency. An improvement goal is a target for students' growth on a given assessment within a specified period of time—for example, to have all students improve their scores by 25 percent on the district mathematics interim assessments between September and May.

By contrast, a proficiency goal is a target for how many students will achieve a level of performance that is considered reasonable and appropriate for students in their grade within a specified period of time. Proficiency goals are not used to measure growth so much as to measure the number of students who have met the performance benchmark. An example of a proficiency goal would be for 90 percent of a school's tenth graders to perform at or above grade level on a district math assessment by the end of the school year.

Establishing both improvement and proficiency goals keeps schools focused on two distinct and important objectives—growth and competence. A school that is pursuing an improvement goal must concentrate on advancing the learning of all students, even those who are currently far below proficient or considerably above proficient. We have worked with schools where most or all of the students are meeting the proficiency mark, but few students are improving markedly. In these schools, improvement goals can be the more relevant measure and a more meaningful motivator for change. However, we've also worked with a school that managed to improve the performance of a large number of students from reading three or more grades below level to reading only one grade below level. This school met its improvement goal because a large number of its students significantly raised their reading scores. However, these students' progress did not help the school meet its proficiency goal because the students remained below the appropriate level for their grade.

Both growth and competence are important for students' real-world success. If students are to be ready to compete in today's economy, it is not enough for their academic performance to show improvement over time. They need to be proficient in problem solving and communication, among other skills. For students whose performance is less than proficient in either area, improvement isn't enough. Schools must insist on educating all of their students for proficiency, and that means regularly setting progress goals for both proficiency and improvement.

In addition to setting aggregate improvement goals, some schools find it useful to set improvement targets for individual students throughout the year. Setting individual student goals can focus teachers', students', and even parents' attention on what needs to be accomplished. We know schools that design individual learning plans with targets and action steps for all students, as well as schools that take a less time-intensive approach of simply setting goals for each student. In schools that involve students and parents in conversations about goal setting, students often surprise teachers by setting goals for themselves that are higher than what the teachers would have set for them.

When the Franklin math department began deliberating about target scores on their poster assessment, they ran into a problem. "It seems like we're shooting in the dark here," said one geometry teacher. "I mean, we've never given this assessment before, so we have no idea how kids are going to do on it. We could sit here and say we want to have 100 percent of the students exceeding expectations by the end of the year, but that's just talk. I don't see how we can set goals for performance on this assessment until we have some kind of a baseline for where we are now. Without that, what's the point?"

Setting realistic and appropriate goals involves first analyzing baseline data to determine where your school currently stands. You may already have done this as part of the data overview or when digging into data that helped you identify your learner-centered problem. Next you need to think about what long-term success would look like. The geometry teacher in the vignette above raises an issue that we have often heard: How do you decide what you are shooting for? We have seen schools that use other schools as a benchmark by which to set their goals. Sometimes schools look to other schools that are having more success with similar student populations for an idea of what they should aim to achieve. We have also seen schools look to schools with different student populations (for example, urban schools looking at suburban schools . . . or vice versa) for the same purpose. This approach of looking externally for benchmarks can minimize the potential to underestimate the level of achievement that is possible based on current data.

The next step is to decide how long it should take to move from the current performance level to a level that would constitute success. With this time frame in mind, you can set intermediate goals that will lead to meeting that long-term success target.

The Goldilocks Problem

Just as Goldilocks found herself trying out beds that were too hard and too soft before settling into one that was just right, so do schools face the difficulty of setting goals that are neither so hard that faculty become demoralized nor so soft that there is little to strive for. It's useful for teachers to set ambitious goals so they are constantly pushing themselves and each other to improve their practice and promote student learning. However, because the improvement process involves ongoing inquiry and learning, schools must keep in mind that progress goals are a means to an end rather than an end in themselves. In other words, missing a lofty target does not necessarily mean complete failure, just as attaining a very conservative goal does not mean you have achieved raging success.

Setting goals offers schools the opportunity to discuss the big picture of what matters to them—like helping students become learners and thinkers, readers and problem solvers, and kind and contributing citizens. Setting goals also offers schools the opportunity to establish high expectations for what students can achieve with the support of teachers. Goals that are set internally are merely benchmarks for measuring progress, keeping faculty members focused, and holding team members accountable to one another, and they should be seen as such. Attaching extraordinarily high stakes to these goals creates incentives to game the system, which (as chapter 2 explains) does not support student learning. Thus, schools should strive to set ambitious but achievable goals, and maintain the perspective that what matters most is not meeting a particular target but constantly self-assessing to determine what is working and what can be done better to meet all students' learning needs. Exhibit 7.4 from Franklin High School shows how goals can be included in an assessment plan. After deciding how, when, and by what standard students' progress will be measured, you are ready to begin implementing your action and assessment plans.

Exhibit 7.4

Franklin High School Math Department Progress Assessment Plan				
MONTH	**ASSESSMENT**	**WHO COLLECTS DATA?**	**WHO SHARES DATA?**	**HOW ARE DATA SHARED?**	**PROGRESS GOALS**
Ongoing	Weekly examination of students' responses to open-response classroom assignments	Math teachers	Math teachers	Small groups—final math department meeting of each month	
January	Open-response mathematics poster assessment (baseline)	Math teachers	Dept. Chair Mallory Golden	Math department meetings	50% of students met or exceeded the standard (baseline)
February					
March	Open-response mathematics poster assessment #1	Math teachers	Dept. Chair Mallory Golden	Math department meetings	65% of students will meet or exceed the standard
April					
May	Open-response mathematics poster assessment #2	Math teachers	Dept. Chair Mallory Golden	Math department meetings	80% of students will meet or exceed the standard
June	End-of-year state test	Principal Roger Bolton and administrative staff	Principal Roger Bolton and instructional leadership team	Data managers will create graphic displays and present data when results arrive in September of next year	Average scaled score in math will improve 3 points or more; 50% of students will meet the proficiency level in math
July	Discussion of progress (reflection on assessment)	Principal Roger Bolton and Math Coach Sasha Chang	Principal Roger Bolton and Math Coach Sasha Chang	Final math department meeting	

Integrating the ACE Habits of Mind into Step 7: Planning to Assess Progress

SHARED COMMITMENT TO ACTION, ASSESSMENT, AND ADJUSTMENT

Chapter 7 addresses the importance of planning to assess the extent to which your action plan improved *student achievement*; chapter 6 stresses the need to develop implementation indicators that allow you to assess the extent to which the plan improved *teaching practice*. Taken together, these two types of assessment give your team the guidelines you need to make a collective impact. You can make this work more personal—and more immediate—by giving teachers time to set their own goals for how they would like to see their practice change over time. To formalize this, you can hand out index cards and ask teachers to each write down a short-, medium-, and long-term goal that they have for their own practice. This can help to reinforce the idea that the team's collective success hinges on each individual making a commitment to improving his or her ability to help students meet ambitious learning goals.

INTENTIONAL COLLABORATION

If you have given teachers an opportunity to write down their personal improvement goals, you can then facilitate intentional collaboration by pairing teachers and having them share their goals and brainstorm ways they can support one another in reaching them. Over the course of implementing the action plan, building in time to allow pairs to reconnect around their goals may help to foster the kind of mutual support that will allow teachers to make meaningful changes in practice. This kind of "buddying up" can even work across schools or districts. Specialists (such as art or music teachers) who do not have a person who shares their role in their building can find it very useful to discuss their goals and their progress toward them with someone who understands well the pedagogical challenges associated with a particular content area.

RELENTLESS FOCUS ON EVIDENCE

Don't overlook the value of the student voice as a potential source of evidence. So far in this book, we have mentioned the importance of conferencing with students about their learning. But we have not yet discussed the possibility of asking students directly about how well they think *a teacher's use of the instructional strategies* supports that learning. As always, it is important to find ways to elicit responses from students that are descriptive and specific so that you will be able to act on them. For example, "Working in small groups feels like a waste of time to me" is not nearly as useful as, "When we work in small groups, I find that I usually know how to do the problem and so it really slows me down to have to get everyone else to understand it."

Interviews and surveys are two ways of collecting student data; which you use depends on your priorities. If you would like detailed information with the possibility of follow-up questions, interviews can be the way to go. In this case, you will need to decide who will do the interviewing. Will teachers ask their own students? Their colleagues' students? Will the information be collected by someone that the students do not know? Or is it possible to have the students themselves collect the information as part of a research project? For any of these, you will need to think about the reliability of the data and the validity of the inferences you can draw from it. Nevertheless, when taken as part of a larger effort to assess the action plan, students can provide an important piece of the puzzle.

Surveys can also be an effective means of learning about student perceptions of teaching. A questionnaire can be as low-tech as a piece of paper with checkboxes or as high-tech as an online survey. The Data Wise Project website provides links to organizations that have produced surveys designed to elicit student views on a wide range of topics pertaining to their level of engagement with content, their peers, and teachers. If properly administered, they can provide an opportunity for allowing students to share their feedback anonymously. Teachers have told us that this information is extremely valuable because it provides them with more information about the target of instruction: the students!

8

ACTING AND ASSESSING

Liane Moody, Mary Russo, and Jonna Sullivan Casey

THE BACK-TO-SCHOOL BUZZ WAS UNMISTAKABLE. CLARK K–8 SCHOOL PRINCIPAL
Sandy Jenkins welcomed many returning teachers and a few new ones as she opened
the first faculty meeting of the year. "What I'm passing out is a one-page summary of the
instructional strategies we developed last spring to improve students' skill at making inferences in a variety of literary genres," she explained. "Since we spent a lot of our time working
in grade-level teams, I thought it would be helpful for us all to see how our work in developing student reading skills connects across the school and gets built from grade level to
grade level."

On paper, the summary of the action plans for each team made a lot of sense. Yet Sandy
had a nagging feeling that bringing these plans to life was going to be a lot harder than
anyone expected. What if the focus on the action plan distracted teachers from all the other
important things they needed to do? What if teachers struggled with the strategies and gave
up quickly? What if teachers didn't implement them with skill and consistency? And, worst of
all, what if the strategies didn't make a difference for student learning?

When teachers have worked collaboratively to develop an action plan for improving instruction, you may find that they have a great deal of momentum behind
their ideas for change. Actively engaging in the improvement process can em-
power teachers, inspiring in them the confidence that they play the critical role in

improving student achievement and the commitment to fulfill this role to the best of their abilities. Nevertheless, as a school leader, you may find that when it comes time to implement the action plan, your faculty needs you more than ever. Teachers will be center stage as they begin implementing instructional improvements in their classrooms, and they will look to you to orchestrate a smooth flow among the various components of the plan and help them regroup when the going gets tough.

The reality of school improvement work is that even with the best planning, when you begin implementation you will inevitably encounter surprises and challenges. Instructional strategies will look different in practice than they did on paper. Students will respond in different ways. As teachers develop more sophisticated knowledge about their practice, new and more complex problems of student learning will emerge. Thus far in the improvement cycle you have been guiding your faculty in an inquiry process; implementation is simply the next logical step in training teachers to look deeply at problems of student learning and develop a disciplined way to respond to them. To capture this spirit, some school leaders describe the action plan as an experiment, a form of action research in which a school tests its theories of how instructional strategies lead to student learning.

Your school teams worked hard to put their action plan ideas in writing. Now that it is time to put the ideas into practice, four questions can guide your work as a school leader:

- Are we all on the same page?

- Are we doing what we said we'd do?

- Are our students learning more?

- Where do we go from here?

ARE WE ALL ON THE SAME PAGE?

While you may wish teachers could put all of their energies into implementing the action plan, the reality is that any plan for instructional improvement will need to occur in the context of your school's ongoing work. For example, Clark K–8 School's new focus on using Think Alouds with third- and fourth-grade students must occur alongside their district's requirement that all schools implement workshop-style instruction. At Franklin High School, teachers will need to integrate the new problem-solving strategy they've developed with a very explicit and detailed pacing guide for the math curriculum. To help teachers bring the action plan alive, school leaders need to communicate the action plan clearly, integrate the plan into the ongoing work of the school, and use teams for support and internal accountability.

Communicate the Action Plan Clearly

How would you like to lead a school where teachers are so focused on student learning that a visitor could ask any one of them about your school's instructional goals and get the same thoughtful answer? Communication prior to and during implementation can help ensure that the goals and strategies of the action plan are well understood and that expectations for teachers and students are clear and consistent across classrooms.

One effective means of communication is the creative use of school documents. While the action plan document itself may comprehensively lay out the steps teachers will follow to implement an instructional strategy, that document is most likely not the best way to communicate the plan to faculty and staff who were not actively involved in drafting it. Offering instead a one-page summary that sets out the key components of school improvement work can be an important step in helping create an environment in which all teachers are able to describe in specific and concrete language how the school is working to improve student performance. A document that distills the important points from a school action plan, like the Clark K–8 School Improvement Plan at a Glance shown in Exhibit 8.1, can be effectively shared with everyone in the school community, including students and parents.

At Franklin High School, the entire math department was involved in the process of identifying problem solving as a major student weakness and in choosing the Problem-Solving Approach as a promising way to deal with it. However, not all math teachers participated in every step of writing up the action plan. Franklin experienced a common problem of communication that arises when schools attempt to move from having a representative team develop an action plan to having a broader group implement it. To deal with this problem, the math department chair worked to bring all faculty on board by making sure that all math teachers understood the goals for student work, the changes in practice designed to help achieve these goals, and how progress toward these goals would be measured. Communicating this information in a large school is an important and ongoing challenge.

Exhibit 8.1

Clark K–8 School Improvement Plan at a Glance

LEARNER-CENTERED PROBLEM: Students have trouble drawing text-based inferences when reading.

PROBLEM OF PRACTICE: As teachers, we do not teach inference explicitly, and we do not help students make connections between the inferences they make in their lives and the inferences they need to make from text.

INSTRUCTIONAL STRATEGIES

(Includes providing students with exposure, modeling, shared practice, guided practice, and independent work to ensure these strategies are taught, demonstrated, practiced, and applied.)

GRADES 1 AND 2	GRADES 3 AND 4	GRADES 5 AND 6	GRADES 7 AND 8
Use oral questions after Read Alouds to push discussion from facts to higher levels of meaning—e.g., What made you say that? How did you know that? Demonstrate and require students to justify or "prove" their answers orally with new information learned.	Continue oral questions and proving your answer techniques from grades 1 and 2, applied to more challenging pieces of writing. Model Think Aloud process for using information from text to back up conclusions and opinions both orally and in writing. Provide students with questions in written format for reference when practicing Think Alouds.	Continue oral questions, proving your answer, and Think Aloud techniques from prior grades, applied to more challenging pieces of writing. Model use of two-column format in Reader's Response notebooks to ask, record, and answer questions about text that require reading between the lines (inferring). In Literature Circles, one-to-one teacher conferences, class discussions, and writing assignments, require students to back up opinions with solid reasons that are both stated and implied in text.	Continue oral questions, proving your answer, Think Aloud, Reader's Response notebooks, and discussion techniques from prior grades applied to more challenging pieces of writing. Apply all of the above techniques to character analysis in literary genres required at grades 7 and 8—e.g., How is the character developed and revealed through what he/she says? What others say about him/her? What he/she does?

ASSESSING PROGRESS

SHORT TERM	MEDIUM TERM	LONG TERM
Observations of discussions in classrooms for each grade; students selected at random can give detailed examples and explanations for opinions.	Student responses on items testing inference skills using district's benchmark reading assessments (Sept./January/June) show increase in correct responses.	Pattern of student responses on items testing inference skills on statewide, end-of-year tests shows increase in number of correct responses.

Integrate the Action Plan into Ongoing School Work

Being clear about what the action plan entails is an important task. But it can be equally important to make sure that your school's other instructional goals are not eclipsed by the new plan. A good way to do this is to work with your faculty to develop a schoolwide curriculum map and describe how your new strategies fit into this overall plan.

At Clark K–8 School, principal Sandy Jenkins and her leadership team had created a schoolwide English language arts curriculum map based on the state curriculum frameworks, district guidelines, and their own action planning. For each English language arts learning standard, the team compared what each grade level would be covering each week of the school year to ensure that teachers would teach all standards to all students over the course of a year. Anyone who consulted this map, which was prominently displayed outside of the school office and posted in individual classrooms, could see what topics would be featured when at each grade level. The map proved extremely helpful when grade-level teams met to figure out how to integrate the instructional strategies from their action plans into their ongoing work.

Use Teams for Support and Internal Accountability

As he looked around at the department meeting, principal Roger Bolton could see that Anne McGovern and Jean Louis felt lost. As teachers of "intensive math" at Franklin High School, their classes were filled with the weakest math students in the building. Both new teachers, they were pleased to be included in the math department's process for analyzing data and brainstorming instructional improvements. They were enthusiastic about the Problem-Solving Approach that the department had chosen. But now that it was time to actually start teaching it, the plan seemed out of reach. "I don't see how we can teach this method," Roger heard Jean mutter at the end of the meeting, "if our students can't actually read the problems we give them or do the most basic calculations that they ask for."

When you first began organizing for collaborative data analysis, as a school leader you worked to build a system of interlocking teacher teams. Now that it is time to implement your action plan, these teams can become an important source of support and inspiration for teachers. As teachers become accustomed to checking in with their colleagues regularly, they make a greater effort to be prepared for meetings. When teachers see their teammates working hard to implement the strategies, they are motivated to do their best to make changes in their own classrooms. And as teachers realize that they eventually will be turning over their students to the next year's teachers—who will expect students to have experienced the teaching practices agreed on in the action plan—they develop an increased sense of personal responsibility for their students' performance.

There may be times, however, when you discover that the team structures you put in place are not enough, and that you may need to facilitate the development of new collaborations. Principal Roger Bolton guessed that one of the reasons intensive math teachers were frustrated was that they needed guidance about how to make the

Problem-Solving Approach more accessible to their students. So Roger arranged to have the math department meet with English as a Second Language specialists and special education teachers to discuss how to provide more instructional scaffolding for student learning, such as breaking the steps of the approach into smaller units that could be taught over a longer period of time. Because Roger had involved all faculty in exploring math performance at the beginning of the year and then later shared the math department's action plan with the whole school, all teachers were quite familiar with the task at hand. Encouraging faculty to work across disciplines to figure out how to connect the instructional goals of the school to their daily lessons can be a powerful way of making sure implementation gets off the ground, especially when considering the learning of at-risk or struggling students.

ARE WE DOING WHAT WE SAID WE'D DO?

As a school leader you can begin to keep track of how things are going almost from the moment teachers start implementing the action plan. Monitoring is critical to ensure a smooth launch and to clearly signal to teachers that this work is so important to you as the school leader that you intend to give it your personal attention. There is no point in waiting until the implementation period is well under way to get a read on whether teachers really integrated the instructional strategies into their practice. If you wait that long and then find out that things did not go well, it's like looking in a rearview mirror—the action is past, and it is often too late to change it. If you stay involved from the beginning, you can become a helpful partner in making sure that instruction really changes. To do this, you may find it helpful to visit classrooms frequently, promote consistency rather than conformity in instructional practices, and adapt professional development plans to meet ongoing needs that emerge from the work.

Visit Classrooms Frequently

Observing practice was something your team needed to do in order to identify the problem of practice that you were committed to addressing with your action plan. Once you start implementing that plan, you will want to get right back into classrooms to see how things are going. In fact, these visits should be part of your plan to assess progress.

As mentioned in chapter 5, the Data Wise Project Team created *Key Elements of Observing Practice: A Data Wise DVD and Facilitator's Guide* in response to feedback from practitioners about the challenge of creating a culture where observing practice is a comfortable part of all teachers' experience.[1] That resource argues that effective classroom-visit routines contain five key elements:

- Focus

- Observe

- Debrief

- Adjust

- Follow Up

When the purpose of classroom visits is to implement and fine-tune instructional improvements assessing progress, then the task associated with the *focus* element is reviewing your problem of practice and understanding how the lessons you will be observing will attempt to address that problem. When you *observe*, you will be collecting evidence about what teaching and learning looks like when the action plan is being implemented, and when you *debrief* you will discuss the evidence that you heard and saw and commit to how you will *adjust* instruction based on what you learned. When you *follow up*, you will discuss what happened when you adjusted instruction and plan new steps.

During your *focus* meeting, you may want to distribute note-taking sheets that remind observers about what the learner-centered problem and problem of practice are and give people space to keep track of what the teacher is doing, what the students are doing, and what task students are actually working on.[2]

One school we know developed a very detailed protocol and schedule for conducting classroom visits. Recognizing that it would be impossible for an individual to observe all aspects of classroom practice at once, the school's protocol involved having four classroom visitors at a time, each charged with making observations about a specific area of practice. Because their action plan focused on improving the use of questioning and conversations in teaching, the four areas of practice targeted by the protocol looked at what types of questions teachers ask, what kind of evidence there is for conversations about learning, physical evidence of improvement strategies, and students' perspectives on their work. Each observer was given a note-taking form unique to the area he or she was observing. The entire classroom visit schedule called for a pre-meeting to give an overview about the day, which consisted of two classroom visits of 15 minutes each, and a post-meeting to debrief the experience.

Promote Consistency Rather Than Conformity

When you visit classrooms, you are bound to find as many variations on the action plan as you have teachers. The challenge for school leaders involves distinguishing between skillful adaptations that move teachers to more sophisticated ways of supporting student learning and unskillful ones that water down or distort the spirit or intent of the original plan.

> **Clark principal Sandy Jenkins** had worked hard to encourage teachers to faithfully implement their action plans. But on one visit to Vivian's fourth-grade classroom, she began to question the value of her efforts. As Sandy observed the teacher leading the class in a Think Aloud exercise, she could see that two students seemed to hold back from the activity. When the teacher called on one of these students, he was clearly uncomfortable and struggled to put his ideas into words.
>
> When Sandy expressed her concerns to the teacher after the visit, Vivian knew just what she was talking about. "Jeffrey struggles with activities that put pressure on him to speak up," she explained. "But if I don't call on him he just tunes out and misses the lesson. I used to work with Jeffrey and several students with similar difficulties separately to show them how to underline key words that helped them figure out the deeper meaning of what they were reading, but with the focus on whole-class Think Alouds, I stopped doing that."

Sandy is faced with a leadership challenge that arises for many school leaders when they work to change instructional practice: the difficulty of promoting consistency while supporting teacher creativity. In communicating the action plan to teachers, Sandy may have overemphasized the importance of consistency in implementing the plan without highlighting the equal importance of allowing room for teachers to employ their knowledge and creativity in responding to the needs of diverse learners, particularly struggling learners. Vivian will not be able to truly improve her practice if she strives simply for conformity—faithful implementation of a plan that may wind up leaving behind some of the students who most need her individualized attention.

Striving for consistency involves getting to the deeper "why" behind instructional strategies, just as you did when you first examined instruction (see chapter 5). For Clark K–8 School the goal of the action plan is to use teaching strategies that encourage students to "think about how they think" as a means of developing inference skills in reading, not to make sure all students participate in a particular activity such as Think Alouds. Consistency involves the deeper question: How can we achieve our instructional goals with all students?

Although achieving consistency may be difficult, it is a worthwhile goal for several reasons. One is that if you think of the action plan as an experiment, the only way to truly test your hypothesis that your new instructional strategies will improve student learning is to faithfully implement those strategies and then see what happens. Another reason is that in striving for consistency, teachers develop a shared understanding of what constitutes effective instruction, and this understanding is essential in making ongoing improvement part of the everyday work of your school. The most important reason, however, is that students can benefit enormously from consistent instruction. It helps them integrate what they learn as they move from teacher to teacher during the school day or from one grade to the next, and it ensures that all students in all classrooms throughout the school have similar opportunities to learn.

Despite the virtues of consistency, it is important to recognize that, given the needs of diverse learners, it is a rare instance when a single strategy or set of strategies will meet the needs of all students. Classroom teachers are perfectly positioned to explore the chosen instructional strategies and try to improve them in the context of solving learning problems. When they report on their adaptations, the whole school can learn what it takes to elevate the learning of all students.

Some examples we've observed of helpful adaptations involved an action plan in which elementary school teachers used a math routine called "number of the day." During a 10-minute segment of instructional time, teachers asked students to brainstorm strategies for computing that day's number and then displayed the strategies on large chart paper in the classroom. The theory behind the plan was that if students have regular opportunities to explore numbers in an open-ended way, guided by the teacher and with other students so they build their knowledge in a social context, they will become more comfortable with numbers and develop an intuitive sense of the many ways numbers can be used. Teachers worked with the class to record the ideas their students generated, and the principal reviewed them during her classrooms visits. One first-grade teacher noted that some students in her class were not as forthcoming with their strategies as others. To inspire these children to see that they were capable of generating strategies that were just as good as those of students who spoke up more readily, the teacher decided to designate certain students the day before to be the first to share their ideas the next day for the number-of-the-day task.

Another teacher made a different modification. When he saw that his students were not producing as many math strategies as he would have liked, he decided to leave the 10-minute math chart paper up all day long and let students add strategies during free times throughout the day, such as lunch or recess. The result was a dramatic increase in the number and quality of strategies students generated. In modifying the instructional strategy, these teachers were able to make changes that made it more likely children would experience the heart of the strategy: stress-free exploration as a way to build comfort and confidence in manipulating numbers.

Adapt Professional Development Plans to Meet Ongoing Needs That Emerge from the Work

Franklin High School math teachers had been using the Problem-Solving Approach in their classes for six weeks. The action plan called for their March professional development session to offer guidance about assigning and grading Poster #2. As math coach Sasha Chang and department head Mallory Golden met with the principal to plan the session, they began by sharing some concerns.

"I'm not so sure we should focus our professional development on the rubric again," began Sasha. "I've been in a lot of classrooms, and I'll tell you what I'm seeing: teachers are using the Problem-Solving Approach, that's for sure. But it seems like it's kind of taken on a life of its own. Instead of focusing on helping students get good at thinking for themselves, they are focusing on helping them get good at following the steps of the process. Teachers seem to be placing more emphasis on evaluating whether the students follow the steps than on evaluating the thinking that actually happens at each step."

"My sense is that quite a few teachers realize this is happening," Mallory responded. "Some people have come up to me and say that they like the approach, but they feel the training on it just hasn't gone deep enough. They find themselves just walking students through the 'understand' phase of the problem, doing much of the work for the kids themselves because they're just not sure how you teach that part of the process."

When you first created your action plan, you took your best guess at what kinds of professional development your faculty would need to support them in the work. Once you begin implementing it, however, you may find that you have to modify your professional development plan, either by changing the content of scheduled sessions or by adding additional ones to make sure teachers get the help they need.

One school we know used a "just-in-time" approach to ensure that teachers were thoroughly prepared to teach each unit of a new math program. They arranged for a workshop to be held just before the teaching of key units at each grade level so that teachers could review the lesson, materials, and teaching moves required immediately before they taught them.

For teachers to make meaningful change in their practice, they may need to make multiple attempts to integrate new ideas. Instead of being discouraged when things do not go perfectly the first time around, as a school leader you can focus your efforts on understanding why teachers are having trouble with certain aspects of the plan. If you structure professional development so it is flexible and provides opportunities for teachers to learn, try out, analyze, get feedback, and reflect on new practices, you can help teachers feel that they will be supported during this hard work.

For example, an action plan for improving writing skills might call for the use of one-on-one conferencing with students about their writing. For teachers unfamiliar with this practice, incorporating it meaningfully into their teaching might require that they have an the opportunity to see another skilled teacher demonstrate key components of conferencing, such as asking appropriate questions, giving specific feedback, and guiding students in editing. After that, teachers would most likely need ongoing opportunities to try out this practice in their classrooms and meet with other teachers to discuss, analyze, and reflect on their implementation and the results they were getting. You can demonstrate the depth of your belief in professional development by participating in sessions along with teachers; you model the importance of professional learning by being a learner yourself. In creating and supporting ongoing opportunities for professional development, a school leader reinforces the idea that the goal of school improvement work is to create a school culture in which everyone is learning.

ARE OUR STUDENTS LEARNING MORE?

Although supporting teachers in improving their practice is an important part of your job during implementation of the action plan, as a school leader your ultimate responsibility is to keep your faculty focused on student learning. After all, the main reason your school developed an action plan was to increase student learning, and the main reason you developed an assessment plan was to be able to measure progress toward this goal. You can keep the focus on learning in the short term by regularly checking in with teachers about learning outcomes. In the longer term, you can help teachers see the big picture and be honest in evaluating what is or is not working.

Regularly Check in with Teachers About Learning Outcomes

Sandy Jenkins had learned a lot by visiting classrooms throughout the fall to observe how teachers were implementing the strategies outlined in their action plans. As part of her visits, she tried to make a point of looking through student work and talking with the children themselves about what they were learning. A couple of days after the winter results of the district's reading assessment were in, Sandy stopped by third-grade teacher Jae Kim's classroom to have a more concrete discussion about how things were going.

"I noticed that your class made some real progress on the December assessment," Sandy began. "Can you tell me more about what you saw in the data and how it affects the way you will approach the next few months?" Jae showed Sandy a spreadsheet that displayed the results of the district test alongside his own assessment of each student's performance from conferencing notes, then explained his findings: "Well, although most students reached or exceeded their targets on the district assessment, you can see that there are three kids who fell pretty far short. For Danny and Keisha, I saw this coming. You can see from my notes that Danny is still at the decoding stage and Keisha just can't seem to get past the literal meaning of the words. As for Marissa, I'm really surprised at her score. If you just sit with her as she reads and talks about a book she's read, she seems to know what's going on. Maybe she has trouble transferring her knowledge into a testing situation? Anyway, I'm a little concerned about how to reach these kids. They all need something different and there just doesn't seem time in the day to give it to them."

In the days before your school was engaged in a process of continuous improvement, it might have been awkward to sit down with a teacher in the middle of the year and ask him what he could tell you about how much his students were learning. But once you have action and assessment plans in place, initiating these kinds of discussions can become much more comfortable. When teachers begin to understand that you are an ally in their quest to help each child reach his or her potential, you may find that they look forward to these encounters and actively solicit your advice in finding solutions.

Sandy and Jae had their conversation about the performance of struggling learners in his class before it was too late. By the end of their discussion, Sandy had offered to have a literacy specialist work with Jae's neediest students intensively over the next several weeks right in the classroom, so that Jae could see some of her teaching moves and begin to use them himself. She offered to join the next third- and fourth-grade team meeting to participate in their discussion about whether Think Alouds were making a difference for students who were still working to master the most basic reading skills. Another strategy she came up with was to ask the school's parent liaison to make a particular effort to reach out to the families of these three students and make sure that they understood the extra support their children would be getting.

Collecting short-term and medium-term data on student learning in the way described in chapter 7 provides direct and immediate evidence about whether students are learning and gives you an opportunity to make midcourse adjustments in the plan if they aren't. When you focus on what multiple data sources reveal about student learning, you can remain true to the goals of the plan while modifying the instructional approach when needed. Maintaining the ability to change midstream requires treating the action plan as a dynamic document, so that teachers don't see it as a straitjacket but as a living, organic process tailored to the school's mission.

Help Teachers See the Big Picture

Math department chair Mallory Golden collapsed into the chair in principal Roger Bolton's office and let out a long sigh. "Take a look at this," she said as she handed over a chart showing Franklin High School's performance on the most recent state math test. "All that work on the Problem-Solving Approach and the percentage of our students scoring in the lowest two proficiency levels has barely budged. According to the rubrics we've been using, our students have made big strides in tackling multistep problems. How do I tell my teachers that all that hard work was for nothing?"

After leading your school through a difficult process of change, it can be frustrating when you don't see results right away. During his regular visits to classrooms, Roger observed firsthand the visible changes in math instruction at Franklin High School that seemed to engage more students in learning. He felt instruction in math was finally on the right track. They still had a long way to go, but he knew it was up to him to make sure that they didn't allow a quick look at the data to throw cold water on their efforts.

Helping teachers see the big picture means encouraging them to think about whether they have really explored the data completely and whether they have taken into account the many other indicators of student learning available to them as a school, as well as the many other ways to present data. When Mallory and Roger looked closer at the numbers, they realized that although the percentage of tenth graders scoring in the "Failing" and "Needs Improvement" categories of the test had not changed much since the previous year, more students were now in the higher of these two categories (see Exhibit 8.2). Students had higher raw scores within each proficiency level than they had in previous years, but because of the way the results were reported, these differences were not readily seen. They also noticed that the percentage of students taking the test was noticeably higher than it had been in previous years. This could mean that some of the weakest students, who traditionally had avoided school and testing days, this year had the confidence to at least give the test a try. By looking at the same data in a more detailed way, they had a more complete picture of the effects of implementing their action plan for math.

Exhibit 8.2

Franklin High School Distribution of Student Proficiency over Time

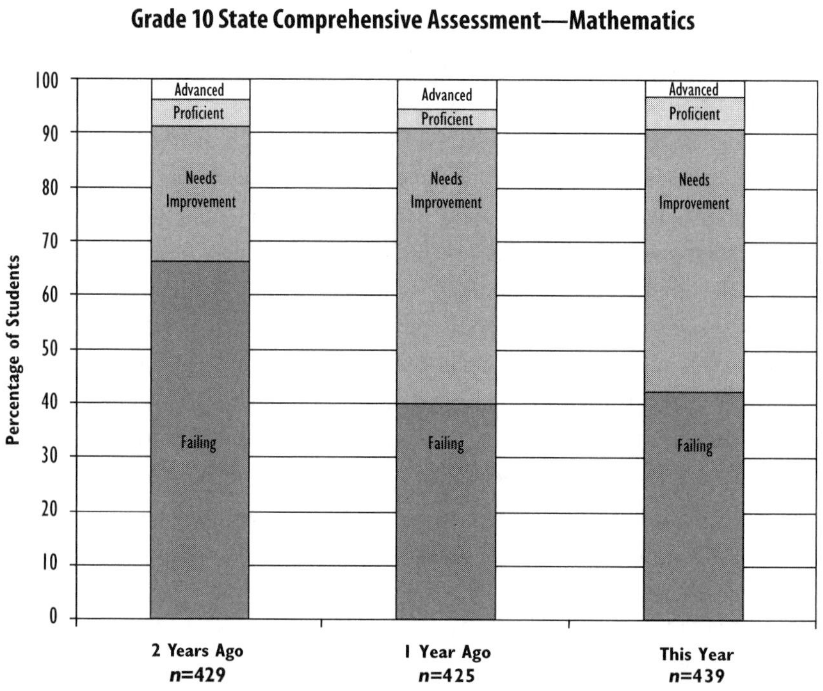

Grade 10 State Comprehensive Assessment—Mathematics

Helping teachers see the big picture also means managing expectations around the question of how soon it is reasonable to expect to see improvements in scores on tests used for accountability purposes. When Roger saw that the math faculty's assessment plan set a target that Franklin High School would meet accountability goals on the state math test, he let them do it. After all, he reasoned, meeting this target was a measure by which many people would judge the school. Nevertheless, Roger knew that it would take time for teachers to develop skill and competence in teaching the Problem-Solving Approach. Also, the plan had only been in effect for the second half of the school year, and there had been some glitches along the way. This meant that in a number of classrooms students had only a month or two of solid training in the methodology. Given these factors, Roger felt that it was too soon to use the state test results to judge whether the plan was successful or not, so he encouraged his faculty to try the approach for another year. He also shared with teachers his own evidence and observations from his classroom visits that instruction in math classes was improving.

Be Honest in Evaluating What Is and Is Not Working

Sandy carefully reviewed the charts that the instructional leadership team had prepared showing changes in student reading performance over the previous school year. Although all grades had made progress, she noticed an interesting phenomenon: the improvement among the fifth and sixth graders was much stronger than that among third and fourth graders. To build each team's commitment to the plan, she'd made the conscious decision to let each grade-level team choose its own instructional strategies for achieving the schoolwide goal of helping students become more skilled readers. But now she wondered: was there a chance that the strategy adopted by the third- and fourth-grade team was not as effective as the strategy adopted by the fifth- and sixth-grade team?

Sandy faces a delicate situation. The third- and fourth-grade team implemented their Think Aloud strategy with zeal all year. Yet student performance on the district-mandated benchmark reading test was not that impressive. As a school leader, you may find that once the data come in you need to help your teachers take a hard look at whether the strategies they have worked so hard to implement really made a difference. This can be difficult, because when people believe strongly in their ideas they often become "pet projects" in which a lot of energy and time is invested, and teachers may become unwilling to look at signs that those strategies are not working with some or all of their students. While we do not want to encourage schools to simply abandon strategies that do not produce results across the board, it is important to take a careful look when learning outcomes are not as robust as you had hoped. As a school leader, your responsibility will sometimes be to point out when a well-designed and well-executed strategy just isn't doing the job.

In the case of Clark K–8 School, the graph of reading test performance (see Exhibit 8.3) would not be enough to tell Sandy whether the third- and fourth-grade strategy was problematic, and certainly would not be enough to tell her why. There are plenty of reasons why the average growth patterns might be different for different grade levels. Sandy would need to consider this graph in combination with other data, such as her observations during her classroom visits that the Think Aloud approach did not seem to work well with certain students, or her observations during classroom visits of the upper grades that might have shown those teachers having particular success with Reader's Response notebooks and Literature Circles. When Sandy begins a conversation with her faculty about whether they might need to supplement or replace their chosen strategy, she can raise questions such as: Are we truly implementing the strategy to the extent we planned? Have we been doing it

Exhibit 8.3

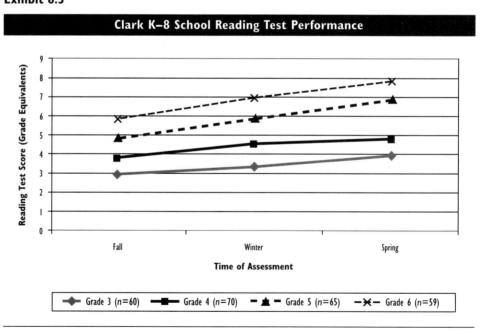

long enough? Is it working for all learners? Is this strategy powerful enough to be our primary focus?

Viewing implementation as an experiment from which the school will learn new things about effective instruction can help school staff approach their own work honestly and critically. As you evaluate the effectiveness of implementation (the extent to which we are doing what we said we'd do) as well as the effectiveness of the strategies themselves (the extent to which students are learning more), it helps if you remain open to the possibility that change may be required. In this way you help your school become invested in student learning rather than in any particular strategy. Sometimes the data will show that it is time to change course.

WHERE DO WE GO FROM HERE?

Once you have implemented your action plan and the ideas and practices embodied in it have been tried out with consistency, it is time to regroup. No doubt you and your faculty have learned a lot—and probably determined that you have a lot more to learn. It's important to ground the next level of work solidly in evidence of student learning. Three things you can do once you have made it around the steps of the improvement cycle are to celebrate success, revisit your criteria and raise the bar, and plan how to keep the work fresh and ongoing.

Celebrate Success

At the final faculty meeting of the year, Sandy surprised her teachers by not passing out a series of data charts. "We're going to talk about a different kind of data today," Sandy began. "We've worked hard all year to try to improve reading instruction in our school. We've had our ups and our downs, but I think every one of us has learned something. On the paper I am distributing, I'd like you to take a few minutes to describe something in your teaching this year with which you were successful. Be sure to write down evidence of its success and the reasons why you think your effort worked. After you've had a chance to jot down your ideas, evidence, and reasons, we're going to divide into cross-grade groups and use a protocol that allows us to really get at the heart of what success looks like, sounds like, and feels like."

So often teachers are asked to look at test scores or their own practice and talk about what went wrong. We have found that tempering this by giving teachers a chance to think deeply about what makes for successful practice can be a very positive learning experience. Using a formal protocol such as the Success Analysis Protocol that

Sandy used at Clark K–8 School can help ensure that the conversation gets beyond simple platitudes and continues the practice of talking about teaching in a fine-grained way.[3] Giving teachers a chance to talk together about their own success and reflect on the reasons for that success does more than give them a well-earned moment of appreciation. It also allows them to begin to internalize the qualities at the heart of best practices, such as evidence, analysis, and reflection, and to think about how to bring these qualities more strongly into their work.

Another way to celebrate success involves simply showing your faculty how far they have come. Sandy used the table in Exhibit 8.4 to show her faculty how they had worked through the eight steps of the improvement cycle, often managing a number of different tasks at once, in order to make progress.

There are, of course, many other ways of celebrating success that may rely more heavily on making public the results of your student assessments. Success can be defined collectively or individually, and progress as well as achievement can be acknowledged for both students and teachers. What is important is that a collective sense of accountability for results is built among teachers. Acknowledgments of

Exhibit 8.4

	Organize for Collaborative Work	Build Assessment Literacy	Create Data Overview	Dig into Data	Examine Instruction	Develop Action Plan	Plan to Assess Progress	Act and Assess
Clark K–8 School Time Line for Completing the Steps of the Improvement Process								
STEP OF THE IMPROVEMENT PROCESS								
Aug.	■	■	■					
Sept.	■	■						
Oct.	■			■				
Nov.				■				
Dec.				■	■			
Jan.				■	■			
Feb.				■	■			
Mar.					■			
Apr.					■	■		
May					■	■	■	
June						■		■
July								■

progress are especially powerful for students when they can be broadly distributed across all student groups, and not just among those who are accustomed to recognition. An authentic way of celebrating success involves thoughtful displays of the student work that meets or exceeds clearly articulated standards. In one school we worked with, each teacher put up a "Wall of Work" in his or her classroom and the principal created schoolwide displays showing the work of every student in the school, together with a statement of the standard the work was intended to demonstrate. In another school, to reward students' efforts to improve their writing, teachers displayed not just the final pieces of writing, but the brainstorming sheets, outlines, first drafts, and edited drafts as well. They did this to show concretely the hard work that it takes to get to standards and to remind students that, with effort, everyone can improve.

Revisit Your Criteria and "Raise the Bar"

Roger met with the Franklin High School math department and talked with them about the disappointing performance of tenth graders on the state math exam. "Let's not let this get us down, folks," he told them. "Some of the posters the kids created, especially for the most recent assignment, are quite impressive. You seem to have hit on a type of assignment that captures their imagination and an approach to tackling word problems that gives kids something to hold on to."

"The second round of posters did go quite well," Mallory added. "In fact, for most steps of our rubric, we met our target of having 75 percent of our students score 'Meets Expectations' or better."

"I wonder," Roger replied, "whether it's time to take another look at that rubric and the way we apply it. Let's be sure that when we say a piece of work 'Meets Expectations' we are talking about high expectations. When we first got into this problem-solving thing we weren't quite sure what it was reasonable to ask of kids. Now that we've seen a little of what they can do, I think we can start asking for more. How about taking a look at the scoring rubric used in the state exam? We want to be sure there is alignment between how we assess students and how the state does."

As teachers gain understanding of the strategies they are implementing, as a school leader, you can help them adjust the criteria by which success is measured to promote the deeper understanding of the material that comes with time. By revisiting the conversations they had when they were first developing shared understandings and expectations for the work, teachers can begin to redefine what is possible. At

Franklin, teachers had very little experience using a systematic approach to evaluate students' demonstrations of their problem-solving strategies. At first, they may have made their rubric too easy or made their grading too lenient. By sticking with the strategies and refining them, they can collectively come to better and more nuanced understandings of what good work really looks like.

For a school that is implementing a new set of instructional techniques, very visible signs of implementation—like the prominent display of student work—may be one way of demonstrating success. For a school in which teachers are refining their practice, the criteria will need to become more refined and more focused on complex teaching and learning skills. For example, a more refined approach could include the student self-assessment on the rubric with each piece of work displayed. As the criteria change, the ongoing feedback teachers receive from their colleagues evolves to push their practice toward higher goals. By continuing the conversations in which teachers reflect on their practice and their goals for student learning, the criteria for success will continue to deepen along with teacher learning.

Plan How to Keep the Work Fresh and Ongoing

The improvement cycle curves back on itself for a reason: once you get to the "end," you continue back around the cycle, but each time you use it at a higher level and apply it to a more complex problem of student learning. As using the improvement cycle to change instruction becomes ingrained in the practice of your school, you may find it becomes easier to know what questions to ask, how to examine the data, and how to support teachers and students. You will also be able to go deeper into the work, asking tougher questions, setting higher goals, and involving more people in the process. The first time around it might have been all you could do to get your faculty to begin thinking about addressing student learning in a proactive way. As you continue, you may find that you need to involve other constituents who have a stake in student learning outcomes, such as families and community members, in the process. By the time you have been doing this kind of work for several years, you may notice that you quite naturally find ways to enlist the support of even more partners in making a difference for student learning.

As you keep the work going, you may also find that you are able to distribute leadership responsibilities more efficiently than you originally could. When your school has developed a solid culture of inquiry, it becomes natural for large numbers of teachers to take active roles in making sure that the school focuses on continuous improvement. Teachers increase their span of interest and responsibility from their own classrooms and grade levels to concern for the school as a whole. The roles of instructional leadership team members—in particular those of data managers—may shift as well. Whereas at the beginning only a few individuals might have been interested in or capable of analyzing data, as more teachers in your building become comfortable with this work, the skills become more widely spread throughout the faculty. The instructional leadership team can then graduate to a role of thinking more broadly about what kinds of assessments and professional development opportunities would best support the school's vision for improving student learning, and the team can engage in evidence-based conversations with your district about what kinds of central support would be most helpful. With that in mind, the next chapter of this book lays out the most effective ways we have seen districts support schools in using data wisely.

Integrating the ACE Habits of Mind into Step 8: Acting and Assessing

SHARED COMMITMENT TO ACTION, ASSESSMENT, AND ADJUSTMENT

We've saved our single most important insight about building this particular habit of mind for this last step of the Data Wise Improvement Process. Here it is: every time you have a meeting or hold a professional development session, set aside five minutes at the end for participants to provide specific, descriptive feedback about how it went. If you have taken one of our courses or read *Key Elements of Observing Practice: A Data Wise DVD and Facilitator's Guide*, you know that the Data Wise Project team's favorite way to do this is to use the Plus/Delta Protocol (see Selected Protocols at the end of the book). You begin by reminding people of what the objectives and the agenda of the session were. Then give them a few minutes to reflect on "pluses." These are things that worked well. To prompt for these, you can ask, "What contributed to our learning and productivity today? What should we keep doing?" Then allow time for people to reflect on the things they wish they could have changed about the session. These are called "deltas" (and often noted with the symbol Δ, which denotes change). Here you can ask: "What detracted from today's experience? What should we do differently next time?"

This protocol nicely connects an **action** (the meeting) and your **assessment** (asking for feedback). The power of the Plus/Delta Protocol lies in your commitment to using the feedback you obtain to **adjust** what happens the next time your group is together. For example, during one meeting, you may learn that people felt uncomfortable that an important discussion about the learning needs of a particular group of students was cut short because you didn't leave enough time for it on the agenda. If you don't ask for feedback about the meeting, some people may walk away with a sense of unfinished business or disillusionment with the process. If you allow space for this comment to arise, but do nothing to address it, you are arguably worse off than if you didn't ask for feedback—people will learn that nothing comes of raising a "delta." But if you take the feedback to heart and directly address it before or during the next meeting, participants will see that when they provide a candid assessment, it does indeed lead to action. Time after time, we've seen how this reflective practice generates a virtuous cycle of continuous improvement, in which a school or team can gracefully recover when something doesn't work.

INTENTIONAL COLLABORATION

Throughout this book, we've argued that protocols can be extremely useful tools for building this habit, and we've pointed you to protocol instructions so that you know how to get started. But protocols become truly powerful when you adapt them to meet your needs and your context. Believe it or not, there is a protocol out there that is designed specifically to help you reflect on the effectiveness of a protocol! It is called "SUMI," and it involves writing the following four letters on a piece of chart paper (or whiteboard, or shared document):[4]

S   What **surprised** you as you engaged in this protocol?

U   How could you **use** this protocol in your teaching and other meetings?

M   How would you **modify** this protocol?

I   What is the **impact** of this protocol?

Then you ask participants to reflect out loud on these four questions. Taking time to debrief each protocol has two important benefits. First, it helps participants to construct meaning for themselves from what they experienced. We've been interested to see that sometimes the person in the room who was most vocally against using protocols ends up having the greatest insights. One principal we worked with told us that the impact of one particular protocol was that "it forced me to listen, which was hard, so it made me wonder if I am not doing enough of it." Second, it gives teachers an opportunity to think about how they might adapt the protocol for use in their classrooms, and teachers can never resist an opportunity to think of new strategies to use with their students. When students *see* the adults in your building modeling intentional collaboration, they get a glimpse at what teamwork looks like. But when students regularly *experience* the rich peer interactions that protocols allow, they can make great strides in developing the kinds of expert thinking and complex communication skills that they will need to thrive.

RELENTLESS FOCUS ON EVIDENCE

One way to capture evidence of team learning is to create "living documents" that keep track of decisions over time. In our own work on the Data Wise Project team, we create one electronic document for each of our major work streams and store all documents online so everyone on the team can access and edit them. Each time we plan a meeting for a particular work stream, we add a new agenda to the top of the appropriate document, and as each meeting unfolds, we take notes directly into the agenda. At the end of the year, the documents contain an easily searchable archive of our previous thinking, reflections, and actions. We strongly recommend that you consider this approach for documenting all the good work you and your colleagues do to use data wisely. You may find it is a rich source of evidence for collective reflection on what you have achieved—and what remains to be done.

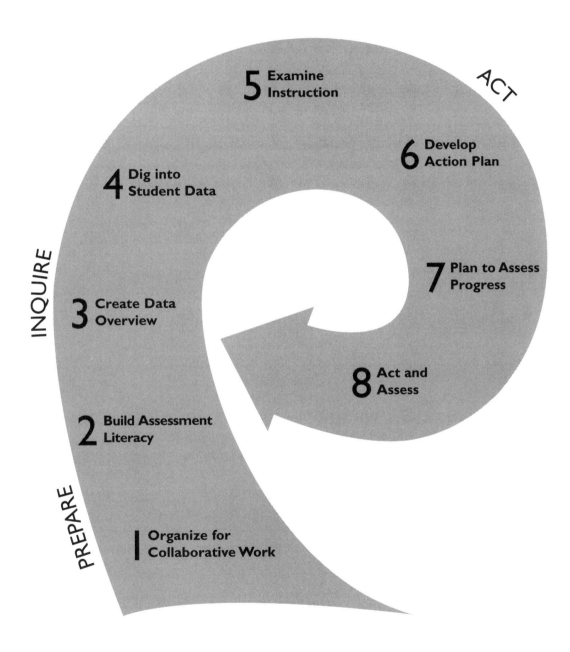

9

ROLES FOR THE DISTRICT CENTRAL OFFICE

Nancy S. Sharkey and Richard J. Murnane

THE PURPOSE OF THIS CHAPTER is to provide school superintendents and their leadership teams with an understanding of the roles that district central offices can play, and in most districts *must* play, if schools are to make constructive use of student assessment results. These roles, which we describe below, include providing a data system and software, incentives, skills, and time to do the work. We also argue that it is important for central office teams to model the work.

THE DATA SYSTEM

Districts and schools must consider numerous factors in establishing and maintaining a data system—what is worth including, how the data should be organized and stored, what software to use and whether to create or buy it, and who has access to what data.

What Should Be Included?

An important first step districts can take to support schools' efforts to use data constructively is to create and maintain a student information system that is accurate and kept up to date. Of course, it makes sense for the data system to contain student-specific, detailed results from assessments used for accountability pur-poses—the results schools are under pressure to improve. However, since analysis of these scores always raises more questions than it answers (see chapter 4), the potential to examine multiple data sources is important. For that reason, many dis-tricts have found it useful to ask schools to administer interim assessments in core subjects over the school year and to store results from these tests in the district's cen-tral database. Other potentially valuable information to store and make available to schools electronically includes results on midyear and end-of-year course-specific tests. As explained in chapter 4, teacher teams often find it valuable to examine not only students' total scores on these examinations, but also skill-specific subscores and responses to individual items. Consequently, it is important that the district data system make this easy to do.

Given that time spent testing children is time taken from instruction, it is impor-tant to verify that test results are useful in diagnosing the strengths and limitations of children's knowledge and the extent to which they have mastered skills included in state learning standards and in the district's curriculum. For example, if the cur-riculum and standards emphasize skill at responding to open-ended questions, it makes sense for the assessments to include open-ended questions. If the curriculum and standards focus on multistep questions, the assessment should as well. We have seen many schools analyze student assessment data only to realize that the district-required assessments were not aligned with the district-required curriculum. For ex-ample, an eighth-grade math test assesses algebra skills not covered in the district's curriculum until ninth grade. If the assessments do not match the curriculum and standards, teachers and administrators are unlikely to believe that the assessment results are accurate measures of what students know and can do and, consequently, that looking carefully at those results is a valuable use of their scarce time.

As we explained in chapter 3, school-based teams often want to examine the relative performance of students with different characteristics. For that reason, it makes sense for the districtwide database to contain information about individual students, including gender, race, and ethnicity, special education status, language-minority status, and free or reduced-price lunch eligibility. Some school teams also want to examine the performance of groups that participate in special programs, such as tutoring or afterschool programs. Having this information recorded on the district database makes these tasks much easier to accomplish. Since enrollment in programs like tutoring changes rapidly, it is important to implement a strategy for keeping the information up to date.

How Should the Data Be Organized?

It makes sense to store student data at the individual level so that school teams have the flexibility to examine assessment results for students grouped in a variety of ways. It is also important that the data system track students over time, as they switch schools and complete additional assessments. To do this, each student must have a personal identification number. Many states assign identification numbers to students when they first enter a public school in the state. When districts use these same numbers, the tasks of following students from district to district and merging results from state- and district-administered assessments become easier. Updating the district's data system regularly so that records accurately reflect the school each student is attending and the classes each student is taking is critical. School teams will persevere in making sense of student assessment results only if they find that the information in the district's database is accurate and up to date.

Districts with relatively small numbers of students may find it sufficient to store student data in a database management program. However, to provide support for a large number of data teams making multiple varied queries about student data, many districts find it necessary to purchase a data warehouse, and some state education agencies are developing their own statewide data warehouses.

What Software Should Be Used?

Once all pertinent information is located in a well-supported data warehouse or database, the district must give schools software to analyze the data. Many districts we have worked with provide all schools with customized software that allows teams to easily create the types of graphs illustrated in chapter 3. It is also becoming more common for districts and states to provide online tools for displaying, charting, and analyzing student data directly through the data warehouse websites.

It is important to recognize that the capacity to analyze student assessment data will vary widely across schools. This creates the challenge of providing tools that satisfy the needs of school teams doing quite sophisticated work and those that are just beginning. This is a challenge because, typically, the more sophisticated the analyses a software system will support, the more complex its design and the more difficult it will be to use.

We have seen districts deal with the "power versus ease of use" trade-off in a variety of ways. Some provide all schools with basic reports that school staffs will likely start with when creating simple data overviews of their schools. These basic reports can be preprogrammed in the district's data system, enabling school staffs to retrieve them easily for their own schools. One district calls these reports the "Top Ten" and distributes paper copies to school administrators as well as making them available online. Once these overviews have been discussed by administrators, members of the instructional leadership team at each school can engage in the deeper data work that discussion of these reports will prompt. A variant of this strategy used by other districts is to create an easy-to-use interface that allows schools to address an important but limited set of questions. Once school teams have mastered this software and demand more powerful tools, the district provides training in accessing more sophisticated features.

As school teams become good at the work, they make greater demands of the data. For example, one school team we worked with wanted to know how students who had been in their building for at least two years had fared on the state assessments. Another wanted to investigate whether students who had math for their first-period class did less well on the state math exam than students who had math later in the day. Designing data and software systems that allow teams to answer such detailed questions efficiently and also engage the novice user after only a little training is a significant design challenge. District staff need to be prepared to support schools at all stages in their learning and to help schools to share novel display strategies and creative and informative analyses.

Make or Buy?

Districts that want to give schools the tools to do the work described in this book need to decide whether to create data and software systems in-house or purchase them from an external vendor. Each alternative has advantages and disadvantages, the importance of which will depend on local circumstances, including in-house technical capabilities. One district that we have worked with created its own web-based database system, which enabled schools to combine student characteristics and state assessment data with benchmark data generated at the school level. An advantage of this choice was that because many central office departments and school representatives were involved in the design and implementation of the data system, many clients were ready to use the product. A disadvantage was that the process was slow. It took more than a year to provide schools the tools for basic analyses like those described in chapter 3, and the development process was ongoing three years later.

Another district we have worked with contracted with a vendor to provide reports and analyses of student assessment data to administrators, teachers, parents, and students. Some vendors provide data warehouse and software systems that will support very sophisticated data analyses. Some also provide benchmark or interim assessments and teacher professional development tailored to meet needs identified in the assessment results. An advantage of purchasing products and services from external vendors is that they are usually prepared to act quickly. Of course, these products come at a cost, which is typically assessed on a per-student basis.

Who Has Access to What Data?

Because student information is confidential, every district with a central data system must have a process for determining who has access to what data for which students. In several districts we work with, teachers could not access the assessment results of their former students. Since results from the state tests administered in May were not available until September, this meant that they could not learn whether students they had taught the previous year were able to demonstrate proficiency on the skills they had emphasized. The importance of remedying this flaw in the access system seems straightforward. However, other access questions are more difficult. For example, should teachers be able to access test scores of the students taught by other teachers in their schools? Should math teachers be able to access reading scores for the students to whom they teach math? These are two examples of the many access questions that arise when school faculties attempt to examine student assessment results. However, as norms in the education sector slowly shift toward giving teachers more access to student data, these questions may become less salient.

INCENTIVES AND SKILLS

We have seen that schools make more progress with this work when they feel that all district policies—especially those that pertain to planning, professional development, and evaluation—support rather than undermine their efforts to use data to improve teaching and learning. An instructional leadership team that has dedicated itself to this practice wants to know that its efforts are being recognized and valued by the central office. When district personnel request to see the improvement process in action during their visits, ask what they can do to make things go more smoothly, and find ways to connect schools that can learn from one another, so school-based educators have strong incentives to deepen the work of improvement.

While incentives are important, they are not enough. To use student assessment results constructively, school faculty need a variety of skills, including the ability to (1) understand, interpret, and use assessment data correctly (assessment literacy); (2) use software or online tools to access data and create and understand graphic displays of assessment results; (3) participate productively in group conversations and decisions where they have to be open to sharing practice and debating ideas; and (4) develop, implement, and assess action plans to improve instruction. The district central office has a major role to play in organizing and supporting the requisite professional development.

Assessment Literacy

To interpret score reports from different tests, teachers and administrators need to understand scales, benchmarks, and percentile ranks. To appreciate what inferences are appropriate to make from assessment results, educators also need to understand other concepts explained in chapter 2, such as measurement and sampling errors, validity, and reliability. In our work with schools, we have observed two strategies that appear to help school teams acquire elements of assessment literacy: modeling good practice and providing expertise on an as-needed basis. One district we have worked with created a sample whole-school improvement plan that modeled the appropriate use of student assessment results. Since every school was required to create such a plan, the model plan attracted considerable attention. This district also had a research office staffed by people with the skills to answer the many questions that arise as school-based teams work to make sense of test score reports.

Using the Data System

In chapter 3, we described the types of data displays that school staffs may find useful in catalyzing conversations about student assessment results. We have seen district central offices engage in several activities to help school-based educators learn to use the district's data system and create effective graphic displays. One is professional development specifically directed to teaching these skills. A second is creating guidelines with instructions for school-based users to easily produce commonly requested graphs for specific groups of students. A third is creating an online help system and having district staff available to answer any questions that arise. Many educators refer to this process as "pulling the data" from the system. They also speak of the need to help other teachers learn to pull the data on their own, rather than relying on the principal or a data manager to help them.

Group Processes and Collaboration

A theme of this book is that to contribute to instructional improvements, the work of analyzing student assessment results needs to be done collaboratively. Some teachers feel uncomfortable participating in many of the activities described in this book, including brainstorming about potential explanations for patterns in student assessment results and discussing their students' work with other teachers. Some teachers are reluctant to be observed by other teachers because this runs so contrary to the closed-door culture of their schools. It is worth remembering that many building and district administrators come out of schools with closed-door cultures and have no experience in creating a culture in which teachers work together as described in this book.

We have suggested that using protocols to structure conversations about student performance and instructional strategies can help create a "data wise" school culture. In our experience, many school leaders are not aware of the value of protocols and how to use them. We see this as a potentially valuable focus of professional development for school leaders and other educators.

As we explained in chapter 3, having all teachers and administrators take the assessments that states require of students has been an eye-opening experience in some schools we have worked with, one that catalyzed constructive conversations about teaching and learning. Districts can facilitate this activity by ensuring that school staffs have copies of previously administered tests and answers available.

Collaboratively creating scoring rubrics and then scoring student papers in groups also builds collegiality and teacher knowledge. Teachers have told us that scoring state assessments was a powerful form of professional development. It not only taught them to understand what the assessment was asking, but also increased their understanding of the curriculum standards and what different levels of student performance actually looked like. This activity can help teachers develop a common language of assessment and instruction. Typically, however, the teachers who have experience grading state tests are the "specialists," or teachers who are already recognized for their skills. Districts might expand the cadre of teachers who participate in grading state tests so that more teachers have access to these learning opportunities and can share what they have learned with other teachers at their schools.

Developing, Implementing, and Assessing Action Plans

Another recurring theme of this book is that analyzing student assessment results is a critical part of effective instructional improvement strategies. Chapter 5, for example, presented ways school staffs can identify *current* teaching practices at their schools, and chapter 6 discussed how teachers and administrators can create instructional action plans that move teachers from analyzing data to developing strategies for improvement. In our experience, however, we have found that many school faculties need help in moving from understanding the learner-centered problem to framing a problem of practice to designing and implementing an effective action plan for improving instruction.

Districts can support the work proposed in both chapters by providing professional development in content and pedagogy. In some districts we have worked with, professional development is provided through coaches (also known as specialists), who receive professional development from the district's central office and then share what they have learned at the schools where they work. These coaches typically spend part of their time working with groups of teachers (for example, leading a session on exploring assessment results). They also spend part of their time in classrooms, modeling, assisting with, and observing lessons. An important and often missing step in using coaches to support instructional improvement is teaching them the skills described in this book. Unless coaches understand how to do the steps of the improvement cycle, they will not be able to help schools carry them out.

Employing coaches is not the only way to increase teachers' instructional capacity. In most schools, there are teachers with the expertise to help other teachers develop greater pedagogical and content knowledge. By creating opportunities for teachers to learn from each other (for example, by visiting one another's classrooms and having structured and safe conversations about teaching and learning), districts can take advantage of the expertise that already exists within schools and the district while increasing capacity still further.

TIME

The school day in most districts does not afford teachers and administrators enough time to work together to systematically examine student assessment results and then translate their acquired knowledge into instructional improvements. One district we worked with negotiated a contract with its teachers union that called for slightly longer school days four days per week and an early release day for students once each week. Teachers meet for professional development after students leave on the early release day. Half of this time each month is dedicated to district-selected professional development topics, and half is set aside for topics selected by school-based decision-making teams. Teachers reported that they had used some of their time creating rubrics together and scoring student work based on the rubrics. Professional development time also was allocated to look at external assessment results and to plan instruction accordingly.

Teachers often need time not only to talk with each other, but also to talk with students. As explained in chapter 4, conversations with students can be an important data source for understanding what they know and don't know and, perhaps more importantly, why. Systematically gathering this type of data from students, however, can be difficult in the typical instructional schedule. If districts value the information gleaned from conversations between students and teachers about student work, they could encourage schools to adopt schedules that build in time for such conversations.

Observing colleagues in the same school can provide teachers with practical instructional ideas, can help foster mentoring relationships, and can further discussions about instructional strategies. For these reasons, many schools we have worked with see this activity as central to their strategy for creating consistent, effective instructional programs. Some school districts facilitate this activity by paying for substitutes to cover the classrooms of visiting instructors.

It is quite possible that there isn't enough common planning time, even if the district has created additional shared professional development time. In these cases, the district might compensate teachers if they spend their own time on professional development activities pertaining to improving teaching and learning. For example, one district negotiated a stipend for teachers who participated in a set number of hours of professional development activities that exceeded the number of hours required by contract. This extra pay provided teachers with the incentive to improve their instructional practice, even when the district could not provide additional time in the school day for this endeavor.

MODELING THE WORK

Perhaps the most important way a school district's leaders can support schools' efforts to improve is to model the process, engaging in each step so that they have first-hand experience in what is involved. A central office leadership team that did this started by setting norms and expectations around how team members would use their collaborative time. They took time to build their own assessment literacy, admitting to one another when they did not know how to read some of the reports they were expecting a typical teacher to understand. Then they analyzed overview data of student performance on state assessments and dug into a wide range of other sources of evidence to help them identify a learner-centered problem that they were particularly passionate about. Then came the tricky part: examining what they were doing as a district that was contributing to the learner-centered problem. With this problem of practice in hand, they created an action plan that called for them to make changes in district policy. They enacted the plan and assessed the extent to which their actions may have addressed the learner-centered problem. Throughout the process, they tried to support one another in cultivating the habits of mind of action, collaboration, and evidence. The work was hard, but they knew that they needed to face it—just as they were asking school teams to do. Their dedication sent a strong message to schools throughout the district about how much the central office leadership valued the work of improvement.

After trying out the process, the district can show its commitment by sticking with it. This includes celebrating the successes, setting new goals, and returning to the improvement cycle again and again. It also includes looking through all of the ACE insights at the end of the preceding eight chapters and thinking about how to apply them to the district context. In short, district central offices that want schools to become data wise need to become data wise themselves.

10

HOW WE IMPROVE

Kathryn Parker Boudett, Candice Bocala, and Elizabeth A. City

ONE DAY A FULBRIGHT SCHOLAR from New Zealand came for a fellowship at the Data Wise Project at the Harvard Graduate School of Education. When she arrived, she brought a card that had a photograph of a fern frond unfolding and a blown glass statue of the same image. "This is the koru, a Maori symbol of great importance in my country," she explained. "It means new beginnings. I thought you might recognize the shape," she said, her eyes twinkling. She held the green glass figure up to a poster of the Data Wise Improvement Process arrow that was hanging on the wall. The resemblance was striking.

From that day onward, the Data Wise Project team began to see things in a new light. Our curved arrow, which had arisen organically out of the combined imaginations of our original group of nineteen authors, had its roots in nature! And, more importantly, nature has done us one better. Ever since settling on the image of the curved arrow, we had a nagging concern. Our team of authors and the schools we worked with had appreciated the simplicity of the image. But we all knew that in reality the process was much more complex, since at any one time there would ideally be many improvement cycles happening simultaneously at different levels of the educational enterprise. How could we capture this complexity in a way that did not overwhelm? We had tried introducing the concept of fractals: mathematical patterns created from the same shape repeating, over and over, combining to make a larger parallel design. But when we shared this idea in words, the explanation always fell flat.

Then we started showing people the photograph of the koru, where the great sweeping spiral of the fern frond was repeated in a similar spiral for each of its leaves. The photograph of the koru did what words could not, revealing the pattern of interrelationship that we had been trying to convey.

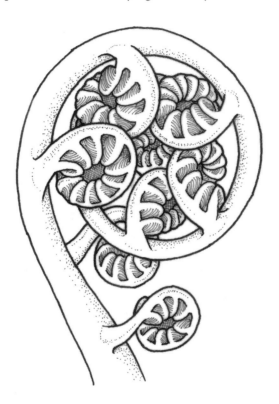

OUR THEORY OF ACTION

In the years since we first published *Data Wise*, we have collected stories about how schools and districts far and wide have brought the book's ideas to life. Through reflecting on these examples, we have developed an informal theory of action—a hypothesis that draws a causal chain between actions and a desired outcome—for how improvement happens in schools and school systems:

IF educators . . .

> **model the Data Wise Improvement Process and ACE Habits of Mind** in daily practice,
>
> **build the knowledge and skill of others** to do the work of improvement,
>
> **think big and focus small,**
>
> **act and adjust quickly, based on evidence,** in order to see real change in learning and teaching, and
>
> **capture and share learning** as it unfolds,

THEN . . .

> this learning will **build collective skill and confidence**
>
> so that everyone can **extend the work of improvement throughout the organization,** and
>
> learning and teaching for all children will improve.

This chapter attempts to put some meat on the bones of this theory, drawing on our experience working with schools and districts to illustrate each of the boldface statements above.

Model the Process and Habits

Mahatma Gandhi encouraged all people to "be the change you want to see in the world." This advice is as relevant to using data to improve learning as it is to any field. Once we developed the Data Wise Improvement Process, we were determined to use it every chance we had. We collected a wide range of data on the teaching and learning taking place in our courses and took deliberate action based on what the data showed us. A consistent piece of feedback we received from our students was that they learned as much from watching *how* our teaching team interacted with one another and the class as they did from *what* we actually said. They noticed little things, like the fact that we started and ended every session right on time: "Data Wise time," as many began to call it. They saw how the lead teachers distributed responsibility across the teaching team and how we positioned ourselves as co-learners, not experts. They were particularly tuned in to how we handled ourselves when we botched a lesson, and they told us later that they valued our transparency in admitting when something didn't work and then adjusting until it did.

So if you are wondering where to begin, try starting with yourself. Regardless of your official job title, to be an effective leader of this kind of change you will need to know what it feels like to actually go through the Data Wise Improvement Process and practice the ACE Habits of Mind. You will need to get comfortable with being a public learner—someone who can try something new, stick to evidence when assessing your actions, and embrace your successes and shortcomings with equal enthusiasm. Your modeling will help make it possible for your colleagues to engage in the work of improvement with humility, confidence, and a professional, student-focused attitude. So make a commitment to action, assessment, and adjustment; resolve to be intentional in all your collaborations; and maintain a relentless focus on evidence every time you make a decision. And be ready to describe where you are in your own improvement process to anyone who asks.

Build the Knowledge and Skill of Others

Modeling how to engage in continuous improvement is a good way to teach these practices to others, but there also comes a time when it is necessary to transfer the work deliberately. After all, you cannot have a collaborative approach to improvement if you don't have a great team (and eventually a whole network) of people working with you! We refer to this process as building capacity—capacity that lies in the knowledge and skill of other people to understand the Data Wise Improvement Process, to enact the ACE Habits of Mind, and to commit to following through on any actions and new questions that arise. To build capacity in others, you often have to teach new knowledge and skills directly. But once you have provided this introduction, the best way to get folks started is to have them jump right in. Learning to work together on a meaningful, challenging task will do more to build your team's capacity than all the team-building activities you could possibly invent.

When first learning the work of improvement, you are guaranteed to run into two kinds of challenges: adaptive and technical.[1] Ronald Heifetz and Donald Laurie use these terms to help make sense of the work of leadership. They describe *technical* challenges as those that can be solved by applying solutions, technologies, or knowledge that already exist, while *adaptive* challenges require changing mindsets, beliefs, and assumptions that allow people to fundamentally change the way they work. In our teaching and writing, we are quick to point out the importance of addressing technical challenges, such as creating a data inventory or designing a schedule that gives teachers time to collaborate. However, we have found that the area in which people most need support is facing adaptive challenges skillfully, so they can manage change when there are no easy answers. In our teaching, we put so much emphasis on norms, protocols, and habits of mind because we believe they help leaders to manage a team where members have diverse perspectives, build trust among teachers to open their doors to observers who will examine their instruction, and keep others committed to acting and adjusting, even if the results aren't immediately evident. You may find it useful to use the distinction between adaptive and technical challenges when discussing the work of improvement with colleagues, so that they have a language to describe how their learning is progressing along both dimensions.

Think Big, Focus Small

Schools often tell us that accountability policies that tie rewards and sanctions to students' performance bring perverse incentives to engage in behaviors and thinking that are actually counterproductive to improvement. Years of being asked to commit to large test score increases in unreasonably short time frames can make educators become accustomed to overpromising. "All children will become proficient writers" sounds a lot more impressive than "all children will be able to support an argument using evidence from a nonfiction text." But the more specific statement is detailed enough to provide grist for rich conversations about what effective use of evidence to support an argument might look like for children of different ages. It suggests a writing genre on which to focus, and it can lead to discrete action steps that teachers can do to help children develop at least some of the skills they will need to make progress toward the more abstract goal everyone is hoping for: proficient writers.

You may feel great urgency to solve a big problem, but you may not be sure what to do. Attempting to improve everything at once—hedging your bets that at least one solution will work—is likely to end in frustration. The Data Wise Improvement Process is designed to help you deliberately refine your focus until you have nailed down a pathway to a specific problem that you can address. Exhibit 10.1 uses the image of a funnel to show how the focus of inquiry gets progressively narrower as you move toward an action plan.

To see what this looks like in practice, consider this example from a high school. For this school (as for most), the top of the funnel was unmanageably wide, with *piles and piles of data* on every subject at every grade level for every student. To

Exhibit 10.1

From Piles and Piles of Data to a Specific Action Plan

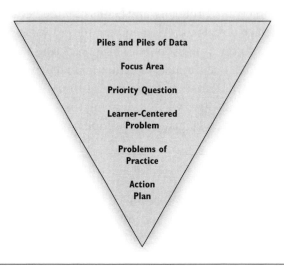

narrow the scope of inquiry, the instructional leadership team identified a school-wide *focus area*:

College-Ready Writing Skills

All departments took up the challenge, each considering the student data pertaining to the type of writing demanded by their discipline. For example, the English language arts (ELA) team discussed a data overview composed of charts showing student performance across a range of subskills. The team observed that students were struggling in a number of areas, including understanding an author's purpose when reading, using appropriate vocabulary and sentence structure, and writing an analysis of complex text. They knew they could not address all of these issues at once, so for this particular improvement cycle they chose to explore a *priority question*:

How are our students using evidence
to support their ideas in their writing?

They then proceeded to dig into multiple forms of data, including scores on formal writing prompts as well as informal homework assignments and student writing journals, to inform their analysis. From this work, the ELA team identified a descriptive and specific *learner-centered problem*:

> Students only give their opinions in their writing
> about text; they do not cite evidence from the text or make
> connections to other texts or real-life events.

With this problem in mind, they examined their own instruction, looking at their various approaches to teaching writing. Specifically, they asked teachers to share all the writing prompts they had used in the last year and they observed one writing lesson at each grade level. From this exploration, they determined that they had the following *problem of practice*:

> We as teachers do not teach students to regularly
> make text-to-text or text-to-world connections or to cite
> evidence from the text; instead, we focus heavily
> on encouraging students to make text-to-self connections.

At this point, the ELA team did some research into strategies for addressing their problem. They realized that they had a few different avenues they could take. They considered creating a minilesson about the different kinds of text-based connections that writers use and then having students write an essay about literature in which they pay particular attention to their text-to-text and text-to-world connections. They also discussed several other promising strategies. Eventually, they decided on the following **action plan**:

> Week 1: Select a sample text and work together as an ELA team to create a model essay that uses evidence and all three forms of text-based connections
>
> Week 2: Develop a lesson plan that allows students to analyze the text themselves, then evaluate and revise one of their previously written essays to incorporate evidence and the three forms of text-based connections

Week 3: Conduct the lesson in our classrooms, with each teacher observing at least one other teacher

Week 4: Have students focus on using evidence and making text-to-text or text-to-world connections in their daily journal writing prompts

Week 5: Administer district writing prompt and collect student work to bring to ELA team meeting

When we talk about action plans, we are *not* talking about the two-inch-thick whole-school improvement binders that many districts require schools to produce one year and implement over the course of the next. While in theory those improvement plans could be action plans for the school's strategy, in practice, they are often compliance documents with lofty goals. Within the Data Wise Improvement Process, action plans are concise, realistic, and evidence-based steps that educators can immediately take to address the demonstrated needs of students. The plans are very specific about how teacher and student actions will change. However, these plans do not come out of nowhere. They should be consistent with your school and school system's overall improvement strategy, and move toward your community's broad goals for children. The balancing act here is between thinking big while acting small—making sure that each set of specific actions links back to your overall strategy.

One way of ensuring that each team's specific actions are part of a coherent school strategy is to foster open communication among the interrelated teams that you put in place when you organized for collaborative work. The high school in the example above chose "college-ready writing skills" as a focus area. We already described the action plan developed by the English language arts department, but it is important to note that, at the same time, the science, social studies, and math departments were also creating very specific action plans around supporting student writing in their subject areas. The instructional leadership team, drawing on its members' knowledge of what was happening in teacher teams, made sure that the various efforts to support students' writing fit into the school's overall strategy for improving writing, as well as consistent with the district's and the community's aspirations for students as successful communicators. They also checked in regularly to see if the whole school had common standards for what college-ready writing looks like across the different disciplines. Your instructional leadership team can play this role by communicating the work being done across teams and clarifying how all the small pieces fit into the big picture.

Act and Adjust Quickly, Based on Evidence

Once you've decided what to do, it is time to take the plunge and do it. But this can be scary. What if the plan doesn't work? We can practically see the shoulders of people in our summer institute relax when we tell them that we have never seen an action plan (including any of our own) that went off without a hitch on the first try. Your action plan is your best guess about what needs to be done, and it will usually point you in the right direction. But the real learning happens when you put the plan to the test, evaluate the evidence about how it is working, and figure out how to adjust to meet the true needs of students.

When we talk with teams that are committed to improvement, many tell us matter-of-factly that they have needed to switch course midway through an improvement cycle. "Turns out our learner-centered problem wasn't the real problem after all," is a common refrain. What impresses us is the confidence with which team members will say this. Instead of feeling embarrassed that they were on the wrong track, they are proud that they were working smart enough to realize it. Finding out what doesn't work and using that evidence to refine the strategy for the next round are key components to learning.

A willingness to adjust can almost guarantee that your action plan will work. It may sound like cheating, but this is how we see it: you keep adjusting both your understanding of the problem (and students' and teachers' roles in the problem) and your understanding of the best solutions to the problem *until you address the problem that students actually have*. For example, after analyzing data, a team might define a *learner-centered problem* as

> Students struggle with calculating the perimeter and area of circles on open-ended problems.

After examining their instruction, they might hypothesize that their *problem of practice* is

> As teachers, we do not give students sufficient opportunities to practice applying their knowledge of geometric formulas to open-ended problems.

But what if teachers provide students with more opportunities to apply their learning, and the problem persists? Perhaps students are struggling with something much more fundamental than teachers originally thought. It may be that students don't have an appreciation of what *pi* is as a concept because they have memorized it as a number. Working through all the sample problems in the world is not going to improve achievement unless the lightbulb comes on, and students realize that *pi* is a ratio that will be consistent for any circle. A necessary first step might be adjusting the action plan to provide hands-on activities for students to work with strings and rulers and developing a conceptual understanding—rather than a procedural understanding—of *pi*. Once there is evidence that students really understand *pi*, the team can proceed to the action plan that gives students more practice in using this ratio when solving applied, complex problems. It may even turn out that they don't need so much practice after all.

Many schools have told us that they find Step 8 of the Data Wise Improvement Process to be the one of the most difficult to complete. But they've also admitted that this step has the biggest payoff. Without acting and adjusting, you end up investing a lot of time in inquiry with very little output for that investment. Remember, it is through adjusting that the Data Wise arrow bends back on itself; actions without adjustments turn the work of improvement into a series of straight lines that might start to operate independently of one another—and probably won't lead to the improvement you are looking for.

Capture and Share Learning

When we ask teams of educators who are using the Data Wise Improvement Process about the extent to which they celebrate success, some teams report they already have a strong and supportive culture in which students and teachers are routinely recognized for their achievements. At this point we are often tempted to push a bit further and ask whether they are celebrating not just what they *achieved* but also what they *learned*. Improving the skills of particular groups of students is laudable, but to make the improvement part of the new way of doing business, it is essential to understand what specific things educators did differently to make the improvement possible. And sometimes, there are no achievement gains to speak of, but there can still be powerful learning if a team takes the time to figure out why. Chris Argyris and Donald Schön argue that in organizational learning, it is not just actions that produce learning, but reflection on that action and gathering feedback about how it went.[2] Jumping eagerly through a series of action steps will not produce real learning unless you also pause to take stock of what you have accomplished and what you would change next time around.

There are several ways to do this. Chapter 8 describes how the Success Analysis Protocol can help your team reflect on the work you have done and provides suggestions for how to harness technology to create shared electronic documents that capture your learning over time. Another powerful approach involves formally recording your journey toward improved learning and teaching. In some of the courses we teach, we ask teams to produce a Data Wise Journey Presentation as they work their way through an improvement cycle, with the eight steps of the Data Wise Improvement Process providing a framework for each team's story. We recommend that schools include three slides for each step, titled as shown in Exhibit 10.2.

In this example, the team members captured their learning about Step 3, Creating a Data Overview. The first of the three slides lists the protocols they used and the types of data they explored. The second slide summarizes what they may have expressed out loud or written on chart paper, whiteboards, or shared documents: capturing their insights electronically ensured that all their good learning does not go to waste. The third slide provides space for reflection; the need to include this slide inspired a conversation about the team's learning that probably would not have taken place otherwise.

You can use your journey presentation in several ways. Your team can return to it right away to help plan your next cycle, or let it sit for a while and then allow it

Exhibit 10.2

An Excerpt from a School's Data Wise Journey Presentation		
Step 3: What We Did	**Step 3: What We Accomplished**	**Step 3: Reflections**
• Used the "What Do We See?/What Do We Wonder" Protocol to discuss overview of science performance in grades 6–8 • Used the Nominal Group Technique Protocol to identify a priority question that each grade-level team would dig into	• We noticed that students: — Scored poorly on questions about the scientific method — Lacked familiarity with basic scientific vocabulary — Frequently left open-response questions blank • We identified the following priority question: — What is students' understanding of the scientific method?	• Removing names from the data made it easier for us to stay descriptive in our analysis • We were suprised that there were so many areas of common stuggle across grade levels • It was really hard to frame a priority question that did not already contain a proposed solution

to serve as a reminder of how far you've come. As new teachers join your team, you can walk them through it to help them understand both where you are and how you got there. Or you can share it with other teams within or beyond your school to inform and inspire.

Build Collective Skill and Confidence

As your team engages in purposeful and collaborative inquiry, uses evidence to drive conversations about learning and teaching, and acts to change instructional practice, you will generate new data to assess your progress and raise questions for further thinking. As you reflect upon the results of your actions, you may begin to feel more responsible—as a *group*, not as individuals—for the learning that is occurring. When this happens, you are building what Roger Goddard, Wayne Hoy, and Anita Woolfolk Hoy call a sense of *collective efficacy*, or the belief that your team and school have the joint ability to successfully bring about changes in student learning.[3]

We've seen how collective efficacy can be self-perpetuating. Success can breed more confidence, more willingness to tackle new challenges, and more belief that what the team does matters. Teachers and principals alike have told us that they experience this as a freeing realization: I am not in this alone. Since no one individual is expected to bear the whole burden of improvement, no one becomes paralyzed by a fear of failure. We on the Data Wise Project team have noticed that we sometimes take turns feeling overwhelmed or inadequate for the task at hand, but there is usually someone who reminds the group: We can do this. We've tried to solve problems before and it's been hard. We know what it feels like to be stuck and frustrated, but we also know that together we can get ourselves unstuck and make progress. We can do this again.

Extend the Work of Improvement

Fortunately, collective efficacy can be contagious, allowing learning to spread systematically from one team to a network of teams and finally to your school—and beyond. This brings us back to the image of the koru, with its spiral shapes repeating at the level of both branch and leaf. Richard Elmore refers to this concept as *symmetry*, or the idea that powerful learning looks the same across all levels of a school, from the individual to the classroom to the organization.[4] Symmetry can occur in many ways, three of which we will describe here.

First, there can be symmetry between the work of the instructional leadership team and the work of all the other teacher teams throughout the building. One way we have seen this play out is for the instructional leadership team to take responsibility for leading the school through one big cycle over the course of the year, with the Prepare phase happening as the school year begins, Inquire occurring before the midyear holidays, and Act taking place as the year winds down. This school-level team may ask a big question that provides a foundation for school teams to pursue many minicycles over the same time period. For example, one instructional leadership team explained that the focus area for the year would be the level of intellectual rigor demanded at the school. In each of their monthly meetings, team members focused on one step of the Data Wise Improvement Process, but they decided to focus their inquiry not on the rigor of the tasks that teachers demand of students, but on the rigor of the tasks the team gave teachers during faculty meetings. This led the team to develop a schoolwide action plan for making faculty meetings more substantive and engaging. As this long, slow cycle progressed at the administrative level, the teacher teams were engaged in frequent, tighter cycles focused on the level of intellectual rigor in their classrooms. Because communication across the school was strong, educators at all levels continued to learn from one another's inquiry and actions around rigor over time.

A second way in which symmetry can occur is across levels of the organization. For example, an instructional leadership team might make a deliberate effort to cultivate intentional collaboration through the use of protocols in faculty meetings. As described at the end of chapter 8, using protocols can be particularly effective when participants are given an opportunity to debrief the experience. If, as part of this debrief, teachers are given time to brainstorm strategies for applying a protocol to the classroom, they may find that there are rich opportunities to let students cultivate the very habits of mind that teachers are working on. We know of classrooms where teachers guide students in developing and enforcing norms, lead students in explicit questioning protocols such as the Question Formulation Technique (described in Selected Protocols), or insist that students maintain a relentless focus on evidence. Habits can also permeate "upward." One of our proudest moments was when we saw a district central office team adopt a formal agenda template for their meeting because they had seen how effective this practice was at one of their schools. Like the multiple spirals within the koru, the work can begin to look the same whether you zoom into the classroom or out to the district.

Third, we have seen symmetry when a school uses a cycle to *improve the way it improves*. Yes, we have seen educators do this, and we do it ourselves! For example, one of the hardest steps of the process for most schools is Step 5, Examining

Instruction. To get a handle on why this is hard, one school decided to do a mini-cycle focusing only on this step. The instructional leadership team collected multiple forms of data to explore educators' attitudes and practices around observing instruction, identifying the equivalent of a learner-centered problem: they discovered that teachers felt they were not receiving useful feedback from previous experiences with observation. Instructional leadership team members then turned the mirror back on themselves, exploring what they were doing that might have made examining instruction less effective than it could have been. They discovered that they had not provided sufficient opportunities for peers to offer specific, actionable, and helpful feedback. The team then developed an action plan for making feedback opportunities a more central part of the peer observation process.

You can expect that no matter how experienced you become with this work, you will always have a growing edge. At this edge, you will be faced with what we call "burning questions"—having reached the limits of your knowledge and skill, you will need to engage in inquiry in order to move forward. Why not let the same process that is guiding your efforts to improve student learning guide your own introspection about the work of improvement?

GET READY FOR SOMETHING BIG

People responded so strongly to the image of the koru that we integrated it deeply into our teaching, using the fern to capture the beauty of new beginnings and the symmetry and interrelatedness of improvement. What we hadn't realized was how that image would go out into the world and then come back to us with new layers of meaning.

At a Data Wise Impact Workshop, we welcomed teams of educators who had been using the Data Wise Improvement Process back to Harvard's campus. When we asked each team to share what they had learned, a team from a primary school in Victoria, Australia, added a new image to the mix. They told us how they had used the koru to convey to their faculty back home how the instructional leadership team and the teaching teams would be using the Data Wise Improvement Process to bring symmetry and synergy to the work of the school. They then explained how they showed their staff members a new image, one the Data Wise Project team had never seen before. It was a photograph of a mature silver fern, growing in a forest of silver ferns, each nearly 10 meters high. When they showed the picture at the workshop, there was a hush in the room. Many of us had never thought to ask whether the koru opened out into anything larger than the knee-high common ferns growing in our home gardens.

Yes, it is true that it takes baby steps to bring about the cultural change necessary to work through the Data Wise Improvement Process while practicing the ACE Habits of Mind at every step. But don't underestimate where those baby steps can lead. This work is transformative—for both students and adults. It is about so much more than data: it is about finding a way to allow every student and every teacher to fulfill his or her potential. So get ready. With proper care, a delicate new beginning can lead to spirals and tendrils of growth that unfold into something bigger than you imagine.

SELECTED PROTOCOLS

THROUGHOUT THIS BOOK, we describe a number of strategies that school leaders can use to increase the effectiveness of collaborative efforts to use data to improve learning and teaching. Many of the strategies use protocols to structure conversations.

In most cases, we describe protocols in the chapters where they are relevant and use chapter endnotes to direct readers to websites where they can obtain more complete information. Here we provide instructions for six protocols that we have found to be particularly helpful in involving groups of educators in meaningful data work. All of these protocols are also available on the Data Wise Project website: http://www.gse.harvard.edu/datawise.

✱ CONSTRUCTING THE IMPROVEMENT PROCESS PROTOCOL

Purpose

This protocol helps a group come to a common understanding of the process of improvement in schools. It allows people to discover for themselves that the improvement process is not linear and that there is no one "right" way to do it.

Notes

* This protocol takes about 45 minutes to complete; feel free to adapt suggested times as needed.

* If necessary, break into groups of three to five people each. (This is a hands-on activity; it is important that groups be small so that everyone can actively participate.)

* Give each group poster paper, tape, markers, and an envelope containing eight sheets of paper, each containing one step of the Data Wise Improvement Process. Also include a couple of blank sheets of paper for participants to add their own steps during the exercise.

Steps

1. **15 MINUTES**. Ask groups to use the supplies given to create a visual representation of how schools engage in the improvement process. Tell them they can feel free to add, change, duplicate, or delete any of the steps included in the envelope.

2. **5 MINUTES**. Ask groups to discuss where their school is in the process they have just described.

3. **10 MINUTES**. Have groups post their creations around the room, and ask people to do a "gallery walk" to see one another's work.

4. **10 MINUTES**. Ask people what they noticed in doing the exercise, and what they noticed during their walk. Ask what steps were missing from the envelope or unnecessary. Key points to bring out are the variety of the processes created and their nonlinear and recursive nature.

5. **5–15 MINUTES**. (optional, depending on circumstances). Come to an agreement about the improvement cycle that the team will use in its work together, acknowledging that any way of modeling the improvement process is artificial but that to make progress, a group needs to agree on how it will approach the work.

✳ THE COHERENCE PROTOCOL

(This protocol was originally developed by Michele Shannon and is used with permission.)

Purpose

After a team has completed the Stoplight Protocol (please see the Data Wise Project website for instructions), the participants may want to use the Coherence Protocol to take stock of the specific things they are already doing to use data to improve learning and teaching. This helps to create a sense of coherence between that work and the Data Wise Improvement Process so that a team can identify a point of entry into the Data Wise Improvement Process.

Notes

*   This protocol takes about 60 minutes to complete; feel free to adapt suggested times as needed.

*   If necessary, break into groups of three to five people each.

*   Give each group a pad of sticky notes, pens or pencils, tape, and one poster-sized Data Wise Improvement Process arrow. (The arrow can be photocopied onto poster paper, drawn on large paper, or even drawn by hand on a whiteboard or chalkboard.)

Steps

1. **5 MINUTES**. Explain to participants that they will be doing a protocol that will help them (1) acknowledge the work they are already doing to use data to improve learning and teaching and (2) connect that work to the Data Wise Improvement Process.

    Ask participants to think about all of the structures, practices, and programs currently in place at the school that support staff members in using data to improve learning and teaching. Give each person five to ten sticky notes and tell them to work independently to write one item per sticky note.

2. **5 MINUTES**. Have each group tape a poster of the Data Wise Improvement Process arrow to the wall. Instruct participants to place each of their sticky notes on the poster near the step of the Data Wise Improvement Process where they feel it belongs.

3. **15 MINUTES**. Give participants time to read through all the sticky notes. Then ask groups to reach consensus about *what is currently happening* at the school. Encourage participants to go through each of the steps in turn and:

    — Condense notes if the same idea is written more than once

    — Add any structures, practices, or programs that are missing

    — Identify (and resolve through discussion, if possible) any disagreements about the placement of notes

4. **15 MINUTES**. Ask the groups to discuss the following questions:

    — What do we notice about this poster? How does it compare to the poster we created in the Stoplight Protocol?

    — At which steps of the Data Wise Improvement process do we already have robust structures, practices, or programs in place? How can we build on our strengths as we integrate the Data Wise Improvement Process into our daily work?

    — Which steps are lacking? Can we identify a particular growth area as a point of entry for integrating the Data Wise Improvement Process into our work?

5. **5 MINUTES**. Ask individuals to work independently to outline a brief "coherence story" that describes how they could see integrating the Data Wise Improvement Process into the work of the school. The story should include:

    — The rationale for choosing the Data Wise Improvement Process to organize the work

    — A current practice that is aligned with the process

    — A suggested point of entry for the launch of the work

6. **5 MINUTES**. Have individuals share their coherence stories with the group.

7. **10 MINUTES**. If participants broke into subgroups, reconvene the full group and allow each subgroup to share the highlights of its discussion. Then guide the whole group in outlining a single narrative that captures the collective thinking about how the Data Wise Improvement Process can support the school in focusing and deepening the work it is already doing.

Tips

*   Sometimes groups have a hard time naming all of the things they do around using data to improve learning and teaching. If they need examples, you could offer the following:

—   Structures: common planning time for a particular group of teachers, goal-setting templates

—   Practices: weekly quizzes, data walls

—   Programs: a science curriculum with benchmark assessments, a mentoring program that allows teachers to observe one another's practice

*   Some groups may be more comfortable finding consensus about where a sticky note goes before placing it on the poster. This can be achieved by going around in a circle, allowing each person to read one sticky note and ask the group's input about where along the arrow it belongs. Other people with similar notes can either discard or place their notes directly on top of that note to avoid redundancy.

*   Some structures, practices, and programs will not fit neatly on the arrow. It is fine to create copies of notes that apply to multiple steps or, if a note applies to all steps, to put the note at the top of the poster. If a note does not seem to apply to any step, it can be placed off to the side.

✳ INQUIRING INTRODUCTIONS PROTOCOL

(This protocol was originally developed by Anne Jones and is used with permission.)

Purpose

This protocol allows participants to practice skills of inquiry, listening, and responding to evidence. As a side benefit, it also gives members of a team an opportunity to get to know one another.

Notes

* This protocol takes about 30 minutes to complete; feel free to adapt suggested times as needed.

* If necessary, break the group into subgroups of three to five people each (four is ideal).

Steps

1. **1 MINUTE**. Tell participants that, in effective collaborative work, team members frequently inquire about the practices, experiences, and beliefs of their colleagues so that they can develop deep and shared understandings of where everyone is coming from. Explain that this protocol will help them develop skills of inquiry, listening, and responding to evidence that they will need in their ongoing collaborative work.

2. **4 MINUTES**. Explain that this protocol involves one round for each person in the group. Ask for a volunteer from each group to get things started. This person will be the "introducer" in the first round. Also ask for a timekeeper.

   Provide the protocol instructions:

   — **The introducer states** only **his or her name, subject taught, and grade level(s) taught.** For example: "My name is Anne Jones. I teach earth science in the eighth grade."

   — **The other people in the group may only respond with questions, and questions must be related to evidence given in the introducer's most immediate statement.** So, in response to the example above, a colleague may ask, "How did you get interested in earth science?" or "What is it like teaching eighth graders?" but not "Where are you from?" or "I used to teach science." This rule is designed to help participants stay with evidence they heard rather than going off on a tangent or connecting the introducer's sharing to something about themselves.

— **Colleagues cannot ask a second question until all colleagues have asked their first question.** This rule is designed to help participants share airtime and listen.

— **When the timekeeper announces that five minutes are up, begin the next round with a new introducer.** Continue with the protocol until everyone in the group has had a chance to be the introducer.

3. **20 MINUTES**. Tell subgroups to self-facilitate the protocol. This exercise takes about 20 minutes to complete with four people in one group; feel free to adapt suggested times for different group sizes. Keep an eye on the clock and remind groups to switch introducers, if necessary.

4. **5 MINUTES**. Ask participants what they noticed during the protocol. This step of debriefing the activity helps people to capture and share their learning about inquiry and listening.

Tip

*   This protocol can easily be modified to help teams explore a variety of topics by changing the introducer's opening statement. For example, if team members need to get a sense of their collective experience in using data, the instruction to the introducer could be to give his or her name and an example of a situation in which collaborative discussion of data helped improve learning and teaching in his or her classroom.

✳ THE QUESTION FORMULATION TECHNIQUE

(Copyright The Right Question Institute, http://rightquestion.org; used with permission.)

Purpose

This protocol helps a group of people fully explore an important issue before jumping into a discussion of what they are going to do about it. It provides a forum in which all voices can be heard, thus increasing the number of ideas generated and leveling the power dynamic.[1]

Notes

* This protocol takes about 45 minutes to complete; feel free to adapt suggested times as needed.

* If necessary, break into groups of five to eight people each and ask for a volunteer scribe for each group.

* Give each group two sheets of chart paper, two markers, and tape. Have extra chart paper on hand in case it is needed.

Steps

1. **2 MINUTES**. Identify the issue. Write the issue you would like the groups to address on chart paper at the front of the room. Issues can be quite general, such as "Using data to improve instruction," or more specific, such as "Our tenth graders are not scoring in the top proficiency levels of our state exam."

2. **5–10 MINUTES**. Produce questions. Ask groups to generate questions about the issue and write their questions on their chart paper. Tell people they have to follow two rules: (1) Phrase all responses as questions, not statements; and (2) The scribe should write questions exactly as stated—no editing questions. As groups work, circulate around the room and remind people to follow these two rules.

3. **3 MINUTES**. Examine. Ask groups to look at their brainstormed list, classifying questions as closed-ended or open-ended. Allow groups to change the form of any questions from closed- to open-ended if they would like.

4. **5 MINUTES**. Prioritize. Ask groups to choose the three questions from their list that they think are most important.

5. **5–10 MINUTES**. Branch off. Ask groups to write the most important of their prioritized questions at the top of a new piece of chart paper. Then tell them to generate new questions about it, again following the two rules noted above.

6. **3–5 MINUTES**. Prioritize again. Ask groups to choose the three questions from this new list that they think are most important.

7. **5 MINUTES**. Share. Go around the room and ask each group to state its prioritized questions.

8. **10 MINUTES**. Debrief. Ask people what they noticed in doing this exercise. Key points that may come up include the way this process keeps a group from jumping to solutions, allows many voices to be heard, and fosters deep consideration of an issue.

Tip

*   The effectiveness of this protocol depends in part on whether you choose a rich issue for discussion, so think carefully about your topic and how you phrase it. Do not phrase the issue itself as a question.

 **AFFINITY PROTOCOL**

Purpose

This protocol helps a group of people explore the causes of a problem that they have identified, allowing all individuals to participate anonymously in hypothesizing about causes.[2]

Notes

* This protocol takes about 30 minutes to complete; adapt suggested times as needed.

* If necessary, break into groups of three to five people each (four is ideal).

* Give each group chart paper, a pad of sticky notes, and markers.

* To do this protocol, a team needs to have identified a shared learner-centered problem or problem of practice ahead of time.

Steps

1. **5 MINUTES**. Ask individuals to work independently to brainstorm hunches and hypotheses about what the causes of the problem might be and write each one on a separate sticky note.

2. **10 MINUTES**. Put people in their groups and give the following instructions:

    — Write the shared problem at the top of the chart paper.

    — Place sticky notes randomly on the chart paper.

    — Work together to sort the items into categories. (If an idea fits in more than one category, it is okay to duplicate the idea on a separate sticky note and include it in two categories; it is also okay for an idea to stand alone. All ideas over which the school has no control can go together in one corner of the chart paper.)

3. **5 MINUTES**. Tell teams to create a header for each category and write it on the chart paper. Large categories can be divided into subcategories with subheadings.

4. **10 MINUTES**. If you broke into groups, have teams share their categories. Ask for a few comments about what people notice and whether there are any patterns. Then have an open discussion about how the results of this protocol can inform the team's ongoing work.

✳ PLUS/DELTA PROTOCOL

Purpose

This protocol helps a team assess what worked well in a meeting or training session and consider what they would have liked to change.

Notes

*   This protocol takes about ten minutes to complete; feel free to adapt suggested times as needed.

*   Give each participant an index card.

*   Draw a two-column chart on chart paper with a plus (+) above the left column and a delta (Δ, a Greek symbol for change) above the right column.

Steps

1. **2 MINUTES**. Review the objectives and activities of the meeting. Explain that a powerful way of practicing the ACE Habits of Mind is to gather feedback about team processes and use this information to refine how the team works together.

2. **2 MINUTES**. Tell participants to copy the T-chart onto their index cards. Ask them to think about what worked well in the meeting and write their responses under the plus column on their index cards.

3. **2 MINUTES**. Ask participants to think about what they would have liked to change about the meeting and write their responses under the delta column on their index cards.

4. **2 MINUTES**. Ask for volunteers to share pluses and write the responses on a chart in front of the room.

5. **2 MINUTES**. Then ask for deltas and write those responses on the chart. Collect all index cards at the end of the protocol.

Tips

*   If participants are hesitant to provide deltas, remind them that deltas will help the team improve its practice (and perhaps put a delta of your own on the list to get things started).

* If you begin each meeting by reviewing the previous meeting's pluses and deltas and explaining how the meeting will take them into account, you are likely to find participants are more forthcoming with their comments at future meetings.

* You can experiment with asking for pluses before deltas at the end of one meeting and then reversing the order in the next. How does this affect the protocol?

* To save time, you can skip the index cards and instead have the whole group offer pluses and deltas out loud. Alternatively, you can have individuals write their pluses and deltas on sticky notes or index cards and leave the notes or cards in the middle of the table, or have someone collect them as they leave. This method allows all the pluses and deltas to remain completely anonymous.

DATA WISE RESOURCES

DATA WISE PROJECT WEBSITE

Please visit http://www.gse.harvard.edu/datawise for information about courses, publications, and other resources designed to support you in learning about and using the Data Wise Improvement Process and the ACE Habits of Mind.

The website contains information about the Data Wise Rubric, a tool for reflecting on the extent to which your school has integrated the Data Wise Improvement Process into your daily work. For each of the eight steps, the rubric lists several key tasks and describes what it looks like when a school is in each of four stages with respect to that task.

BOOKS

Kathryn Parker Boudett and Jennifer L. Steele, eds., *Data Wise in Action: Stories of Schools Using Data to Improve Teaching and Learning* (Cambridge, MA: Harvard Education Press, 2007).

This book tells the stories of eight very different schools that are following the Data Wise Improvement Process, highlighting the leadership challenges that schools can face at each step of the work and illustrating how staff members use creativity and collaboration to overcome those challenges.

MULTIMEDIA

Kathryn Parker Boudett, Elizabeth A. City, and Marcia K. Russell, *Key Elements of Observing Practice: A Data Wise DVD and Facilitator's Guide* (Cambridge, MA: Harvard Education Press, 2010).

This resource contains a series of short videos that invite you into classrooms and meeting rooms at the Richard J. Murphy School in Boston, a school that uses data wisely. The *Facilitator's Guide* lays out a professional development sequence in which teacher teams use these videos as a springboard for working together to design their own process for learning from classroom observation.

TEACHING CASES

Kathryn Parker Boudett, David Rease Jr., Michele Shannon, and Tommie Henderson. *Data Wise at Poe Middle School in San Antonio, Texas* (Harvard Education Press, 2013).

This case tells the story of how a team of educators from Edgar Allan Poe Middle School in San Antonio, Texas, began integrating the Data Wise Improvement Process and the ACE Habits of Mind into the work of their school after attending the Data Wise Summer Institute. It is designed to help school teams think about their theory of action for how using data will improve teaching and learning.

Kathryn Parker Boudett, Susan Cheng, Samantha Cohen, Nancy Gutierrez, Karen Maldonado, Kimberly Noble, Maren Oberman, and Michele Shannon. *Data Wise District-Wide in Evansville, Indiana* (Harvard Education Press, 2013).

This case describes how the superintendent and district leadership team in the Evansville Vanderburgh School Corporation integrated the Data Wise Improvement Process into their district. It is designed to help district teams think about how to build strong learning organizations.

ARTICLES

Kathryn Parker Boudett, Elizabeth A. City, and Richard J. Murnane, "The 'Data Wise' Improvement Process: Eight Steps for Using Test Data to Improve Teaching and Learning," *Harvard Education Letter,* January/February 2006, http://www.hepg.org/hel/article/297.

This article provides an overview of the Data Wise Improvement Process, and outlines the eight distinct steps school leaders can take to use their student assessment data to improve instruction and achievement.

Jennifer L. Steele and Kathryn Parker Boudett, "Leadership Lessons from Schools Becoming 'Data Wise,'" *Harvard Education Letter,* January/February 2008, http://hepg.org/hel/article/203.

> This article provides an overview of evidence from case studies of eight schools using the Data Wise Improvement Process. It documents the leadership challenges that school leaders typically face during each step of the improvement process, as well as the strategies they use to address them.

PROFESSIONAL DEVELOPMENT

Data Wise Summer Institute at the Harvard Graduate School of Education

> Teams of educators from around the United States and the world gather for a week on Harvard's campus for an intense training experience led by Data Wise Project team members and featuring schools that have built wise data practices into their daily work. It also includes live online sessions with Data Wise faculty that are designed to support school teams in incorporating the Data Wise Improvement Process in the year after attending the institute.

Data Wise Impact Workshop at the Harvard Graduate School of Education

> Practitioners who have been integrating the Data Wise Improvement Process into their work come to campus to participate in a two-day workshop to share their successes and learn from faculty and peers about how to address their challenges.

Online Course: Getting Started with Data Wise

> Teams of educators from around the United States and the world gather in cyberspace for an introductory course that presents the Data Wise Improvement Process and supports teams in planning how to integrate ongoing, collaborative, evidence-based inquiry and action into their work.

Online Course: Putting Data Wise into Action

> Graduates of the introductory online course or the on-campus institutes enroll in this course, which supports school teams as they implement each of the eight steps of the process and document their journey.

NOTES

Chapter 1

1. All of our protocols are available on the Data Wise Project website: http://www.gse.harvard.edu/datawise.

2. See J. Cunningham, ed., *Creating Professional Learning Communities: A Step-by-Step Guide to Improving Student Achievement Through Teacher Collaboration* (Dorchester, MA: Project for School Innovation, 2004): vol. 12, pp. 34–37.

3. For further guidance about using norm-setting protocols, see http://www.turningpts.org/tools.htm and J. P. McDonald, N. Mohr, A. Dichter, and E. D. McDonald, *The Power of Protocols: An Educator's Guide to Better Practice* (New York: Teachers College Press, 2003): pp. 26–28.

4. For a description of this protocol, see http://www.turningpts.org/tools.htm.

5. This protocol was developed by Anne Jones. It is available in the Selected Protocols section of this book and also on the Data Wise Project website.

Chapter 2

1. Massachusetts Department of Education, *Guide to Interpreting the Spring 2001 Reports for Schools and Districts* (Malden, MA: Author, 2001): p. 7.

2. H. D. Hoover et al., *Iowa Tests of Basic Skills Interpretive Guide for School Administrators* (Chicago: Riverside, 1994): p. 14.

3. J. D. Braswell, A. D. Lutkus, W. S. Grigg, S. L. Santapau, B. Tay-Lim, and M. Johnson, *The Nation's Report Card: Mathematics 2000*, NCES 2001-517 (Washington, DC: U.S. Department of Education, National Center for Education Statistics, 2001): p. 54.

4. A. Biemiller, "Teaching Vocabulary: Early, Direct, and Sequential," *American Educator* 25, no. 1 (2001).

5. Massachusetts Department of Education, *Guide to the 2000 MCAS Parent/Guardian Report* (Malden, MA: Author, 2000): p. 5.

6. Braswell et al., *The Nation's Report Card: Mathematics 2000*.

7. For a more thorough discussion of value-added models, see D. Koretz, "Value-added Models Are a Promising Improvement, But No One Measure Can Evaluate Teacher Performance," *American Educator*, Fall 2008: pp. 18–27, 39; and D. F. McCaffrey, J. R. Lockwood, D. M. Koretz, and L. S. Hamilton, *Evaluating Value-Added Models for Teacher Accountability*, MG-158-EDU (Santa Monica, CA: RAND, 2003).

8. D. Koretz, "Preparing Students for the MSPAP Assessments," in Assessment-Based Educational Reform: A Look at Two State Programs, part 2, symposium presented at the annual meeting of the American Educational Research Association, J. Pollack, chair, New York, April 1996.

9. For example, D. Koretz, S. Barron, K. Mitchell, and B. Stecher, *The Perceived Effects of the Kentucky Instructional Results Information System (KIRIS)*, MR-792-PCT/FF (Santa Monica, CA: RAND, 1996); L. A. Shepard and K. C. Dougherty, "Effects of High-Stakes Testing on Instruction," paper presented at the annual meeting of the American Educational Research Association and National Council on Measurement in Education, Chicago, April 1996.

10. B. M. Stecher, S. L. Barron, T. Chun, and K. Ross, *The Effects of the Washington State Education Reform on Schools and Classrooms*, CSE Tech. Rep. No. 525 (Los Angeles: University of California, National Center for Research on Evaluation, Standards, and Student Testing, 2000).

11. Adapted from D. Koretz, R. L. Linn, S. B. Dunbar, and L. A Shepard, "The Effects of High-Stakes Testing: Preliminary Evidence About Generalization Across Tests," in The Effects of High-Stakes Testing, symposium presented at the annual meetings of the American Educational Research Association and the National Council on Measurement in Education, R. L. Linn, chair, Chicago, April 1991, and reprinted here with permission of the first author.

12. For example, B. Jacob, *Accountability, Incentives and Behavior: The Impact of High-Stakes Testing in the Chicago Public Schools*, Working Paper W8968 (Cambridge, MA: National Bureau of Economic Research, 2002); S. P. Klein, L. S. Hamilton, D. F. McCaffrey, and B. M. Stecher, *What Do Test Scores in Texas Tell Us?* Issue Paper IP-202 (Santa Monica, CA: RAND, 2000), accessed January 12, 2004, from http://www.rand.org/publications/IP/IP202/); D. Koretz and S. I. Barron, *The Validity of Gains on the Kentucky Instructional Results Information System (KIRIS)*, MR-1014-EDU (Santa Monica, CA: RAND, 1998).

Chapter 3

1. To increase clarity, in this revised and expanded edition we have sharpened the language pertaining to this task. The instructional leadership team chooses a *focus area* for the data overview, and then brings *questions* to the data that help shed light on what is happening within the focus area. (We are no longer use the term "educational question," which we had used in the first edition to refer to both of these ideas.) The goal of the data overview discussion is still to engage a wider group in agreeing upon a *priority question* that will inform where teachers will dig into data.

2. This process was originally described in A. L. Delbecq and A. H. VandeVen, "A Group Process Model for Problem Identification and Program Planning," *Journal of Applied*

Behavioral Science VII (July/August, 1971): pp. 466-491.We use a version of this protocol adapted by the Centers for Disease Control (CDC), available at www.cdc.gov/HealthyYouth/evaluation/pdf/brief7.pdf.

3. P. Senge et al., *Schools That Learn: A Fifth Discipline Fieldbook for Educators, Parents, and Everyone Who Cares About Education* (New York: Doubleday/Currency, 2000): p. 71.

Chapter 4

1. There are many useful protocols for looking at student work, including the Collaborative Assessment Conference, Consultancy, and Standards in Practice. For more information, see http://www.lasw.org/methods.html.

2. For a description of this protocol, see http://www.lasw.org/Slice_descript.html and McDonald et al., *The Power of Protocols*: pp. 84–91.

Chapter 5

1. We are indebted to Harvard Graduate School of Education professor Richard Elmore for many conversations about problems of practice and what it means to examine and improve instruction.

2. This "why-why-why" diagram is from the Thomas A. Edison Middle School in Boston, Massachusetts. We are very grateful to the Edison School for permission to include an example of their improvement work in this chapter.

3. We learned this concept of the instructional core from Richard Elmore. For further elaboration of the idea, see Elmore's essay, "Getting to Scale with Good Educational Practice" in his book *School Reform from the Inside Out: Policy, Practice, and Performance* (Cambridge, MA: Harvard Education Press, 2004).

4. For a good description of the Think Aloud process, see R. Schoenbach, C. Greenleaf, C. Cziko, and L. Hurwitz, *Reading for Understanding: A Guide to Improving Reading in Middle and High School Classrooms* (San Francisco: Jossey-Bass, 1999).

Chapter 6

1. We would like to thank and credit Richard Elmore for clarifying the connection between the problem of practice and the school's overall strategy for improvement.

2. For a complete description of how to set up World Café Conversations, see http://www.theworldcafe.com/twcrg.html.

3. G. Polya, *How to Solve It: A New Aspect of Mathematical Method* (Princeton, NJ: Princeton University Press, 2004).

4. For an excellent description of the value of articulating these kinds of theories, see C. Weiss, *Evaluation: Methods for Studying Programs and Policies*, 2nd ed. (Upper Saddle River, NJ: Prentice-Hall, 1998): ch. 3.

5. This description of professional development draws on work by Elizabeth A. City and Sara Schwartz in which they reviewed research on the characteristics of professional development that make a difference in student achievement. E. A. City and S. Schwartz, *Rigorous, Relevant Research*, unpublished manuscript, 2004.

6. For instructions for this protocol see http://www.nsrfharmony.org/protocol.

Chapter 7

1. Educators used to refer to these tests more generally as "formative assessments," but formative assessment has come to indicate a process of gathering and using evidence to inform instructional practice and provide feedback to students on progress. See, for example, P. J. Black and D. Wiliam, "Inside the Black Box: Raising Standards Through Classroom Assessment," *Phi Delta Kappan* 80 (1998): pp. 139–148; and M. Heritage, *Formative Assessment and Next-Generation Assessment Systems: Are We Losing an Opportunity?* (Washington, DC: Council of Chief State School Officers, 2010), http://www.ccsso.org/Documents/2010/Formative_Assessment_Next_Generation_2010.pdf.

2. For more information about this model, see http://educationnorthwest.org/traits. (Note that NWREL is now called Education Northwest.)

Chapter 8

1. For an alternative resource offering practical tips for getting this type of observation going in schools, see chapter 3 in J. Cunningham, ed., *Creating Professional Learning Communities: A Step-by-Step Guide to Improving Student Achievement Through Teacher Collaboration,* vol. 12 (Dorchester, MA: Project for School Innovation, 2004). Available through http://www.psinnovation.com.

2. Richard Elmore suggests these three key areas can serve as the foundation for any instructional observation protocol.

3. For complete information about the Success Analysis Protocol, see http://www.smallschoolproject.org/PDFS/success.pdf; http://www.nsrfnewyork.org/articles/SuccessAnalysisProtocol.doc; http://www.smp.gseis.ucla.edu/downloads/success_analysis_protocol.pdf; and McDonald, et al. *The Power of Protocols*, pp. 60–62.

4. The SUMI protocol was created by Anne Jones and Susan F. Henry and is used with permission.

Chapter 10

1. R. A. Heifetz and D. L. Laurie, "The Work of Leadership," *Harvard Business Review*, January–February 1997: pp. 124–134.

2. For further reading about organizational learning, see C. Argyris and D. A. Schön, *Theory in Practice* (San Francisco: Jossey-Bass, 1987); and A. Edmondson, "The Local

and Variegated Nature of Learning in Organizations: A Group-level Perspective," *Organization Science* 13, no. 2 (2002): pp. 128–146.

3. R. D. Goddard, W. K. Hoy, and A. Woolfolk Hoy, "Collective Efficacy: Theoretical Developments, Empirical Evidence, and Future Directions," *Educational Researcher* 33 (2004), no. 3: pp. 3–13.

4. R. F. Elmore, "Culture and Strategy" (unpublished manuscript, n.d).

Selected Protocols

1. The most updated version of the Question Formulation Technique can be found at http://www.rightquestion.org and is described in D. Rothstein and L. Santana, *Make Just One Change: Teach Students to Ask Their Own Questions* (Cambridge, MA: Harvard Education Press, 2011).

2. Other versions of this protocol can be found in V. L. Bernhardt, *Data Analysis for Continuous School Improvement*, 2nd ed. (Larchmont, NY: Eye on Education, 2004): pp. 150–152; and B. Andersen and T. Fagerhaug, *Root Cause Analysis: Simplified Tools and Techniques* (Milwaukee, WI: ASQ Quality Press, 2000): pp. 99–102.

ABOUT THE EDITORS

Kathryn Parker Boudett is a lecturer on education at HGSE and director of the Data Wise Project, where she works to support a community of educators in developing and using resources for working collaboratively to use data to make real and lasting improvements in teaching and learning. Working with graduate students and teams of educators who enroll in her courses, Kathy enjoys bridging the worlds of research, practice, and policy.

Elizabeth A. City helps educators advance learning for all students through strategy, leadership development, and improvement practices. Liz has served in many roles, including teacher, principal, instructional coach, and consultant. She is currently director of the Doctor of Education Leadership (Ed.L.D.) Program and lecturer on education at the Harvard Graduate School of Education (HGSE).

Richard J. Murnane, an economist, is Thompson Professor of Education and Society at HGSE and a research associate at the National Bureau of Economic Research. In recent years he has pursued two lines of research. One examines how computer-based technological change has affected skill demands in the U.S. economy, and the other explores how growth in family income inequality in the United States has affected educational opportunities for children from low-income families and the effectiveness of alternative strategies for improving life chances for these children.

ABOUT THE CONTRIBUTORS

Candice Bocala is a doctoral candidate at HGSE, where her research focuses on teacher and school leader learning, collaboration and teamwork, and school improvement. She also conducts program evaluation and policy research and provides professional development for schools and districts. She previously taught elementary school in Washington, DC.

Tom Buffett is the associate for strategic instructional improvement for the Michigan Fellowship of Instructional Leaders located at Michigan State University's Office of K–12 Outreach. He has worked to support schools, districts, and state departments of education. Tom holds a doctorate in education from HGSE.

Jonna Sullivan Casey is program director at the Richard J. Murphy School and the Murphy Satellite BEST Program. She also directs an extensive array of out-of-school programs, including Prime Time After-School, Summer Stars, and Saturday Scholars. Prior to joining Boston Public Schools, Jonna served as purchasing director for Sodexho, USA. She holds a doctorate in education from Boston College.

Sarah E. Fiarman has worked as a National Board Certified teacher and a staff developer and is currently a principal in the Cambridge Public Schools, where her school includes the city's Sheltered English Immersion program. Sarah holds a doctorate in education from HGSE. With Elizabeth City, Richard Elmore, and Lee Teitel, she is coauthor of *Instructional Rounds in Education* (Harvard Education Press, 2009).

Shannon T. Hodge, a graduate of Stanford Law School, is a law clerk to the Honorable Ann Claire Williams of the United States Court of Appeals for the Seventh Circuit. A former high school counselor and testing coordinator, Shannon is also a doctoral candidate at HGSE, where she researches standardized testing and education policy.

Melissa Kagle graduated from HGSE with her doctorate in administration, planning, and social policy. She is currently an assistant professor of education and director of the math/science teacher education program at Colgate University.

Jane E. King works for the Boston Public Schools, where she has served as the principal of McCormack Middle School. A career-change educator, she is a former Boston Public Schools parent and activist.

Daniel M. Koretz is the Henry Lee Shattuck Professor of Education at HGSE. His research focuses on educational assessment and policy, particularly the effects of high-stakes testing on educational practice and the validity of score gains. His current work focuses on the design and evaluation of test-focused educational accountability systems. Before obtaining his degree, Dan taught emotionally disturbed students in public elementary and junior high schools in Parkrose, Oregon.

Gerardo Martinez served as principal at the Mary E. Curley Middle School in Jamaica Plain, Massachusetts, for five years before taking over the Edward Devotion School in Brookline, Massachusetts, where he also spent five years. He is currently principal at the Schofield Elementary School in Wellesley, Massachusetts. He had done extensive work in developing adult learning communities and improving teacher practice through meaningful learning and professional development opportunities. Gerardo holds a master's degree in educational administration from the University of Massachusetts Boston.

Ethan Mintz was the codesigner of the Formative Assessment of Student Thinking in Reading (FAST-R), a tool that Boston Public Schools teachers used to inform instruction. He is coeditor (with J. T. Yun) of *The Complex World of Teaching: Perspectives from Theory and Practice* and has consulted with several school districts to help schools, teachers, and school leaders understand and analyze data for the purpose of making instructional decisions. Ethan holds a doctorate in education from HGSE.

Liane Moody worked for the Boston Plan for Excellence, where she helped design and implement MyBPS Assessment, an online assessment data analysis tool for the Boston Public Schools. Liane holds a doctorate in education from HGSE.

Jennifer Price is principal of Newton North High School in Newton, Massachusetts, where she is committed to excellence and equity for all. Her doctoral dissertation at HGSE focused on the impact on student achievement of sharing student background information with faculty.

Mary Russo is a lecturer on education in the School Leadership Program at HGSE and principal of St. Catherine of Siena School in Norwood, Massachusetts. Prior to that, she was principal of the Richard J. Murphy School, a 950-student K–8 school in Boston, and the Samuel W. Mason School in Roxbury. She has been a principal for over 20 years, is a National Distinguished Principal, and was named Massachusetts Principal of the Year in 2004. She has taught at all grade levels—elementary, middle, and high school.

Nancy S. Sharkey is a program officer for the Statewide Longitudinal Data System (SLDS) program at the National Center for Education Statistics (NCES). As part of that work, Nancy manages a portfolio of states that are creating and expanding their student-level data systems to include teacher data, early childhood data, postsecondary data, and workforce data. She has also worked as the data quality lead for the DC Office of the State Superintendent of Education and worked on the District of Columbia's longitudinal data system project. Nancy holds an Ed.D. in administration, planning, and social policy from HGSE.

Jennifer L. Steele is a policy researcher at the RAND Corporation in Washington, DC, where she is leading a federally funded random-assignment study of dual-language immersion in Portland, Oregon, and co-leading two studies of technology-enhanced school reforms. Her work has appeared in the *Journal of Policy Analysis and Management*, the *Journal of Research on Educational Effectiveness*, and *The Future of Children*. Jennifer holds a doctorate in education from HGSE.

Mark B. Teoh taught history for six years in Texas and Pennsylvania. He has served as an administrator in urban school systems, including as executive director of research, evaluation, assessment, and development in Seattle Public Schools. Mark holds a doctorate in education from HGSE and is currently the director of research and knowledge for Teach Plus.

John B. Willett is Charles William Eliot Professor at HGSE. He is a certified high school science teacher, having taught high school physics and mathematics for almost a decade before entering academia. John teaches courses in intermediate and advanced applied statistics and specializes in quantitative methods for causal inference, for measuring change over time, and for analyzing the occurrence, timing, and duration of events.

INDEX